CONTRIBUTIONS
TO
ECONOMIC ANALYSIS

165

Honorary Editor:
J. TINBERGEN

Editors:
D. W. JORGENSON
J. WAELBROECK

NORTH-HOLLAND
AMSTERDAM · NEW YORK · OXFORD · TOKYO

A HISTORY
OF ECONOMETRICS

Roy J. EPSTEIN
University of Illinois at Chicago
USA

1987

NORTH-HOLLAND
AMSTERDAM · NEW YORK · OXFORD · TOKYO

© ELSEVIER SCIENCE PUBLISHERS B.V., 1987

ISBN: 0 444 70267 9

Publishers:
ELSEVIER SCIENCE PUBLISHERS B.V.
P.O. Box 1991
1000 BZ Amsterdam
The Netherlands

Sole distributors for the U.S.A. and Canada:
ELSEVIER SCIENCE PUBLISHING COMPANY, INC.
52 Vanderbilt Avenue
New York, N.Y. 10017
U.S.A.

PRINTED IN THE NETHERLANDS

Introduction to the Series

This series consists of a number of hitherto unpublished studies, which are introduced by the editors in the belief that they represent fresh contributions to economic science.

The term 'economic analysis' as used in the title of the series has been adopted because it covers both the activities of the theoretical economist and the research worker.

Although the analytical methods used by the various contributors are not the same, they are nevertheless conditioned by the common origin of their studies, namely theoretical problems encountered in practical research. Since for this reason, business cycle research and national accounting, research work on behalf of economic policy, and problems of planning are the main sources of the subjects dealt with, they necessarily determine the manner of approach adopted by the authors. Their methods tend to be 'practical' in the sense of not being too far remote from application to actual economic conditions. In addition they are quantitative rather than qualitative.

It is the hope of the editors that the publication of these studies will help to stimulate the exchange of scientific information and to reinforce international cooperation in the field of economics.

The Editors

PREFACE

During the years that this book was in preparation I was frequently asked, and sometimes challenged, about what could be gained from a history of econometrics. To the extent that one can rationally (or frankly) account for a particular research interest, the answer for me lies in the original impulse that caused me to study economics itself. As I was coming of age nearly a generation ago I became inescapably involved in debates over social questions whose range and urgency had a decisive effect on my choice of profession. Economics attracted me as a realm where such problems could be studied from both an intellectual and a practical point of view, and where one could cultivate interests that were at once mathematical, historical, and political. I approached econometrics with this complex of motives and soon became absorbed in a wide variety of academic research projects and consulting work. With time, however, I started to develop serious questions about the general scientific status of empirical econometrics. There was an obvious disparity between the statistical procedure typically followed by published studies and the theory of inference as expounded in the textbooks. I knew that others in the field harbored similar doubts regarding the interpretation of applied econometric work although it was not very common to express them publicly. I felt it was important to explore the problem more deeply in the context of the studies and methodological arguments developed by the researchers who were most influential in shaping econometrics as we know it today. To my surprise, I discovered a long history of substantive debates over methodology that complements, and even extends, the critiques put forth recently by some of the most respected modern practitioners. It is my hope that readers will find this history as relevant and enlightening as I did in understanding the current state of econometrics.

In its original form this book was presented as my PhD dissertation at Yale University in 1984. I am greatly indebted to P. C. B. Phillips, my principal advisor, for extremely helpful criticisms at each stage of my work while encouraging me to approach it in my own way. He was also generous in sharing with me some of his own reflections on the scientific standing of econometrics. He was always open to my many questions and ideas about econometric methodology. The present manuscript also benefitted from valuable suggestions by a host of other readers. In particular, I wish to thank William N. Parker, my learned teacher and humane friend. He was a constant stimulus for my own thinking in economic history and I hope he enjoyed our frequent talks as much as I did. Sidney Winter was an astute critic who helped me clarify the arguments at various points. Seminar participants at Yale and the University of Illinois at Chicago offered significant insights that influenced my own thinking. Finally, I thank Dale Jorgenson who, as editor, gave unstinting advice and encouragement that led to many improvements in the text. I am pleased to acknowledge their contribution to the final product but responsibility for all errors, omissions, and the like remains my own.

I am grateful to the library of the Cowles Foundation for Research in Economics at Yale University for granting me access to the archive of the original Cowles Commission. T. W. Anderson, Kenneth Arrow, Milton Friedman, Leonid Hurwicz, Lawrence Klein, Don Patinkin, and John Tukey were most obliging in permitting my use of some of their unpublished papers and memoranda kept there. The Yale University Library made available the following collections of unpublished manuscripts: the Chester Bowles papers, the Irving Fisher papers, the Walter Lippmann papers, and the James Harvey Rogers papers. The Rare Book and Manuscript Library of Columbia University allowed me to cite from the Henry L. Moore papers. Tjalling Koopmans and T. W. Anderson each graciously allowed me to ask them about their econometric work at the Cowles Commission but they are not responsible for the views set forth below.

Financial support to prepare the original manuscript was provided by a graduate fellowship from the National Science Foundation and Yale University teaching fellowships. The revisions leading to publication were greatly facilitated by a research grant from the University of Illinois at Chicago. The staff of the University of Illinois Office of Publication Services rendered invaluable assistance in this era of author-supplied camera ready copy.

But most importantly, I must also thank my wife, family, and friends, particularly Bernard Smith and William Sledge, for their steady confidence in me when it seemed most difficult to bring this project through to completion.

Roy J. Epstein

Chicago, Illinois
January 1987

CONTENTS

INTRODUCTION

In quantitative economics forecasts are made each year with confidence on the basis of new methods, old methods are abandoned
and presumably repudiated, but no systematic attempt is made to
appraise trends of method in terms of experience.[1]

Purpose of the Study

This book is a comparative historical study of econometrics as it developed after 1914. The topic has not previously been a focus of research for
historians of economic thought. Nor has it been examined in much detail
by practicing econometricians. My interest in the area was stimulated by
the intense debate among econometricians in recent years over the scientific foundations of current methodology.

I felt that these debates were extremely important yet difficult to evaluate. My own experiences as a participant in several large modeling projects
were no doubt typical for a practitioner in the 1970's in offering stark contrasts between conventional textbook econometrics and actual practice. It
was not difficult for me to question the scientific value of my work and—to
paint with a broad brush—the empirical literature in general. At the same
time, I was greatly impressed by the formal analysis of theoretical models
and the intellectual challenges they posed for statistical inference. I felt it
was imperative to rethink how one should "do" econometrics to restore a
greater measure of confidence in whatever results one might obtain.

In approaching this problem I chose to focus on structural models formulated as systems of simultaneous equations with exclusion restrictions.
Although they were the basis for my own training in econometrics, I actually knew little of the origin of such models, other than the usual footnotes
in textbooks that referred to work done in the 1940's by the Cowles Commission for Research in Economics. It seemed clear to me, however, that an
investigation along these lines might have several advantages. First, many
current writers have specifically attacked the economic validity of this
model so, while familiar, it still seemed deserving of scrutiny. Second, the
theoretical problems of equation specification have finally interested a large
number of econometricians in recent years and the simultaneous model
provides a clear and general framework for this kind of analysis. Third, I

suspected that the Cowles Commission itself must have addressed nearly the same kinds of methodological issues that concern modern investigators. The simultaneous model was open to a wider variety of conceptual problems than any single equation and I wondered how the Cowles researchers understood and defended their own work. The present contribution was undertaken in the belief that careful historical examination of the origins of structural estimation would help provide constructive insight into some of the principal points at issue today.

The idea of structural estimation also provided a unifying theme to study other periods and styles of econometrics. Earlier work by Moore, Schultz, Frisch, and Tinbergen culminated to a great extent in the simultaneous model, although I have also tried to preserve the individuality of these authors. Notwithstanding the famous objections of Keynes to econometrics, an active research group grew up in England after World War II that had a significantly different orientation that bears useful comparison to the Cowles program. And for the United States, at least, I found ample material for analysis in the reaction of later schools of econometricians to the legacy of the Cowles Commission.

Econometrics of course is a very broad field and I would like to make clear at the outset that this book is not intended as an exhaustive history of the subject. I wanted very much to illuminate the connections between the development of econometrics and debates over the formulation of actual economic policies. The reader will soon notice my emphasis on the history of methods in their application to macroeconomic problems, concentrating particularly on the debates over Keynesianism. This decision was influenced by the availability of source materials that permitted an interesting and detailed story to be reconstructed in this area. But one does have to begin with the microeconomic foundations, as it were, since the methodological difficulties connected with the estimation of demand and supply curves in the era before World War II significantly motivated the Cowles Commission and also other schools of research. Structural estimation is interpreted as a synthesizing methodology that only incompletely resolved the economic and statistical issues that impeded scientific consensus on solutions to policy problems.

Accordingly, this book is neither a chronology of statistical methods nor a conventional attempt at economic history.[2] I have tried to capture the central features of the intellectual arena (or perhaps marketplace, to use George Stigler's term) in which reality was mediated by econometric theory. My story has a variety of themes and sub-plots. Perhaps the reader, like me, will be moved to discover a sympathy with the idealism and aspirations, as well as the naiveté, of the early workers in this field.

The Setting of the Problem

The recurrent theme is the persistent gap between the theoretical and empirical achievements of structural estimation. This problem has caused this study to employ two rather different perspectives. They are discussed here to help guide the reader through the later arguments.

Empirical Experience

The founders of structural estimation had all been extremely optimistic about the usefulness of the econometric business cycle investigations by Tinbergen in the mid 1930's. This work was expected both to provide accurate general economic forecasts and to guide government policies intended to control the business cycle. Although many critics offered explanations for Tinbergen's lack of success in this period, the Cowles group was convinced that his approach was sound and only needed reformulation to avoid what they recognized as simultaneity bias and the identification problem. They held high hopes that similar aggregate linear difference equation models could be estimated to yield convincing scientific solutions to the difficult technical and political problems of devising actual economic policy. It also seemed plain to them that their methods would clear up familiar problems of interpretation of earlier demand studies.

Evidence is presented to suggest that the empirical work of the Cowles Commission between 1946 and 1952 was no better than Tinbergen's in accurately forecasting beyond the sample period. Furthermore, their often repeated goal of providing useful analyses of "structural change" seemed hopelessly out of reach. Ironically, they came to believe that many of the basic problems with their models were the ones that the other critics had emphasized in Tinbergen's results. They also felt the force of their own criticisms of poor identification and dubious exogeneity assumptions. These empirical problems seemed so overwhelming that the Commission believed it more worthwhile to devote their energies to other areas in mathematical economics, particularly activity analysis.

It is then suggested that this experience was relived by the next generation of applied econometricians. The argument presents evidence, however, that many of these later workers did not share the Cowles Commission's emphasis on exposing models to critical statistical tests to the greatest possible extent. As a result, they tended to foster an unfortunate illusion of empirical knowledge, the extent of which was never fully determined when the large macro models were jolted by the events of the 1970's. Even where the best statistical practices have been followed, however, it is argued that the present state of the science would still support only very modest claims for the stock of empirical results they have so far produced.

Estimation Theory

The narrative interweaves this theme of empirical disappointments with the remarkable successes in discovering the formal statistical properties of simultaneous equations models. The Cowles Commission solved the basic identification problem and derived an asymptotic theory for statistical tests. Memoranda are cited that indicate their future research program in econometric theory as of early 1947. It is shown how this program was abandoned by the Cowles staff but was largely brought to fruition by other researchers in the 1970's and 80's.

The discussion focuses on the contrast between these achievements and two broader, unsettled problems of econometric modeling. First, it traces debates over the economic meaning of the coefficients of the difference equations linking aggregate economic data. Second, it emphasizes the central problem of model selection, or "multiple hypotheses," with small samples of non-experimentally generated data. These were major objections raised by economists and mathematical statisticians in the 1940's against Tinbergen and the Cowles methodology. The argument throughout is that aggregate linear difference equations are a very limited model for the the purposes of many economic policies. It is also suggested that the model selection problem is as pressing now as two generations ago but has tended to be suppressed in published reports of empirical investigations.

Briefer attention is paid to errors in variables and factor analysis models in the comparative sections on other schools of econometric research.

Use of Original Source Material

Of special importance in a contribution to this methodological reassessment, this book has been able to draw on valuable but previously unknown manuscript material from the archives of the Cowles Commission stored at Yale University. These papers comprise unpublished research, internal memoranda, correspondence, and minutes of conferences from the years 1933–1954. They yield a candid and important background to the Commission's now classic official publications. The range of views recorded in these documents offers uniquely detailed and nuanced evidence for the intellectual history of structural estimation.

The comparative sections on English and Dutch research would have benefited if visits to those countries had been possible. For England, one would certainly like to explore surviving records of the Department of Applied Economics, Cambridge and also to research Keynes's role in econometrics more systematically. The Dutch Central Planning Bureau merits more attention than it has received here for its emphasis on central planning without heavy reliance on the methods of structural estimation. Indeed, the techniques of administration of direct planning in post-World War II Holland and Scandinavia could well be the subject of a separate investigation.

The virtual absence of secondary material on the history of econometrics makes this a very preliminary study that undoubtedly will be improved upon in later work. I confess at the outset to three important topics that receive almost no attention. The first is Bayesian methods. I have little to add to the purely methodological debates over them and, moreover, I have no evidence that they figured significantly in the macroeconomic models I discuss.[3] The second is time series techniques. My story really is oriented around structural estimation as an alternative. I suspect that current developments in the theory of time series ultimately will have a profound influence on our conception of econometrics but this lies outside my "sample period." The third is the influence of recent English econometricians, particularly Denis Sargan and David Hendry. This is a gap that fortunately has begun to be filled by the work of others.[4] In any case, it is hoped that the material uncovered here will prove a useful basis for future research.

Summary of Principal Recent Critiques

The attitudes of modern econometricians to structural estimation are well represented by the writings of five leading practitioners. They are briefly discussed here as a backdrop to the present work in increasing order of their conformity to the original Cowles approach. More references to these authorities and others are made throughout the following chapters.

The basic rejection of the Cowles Commission approach is evident in the work of Christopher Sims (1980a) and Clive Granger (1969). Sims doubts that identification of simultaneous behavioral equations in macroeconomics is practicable. Granger denies that economic relations are really governed by simultaneity. Both authors refuse to allow the concept of an exogenous variable into their work. Their models mimic time series methods "without pretending to have too much [prior economic] theory."[5] The principal difference with the Cowles approach is that by not stressing tests of economic hypotheses they also do not seem likely to develop a reliable theoretical base in the future. Perhaps as a corollary, these investigators do not emphasize that statistical inference in their work is highly contingent on the adequacy of asymptotic approximations to the true finite sample distributions of estimators in models with lagged dependent variables. They retain the use of linear difference equations, similar to Tinbergen's "final forms," but seem less concerned with problems of model selection in this framework than many other schools of econometricians. The approach tends to stress forecasting and prediction with little regard for changes in underlying economic structure.

A different strand of criticism is the work of Leamer (1978, 1983). Leamer is not opposed to the estimation of structural models but emphasizes the even greater problem of model selection compared to the single equation context. His "extended bounds analysis" finds the greatest variation in estimated parameters of interest obtainable from the different possible models with a given data set. He has advocated Bayesian methods in this context that are intriguing but seem to replace the selection problem with the choice of prior distributions. Leamer differs from the Cowles approach by not emphasizing the development of critical statistical tests to reduce the number of plausible competing models. His time series work demonstrates this strongly. Many of his most provocative examples of ambiguity in econometric inference are drawn from cross section models where fewer diagnostic tests are available.

A more traditional, though also ambivalent, position is represented by Hendry (1980). Hendry reflects the commitment of English econometricians to the primacy of hypothesis testing. He especially recognizes the often tenuous nature of exogeneity assumptions in solving identification problems. Like the Cowles researchers, however, he sees econometrics as valuable for examining the testable implications of economically interesting theories. With the benefit of the accumulated experience in estimating structural models, Hendry advocates extensions to nonlinear disequilibrium models using panel data. He approaches model selection by seeing if a favored hypothesis that is statistically significant is also capable of explaining competing results. This so-called "encompassing principle" is in large part a strategy for dealing with multicollinearity that tests the significance of the components of alternative structures that are orthogonal to the hypotheses of interest. Hendry's methodological position is well argued but it does not seem consistently evident in his applied work. He does not emphasize the lack of existing distribution theory for proper hypothesis testing with small samples. Moreover, he frequently remains with single equation linear difference equation models that employ transformations akin to principal components to eliminate collinearity in the sample. It is not always clear what economic theories are being tested with this procedure.

Malinvaud (1981) combines a certain ambivalence about the economic relevance of the simultaneous equations model with the highest standards of mathematical rigor in its application. He frankly acknowledges the tension in the field by asking "how the message sent by Cowles people to the world in 1950 stands today. Should it be replaced by a different one?"[6] Of the econometricians discussed here, Malinvaud retains the greatest interest in devising operational economic policies. Perhaps for this reason he, like the Cowles Commission, stresses the need for a priori assumptions to allow construction of multi-equation models with large numbers of variables but small data sets. He approaches model selection in the same spirit by testing the restrictions of a given specification as much as possible with existing distribution theory to map out their compatibility with the available data. These tests have objectively demonstrated to him the need for other kinds of structures, possibly using panel data to model disequilibrium effects, to generate forecasts and to guide effective intervention policies.

Outline of Following Chapters

Chapter 1 traces the origins of econometrics in the United States starting with Henry Moore and Henry Schultz, Holbrook Working, Elmer Working, and Sewall Wright. I then examine the somewhat later activities of Jan Tinbergen, Ragnar Frisch, and Tjalling Koopmans in Europe. This list is obviously short but I believe these figures are the most significant ones from a methodological point of view.

Chapter 2 is a discussion of the origins of "complete" systems of equations in the 1930's and the statistical problems that were suggested by them. I emphasize here what has been considerably de-emphasized in subsequent decades, namely, the central belief that economic policy should in some way change the fundamental economic structure of society. The first macro econometricians were far more concerned with introducing structural changes than in merely producing economic forecasts. Discovering existing structure was accordingly the highest priority on their agenda.

Chapter 3 puts these efforts in the context of the kinds of policy discussions then taking place in the United States. The econometricians felt their methods would not simply help guide Keynesian policies. In their view, structural estimation promised an objective and politically neutral means of resolving fundamental economic and social divisions that had become apparent in the aftermath of the New Deal and the trauma of the Second World War.

Chapter 4 is an account of the actual experience of the Cowles Commission in constructing models during the 1945–1952 period. Memoranda from the archive detail the practical obstacles of data and computation and also the more fundamental problems of identification and model selection. Fierce criticisms came not only from other economists (Friedman being probably the most steadfast opponent) but also from the most prominent statisticians of the day. Hopes for discovering structure and designing effective policies of structural change began to fade nearly continuously from the onset of empirical work. As a partial consequence, work in the associated statistical distribution theory nearly halted after 1948, with the result that two later generations of econometricians grew up largely satisfied with an asymptotic theory that the Cowles Commission itself viewed as very provisional. The second half of the chapter traces developments subsequent to the Cowles Commission, including the work of Lawrence Klein, Milton Friedman, and the Brookings project. The chapter closes with some observations on the general approach of the 1950's and 60's that emphasized the production of forecasts, while accepting the institutional framework and even downplaying the critical testing of the theories implied in the models.

Chapter 5 surveys concurrent econometric work that was not a product of the "structural estimation" movement. Research in England tended to shun estimating simultaneous equations models in general and macroeconomic models in particular in favor of testing single equation micro models of behavior such as consumer demand. English work also stressed research in distribution theory, statistical hypothesis testing, and time series methods that was largely complementary to the Cowles program.

The Dutch maintained a research effort in econometric theory but Tinbergen led a new movement after the Second World War that turned instead to the study of centralized economic planning that placed minimal reliance on advanced statistical techniques. In Sweden, Wold unceasingly opposed simultaneous equations on methodological grounds as being based on equilibrium notions and proposed instead the "causal chain" approach. In his most recent writings he has gone further and has abandoned both econometric and formal economic theory in constructing social models using the methods of factor analysis.

Chapter 6 discusses the more specialized problem of exogeneity in econometric models. This issue is at the root of many problems in interpreting econometric models: it is often not even clear what a given author means by the term. The chapter clarifies the different uses of the concept. It discusses in this connection a fundamental problem in establishing the a priori validity of an economic forecast. The last section discusses exogeneity and rational expectations, drawing on early Cowles Commission documents and concluding that rational expectations has been valuable in serving to refocus attention in econometrics on structure.

Chapter 7 also discusses a more specialized topic: the recent interest in vector autoregressions as an alternative to conventional "structural" models. The VAR constitutes a remarkable return to a model that antedates the research of the Cowles Commission. As is argued in some detail, the problems that have become manifest in much econometric work are not likely to be satisfactorily solved in this way.

Chapter 8 offers concluding comments on methodological trends and makes some suggestions for future research.

NOTES TO INTRODUCTION

[1]Jacob Viner to Jacob Marschak, 7 July 1947, Cowles Commission Archive, Yale University, (hereafter cited as CCA), folder: Cowles Commission Research programs.

[2]The *Handbook of Econometrics*, ed. Zvi Griliches and Michael Intriligator, 3 vols. (Amsterdam: North Holland, 1985) is the most authoritative source for information on purely statistical matters. A recent paper by Cooley and LeRoy (1985) also bears on some of the methodological issues I discuss below, particularly in chapters 6 and 7. Hildreth (1986) discusses the activities of the Cowles Commission from a somewhat different perspective. I do not know of a study besides the present one that attempts to study the historical development of econometric models in relation to broader economic policy.

[3]Zellner (1985) is an indefatigable proponent of Bayesian methods in econometrics. Hill (1986) and the accompanying replies refer to additional recent literature.

[4]See, in particular, the interview with Sargan by Phillips (1985) and the paper by Gilbert (1986).

[5]See, e.g., Sargent and Sims (1977).

[6]From Malinvaud (1983).

CHAPTER 1

THE DISCOVERY OF "HIGHER STATISTICS" IN
ECONOMIC RESEARCH

1.1 Background

The marginalist revolution in economic theory, which began in the 1860's with the work of Jevons, Walras, and Menger, was reaching a critical intellectual stage by the turn of the century. The neoclassical theory of value and distribution had been largely worked out but it had to confront pressing questions on two fronts. The most fundamental problem was whether its abstract claims for the efficiency and equity of a capitalist economy could be substantiated empirically. To be sure, the countries where capitalism was most highly developed experienced spectacular rates of growth of real output. But at the same time, these societies suffered from new economic and social evils that recalled 18th century fears that a free market state, far from tending towards equilibrium, would fly apart from conflicting internal forces. Downturns of the business cycle and mass unemployment, phenomena that dated only since the 1830's, usually occurred as spasmodic "panics" but depressions lasting nearly a decade were not unknown. Rapid industrialization also brought an enormous range of social problems that challenged the world view of classical liberalism.

The most serious attacks on marginalist theory came from the Socialists, who despite their differences were united in the belief that the private property relations that underlay capitalism and competitive markets had to be revolutionized. Alternative economic schools such as American Institutionalism, German Historicism, and the British Reform movement were not as theoretically cohesive as the neoclassicals, but they accorded far greater emphasis to "nonrational" psychologies of behavior, noneconomic market forces conditioned on historical factors, and imperfect markets. These critics, Commons and Veblen in the U.S. and the Webbs in England among the most well known, began to argue for a broad variety of market interventions and criticized neoclassical theorizing as too remote from reality.

The true extent of the influence of classical economics on actual 19th century policy problems is still debatable. At no time did the ideal of atomistic competition command general intellectual or political support, although economic arguments did contribute vitally to the triumph of such principles as free trade, the abolition of slavery, and the extension of suffrage and other rights. Over time, however, neoclassical economists had to vie more and more with the alternative schools on a quite different range of issues that very often amounted to calls for renewed involvement of the state in economic affairs. As they started to develop an analytical framework for reform, epitomized by Pigou's treatment of externalities, it became apparent that carrying out actual policies required the quantification of basic concepts such as elasticity of demand and marginal cost.[1]

The style of most marginalists, however, was not very empirical. The mathematical work of Walras and Pareto grounded the central neoclassical premise of the optimality of competition but used arguments that seemed beyond empirical test. Even the English, so demanding of experimental proof of key propositions in other fields of science, doubted that the theory of demand could be convincingly applied to estimate actual curves. Marshall and Edgeworth believed that the ceteris paribus conditions necessary for the validity of partial equilibrium theory would not hold for actual data gathered outside a laboratory setting. Edgeworth was especially insistent that, since the prices of substitutes had to vary jointly with the quantities demanded of a good in question, any empirical curve would shift in an intractable manner. He went so far as to write, "It may be doubted whether Jevons's hope of constructing demand curves by statistics is capable of realization."[2] When academic economists such as Marshall, Jevons, and Menger became involved in policy debates they tended to concentrate on macroeconomic issues such as the currency system, where they could draw upon many years of actual experience to set up viable institutional frameworks. Effective empirical work in fact relied heavily on the skills of the historian and the jurist. Economic series were collected and plotted for trends but even at the turn of the century it was almost unknown to use such data to derive specific causal relationships. Indeed, few sets of data of any kind were available in the form of lengthy, accurate, or relevant time series. To the extent that neoclassical analysis, particularly in a more microeconomic context, was framed in terms of empirical marginal products, elasticities, and other parameters, a practical person had to wonder whether proposed reforms could be made quantitatively operational with a reliable determination of signs and magnitudes.

1.2 American Developments 1911–1930

1.2.1 *Henry Ludwell Moore*

Modern econometrics really began with an analysis of the labor market by the American Henry L. Moore (1911). His book aimed at a statistical verification of J. B. Clark's marginal productivity theory of wages in order to frame a policy towards unions and also to refute Socialist notions of labor exploitation. Such questions had been debated for years and were reaching a new level of urgency in the United States at that time with the growth of working class economic and social radicalism, epitomized by the activities of the Industrial Workers of the World (IWW) and other militant organizations. Moore attacked the subject zealously with the new theory of the "higher statistics" being developed in England by Pearson, Galton, Yule, and others. He was very proud of his facility with the then unfamiliar techniques of multiple correlation and contingency tables. With missionary conviction Moore set out to prove to the community of economists that complex mathematical theories could in fact be given substantive empirical content to yield concrete results for social policy.

This first bit of econometric research, however, was extremely crude compared to the detailed verbal arguments presented in a work like Marshall's *Principles*. Moore's greatest strength was a keen statistical intuition that was at its best in justifying simplifications of economic theory to bring it within range of his new methodological artillery. He specifically investigated relations between wages and (1) marginal productivity, (2) personal ability (related to Marshall's notion of the efficiency wage), (3) strikes, and (4) industrial concentration. His most important innovation, and the basis for much of his subsequent work, was to approximate the unobserved marginal changes in the real variables by expressing wages and output in terms of deviations from exponential trends. He generally worked with grouped data for computational simplicity but perhaps he also sensed that such averaging partially corrected for observation errors. These errors were certainly present due both to poor samples and to the lack of a price deflator for the available nominal data. For the case of the French mining industry, he found a significant positive correlation between wages and output after these transformations which he took as confirmation of Clark's theory. Suggestive as this was, Moore's often loose handling of formal theory could create its own share of confusion. For example, he insisted that a rising capital to labor ratio implied a rising share of labor, which is obviously not true in general.

Moore greatly admired work such as Pearson's (1900), which showed brilliantly how probability theory could be applied to many scientific problems. He required some courage to think that similar methods could resolve economic questions nearly as well, since Pearson usually had hundreds of observations obtained under stable laboratory conditions. But Moore did not shrink from drawing strong conclusions from his data. He contended, on the basis of a 6 cell contingency table analysis of 39 strikes, that strikes for higher wages were more likely to succeed when wages were below the trend of marginal productivity than if they were above. His broader point was that the proper role of a union was to promote efficiency in production and to protect workers from exploitation in Clark's sense (i.e. when the money wage is below the marginal revenue product). A spread in competitive wages was to be expected through his assumption that differential ability followed a probability distribution in the population of workers. Most importantly, Moore argued that his findings proved that the Socialists were misguided because:

> If a collectivist state is to have any degree of stability, the principles followed in the apportionment of labor and capital . . . must be the same as in the present industrial state.

> Concentration of industry is no ground for the socialization of industry but . . . illustrate[s] how the increasing welfare of the laborer is dependent upon the skillful management of large capital.[3]

Such conclusions indicated the scale of the questions Moore hoped to answer with the use of "higher statistics."

His next work (1914) was a remarkably ambitious study of the business cycle that had an enormous impact as the first attempt to derive demand curves using multiple regression. The level of economic and statistical sophistication presented in this book immediately set the methodological standard for later econometric practitioners. At the same time, perhaps because of his "outsider" empirical methods, Moore increasingly came to view himself as a kind of rebel in economic theory. His admiration for the neoclassical analysis of the labor market did not extend to the full model of general equilibrium. In a pragmatic, American style he argued instead that the "a priori" theory of demand in the form of simultaneous equations was "hopelessly remote from reality" and claimed that "imaginary theoretical difficulties are dispelled by solving real problems." Moreover, aiming his remarks at Edgeworth, Moore claimed that "for most of the problems of actual life, it is unnecessary to face the complex possible interrelation of phenomena contemplated in the theoretical treatment."[4] Moore saw no sense to theory as an end in itself but at the same time he recognized the a priori appeal of the general equilibrium concept. The question was whether additional, plausible economic assumptions could be made that would allow empirical work to go forward.

This work, too, was notable as a further empirical refutation of Socialist doctrine, and the problem was set up in the opening paragraphs:

> [When] each factor in production receives an augmenting income the mutual adjustment of interests in the production process is brought about in a natural way. The period of decline in the cycle presents a sharply contrasted aspect of industry. With the organization of capital and labor first unchanged, the amount of the product falls; each of the interested factors seeks at least to retain its absolute share of product; friction and strife ensue with a threatening of the disruption of industry.[5]

In reading this one has to think of the context of industrial relations in the United States during the first decade of this century, with three sharp recessions and a remarkably wide spectrum of militant labor ideologies. If the Socialists attributed the "friction and strife" of the business cycle to flaws within capitalism as such, Moore's explanation located the source of the cycle completely outside the economic system. Nature itself, with a cyclically changing climate, caused the fluctuating crop yields which in turn influenced total output. Its key economic implication was that the cycle is driven by exogenous real supply shocks but is independent of systemic factors. These shocks would determine agricultural prices via the demand functions and so affect the rest of the economy.

Theories of this sort were first put forth by Jevons and they were certainly plausible when agriculture was the largest sector in the economy. But no doubt the analysis was heavily influenced by the fact that data available for a sufficient number of years for correlation analysis were limited largely to meteorological records and agricultural reports. The modern system of national accounts did not begin to take shape in the United States for another decade. If one wished to construct statistically testable economic theories, the choice of raw materials would clearly affect the final product. In fact, one of Marshall's main objections to Moore was that "nearly a half of the whole *operative* economic causes have refused as yet to be tabulated statistically."[6] Moore continued to work on weather based cycles for many years but it was the analysis of demand that most captured the imaginations of his followers.

It is interesting to note that Moore also used time series methods in conjunction with multiple correlation. His modeling strategy was based on the belief that supply, at least for his agricultural commodities, was primarily determined by the summer rain. Moreover, he assumed that the entire crop had to be brought to market (with any storage function per-

formed off the farm), so that supply equaled production and was independent of current period harvest price. Making supply a function of rainfall,
Moore used Fourier and periodogram analysis (in effect finding the transfer
function) to uncover damped cycles of 8 and 33 years in farm output. No
economic structure for supply had to be specified.

It was well understood at the time that completely static supply and
demand curves would result in only a single observation of price and
quantity. Although he did not say so directly, it seems evident that Moore
assumed the exogenous changes in supply would trace out the demand
curve. He fully recognized, however, that certain refinements were necessary before the estimation of demand became possible from the published
data. At the very least, the demand curve was subject to shifts from cyclical
trends in the price level and quantity trends arising from population
growth. One could also assume a simple trend in demand due to changing
tastes. Moore wanted to reduce these "dynamic" shifting demand curves
to the static situation of a textbook diagram. His solution was to express the
data as percentage changes and to assume further that prices are observed
over a complete cycle. If the population grew smoothly along trend then
the transformation should make the curve relatively motionless in the
quantity dimension. Prices could behave more erratically but the average
location of the demand curve would still be well defined.[7]

These adjustments seemed to work quite well for Moore's chosen agri-
cultural commodities, in so far as plots of $\Delta P/P_{t-1}$ vs. $\Delta Q/Q_{t-1}$ clearly traced
out curves with a negative slope. His examples included corn, hay, oats,
and potatoes. There was a ready explanation for the unobserved supply
curves. Current period price, defined as the (post harvest) spot price on
December 1, would only affect supply through the acreage planted in
period $t + 1$. Since supply was not explicitly modeled, it was not necessary
to specify the exact mechanism that determined the expected future price.

It was then simple to regress the price term on quantity. Moore did not
explain why he always made price the dependent variable and, as discussed below, the implications of this choice were quite important. One
supposes he was merely following the convention adopted by Marshall. In
any case, the functional form was determined by the plots. The annual data
for corn from 1867–1911 yielded:

$$\Delta P/P_{t-1} = 7.8 - 0.89 \Delta Q/Q_{t-1}$$

$$R^2 = 0.61, \qquad s = 16 \tag{1.1}$$

and, alternatively:

$$\Delta P/P_{t-1} = 1.6 - 1.1\Delta Q/Q_{t-1} + 0.02(\Delta Q/Q_{t-1})^2 - 0.0002(\Delta Q/Q_{t-1})^3$$

$$R^2 = 0.71, \quad s = 14 \tag{1.2}$$

Elasticity was then calculated as either $1/.89$ or $1/1.1$, with the latter preferred on grounds of a better fit. Graphs of predicted prices appeared to follow actual prices closely, although standard errors were not computed to evaluate the significance of individual regression coefficients.[8]

This was a genuine triumph for Moore, who by this time was suffering considerable intellectual isolation from his fellow economists. The simple idea of using data in percentage change form suddenly made it much more plausible to apply multiple correlation to textbook theory. Moore termed this the "link-relative" method. He soon developed a more elaborate correction called the "trend ratio," where each variable was measured as a percentage deviation from a polynomial trend, which sometimes yielded superior results.[9] Skeptics of course would repeat Edgeworth's contention that these demand curves were surprisingly simple given the underlying economic theory. By concentrating on major agricultural products Moore seemed to have found goods for which income and substitution effects were either relatively small, or had been eliminated through the transformation. But the special structure of supply could still make it difficult to use the same analysis for other markets.

The first objection could of course be met by including more terms in the equation. One can speculate that Moore attempted this and found that cross-price elasticities were small, as might be expected for goods such as hay and potatoes.[10] He only asserted that the fit would not be improved as part of his polemic against estimating a complete general equilibrium setup. Later on, Moore (1926) returned to this problem and showed how estimation of cross-partial elasticities followed from his basic approach.

Concerning the second point, Moore achieved a certain notoriety by claiming to have discovered a positively sloped demand curve for producer goods, specifically pig-iron. His regression of price on quantity in this case was:

$$\Delta P/P_{t-1} = -4.48 + .5211\Delta Q/Q_{t-1} \tag{1.3}$$

He offered a weak rationalization for this result that turned out not to convince anyone, possibly not even himself. It has become part of the folklore of econometrics that Moore did not know that a shifting demand curve could trace out a static supply curve, a more obvious explanation that was made immediately by Philip Wright (1915) in a review of Moore's work. The sheer intensity of the effort to vindicate the project and the method seems a more likely reason for his odd interpretation. Moore was certainly aware, for example, that changes in income would shift the demand curve. But in the absence of any GNP series at that time (indeed, pig iron production itself was often used as a proxy for national income) he must have wanted to believe that the link-relatives were sufficient to eliminate this effect.[11] Nevertheless, this was an early sign that an important class of goods existed for which more sophisticated models than (1.1) were needed for a sensible interpretation of the price-quantity scatter.

By nature Moore had an extreme dislike of controversy which masked his anxiety over the hostile judgments towards him by leading figures in the profession. Already in 1912, as the demand studies were taking shape, Marshall wrote bluntly that "Moore is a nightmare to me."[12] At different times he was nearly mocked by Edgeworth, F. W. Taussig, and Paul Douglas.[13] The stress of defending new methods and apparent errors like the pig iron analysis led to his complete avoidance of professional meetings. He continued to publish actively but, save for J. B. Clark (whom he affectionately called "padre carissimo") and a few others, he did not care to associate further with academic economists.

During the 1920's Moore's interest turned to the supply problem but he attacked it in such a way as to leave his original analysis of demand unchanged, despite Wright's criticism. A methodology for estimating supply curves was desirable theoretically but it was also motivated by the practical goal of rigorously analyzing both the tariff and farm policy, two of the great issues of the day. Derivation of industry supply curves had also been a major problem for price controllers during World War I which they only imperfectly solved with the so-called "bulk line" method. Analysis of marginal cost via multiple correlation promised to shed light here as well.[14]

Moore continued to focus on the cyclical relation between climatic shocks and agricultural output but he now estimated the dependency of acreage on lagged price directly. He arrived at a typical result in his (1919) study of cotton farming:

$$\Delta Q/Q_{t-1} = 2.76 + .375\Delta P_{t-1}/P_{t-2} \qquad (1.4)$$

He made it clear that the lagged price was to be interpreted as the expected current price in the behavior of suppliers. The positive sign on the variable was taken as confirmation of the overall logic of the approach. His results naturally led to a model for joint determination of price and quantity. In the "moving equilibrium" presented in Moore (1925), the two variables grew in the first place along the secular trends fitted for the trend ratio. A second movement was a cycle that stemmed from the adjustment to a supply shock: the famous cobweb model. Moore intended this work to culminate in his own version of a general equilibrium model which, unlike the Walrasian conception, was supposed to have a clear and empirically verifiable form.

This first dynamic model in economics inspired an enormous literature in the following years. Moore's pride in this model was reminiscent of his 1914 work, particularly in his dislike for exceptional cases. Critics quickly pointed out that the cycles implied by the cobweb for many markets were extremely unrealistic. Not only could the periods be extremely long, it was frequently observed that the estimated demand and supply slopes implied *instability* and failure to regain equilibrium after a disturbance. Moreover, the assumption which determined price expectations was quite strong in that it implied a systematic error in the forecast. Suppliers assumed that prices above equilibrium would persist when the model clearly indicated that they should fall below equilibrium in the next period.[15] Moore did not respond to these points and soon retired from Columbia University in 1929 at the age of 60, citing poor health. He wrote no more on econometrics until his death in 1958.

The common view that Moore was ignorant of the consequences of shifting demand curves for estimating economic relations is too simple. It is more likely that he recognized the problem but was unable to find a general strategy to deal with it. Still, he thought in terms of an equilibrium market model and was consistent in focusing on markets where technological factors made supply relatively independent of current period price. No method other than lags was available to allow estimation of two different curves, demand and supply, from the same data. But it soon became apparent that many market structures involved simultaneity in an essential way and that Moore's methods were not always reliable tools to solve the problems of interest.

1.2.2 *Choice of Regression: Henry Schultz and Holbrook Working*

One of Moore's most devoted undergraduate students was Henry Schultz, who in October 1922 was a 24 year old statistician with the Institute of Economics in Washington, D.C. (now the Brookings Institution). Schultz came into conflict with the Director, Harold Moulton, over the Institute's many analyses of the tariff. He declared the work of his colleagues to employ "utterly fallacious methods . . . in testing the effect of the tariff on prices."[16] Schultz saw this problem as a natural one for the application of Moore's methods of estimating demand and supply curves. Empirical elasticities could be substituted into Pigou's well known theoretical results to yield operational predictions of tariff-induced price changes.

This was not an easy time for Schultz. He was putting most of his efforts into an analysis of the sugar market that was intended both to refine Moore's procedures and to supplant the "institutionalist" studies of other applied economists. His more senior colleagues, including the same Philip Wright who critiqued Moore in 1915, criticized this project quite severely, doubting that the complexity of the sugar market could be satisfactorily summarized by a regression in two variables. Institutionalists, almost by definition, were preoccupied with many forces other than price and quantity in the analysis of market outcomes. Schultz, like Moore, knowingly relegated all such factors to the error term in so far as they were not eliminated by taking trend ratios. It is doubtful, however, that either he or his critics recognized the possibility of a bias in his estimated coefficients. The major methodological problem from Schultz's point of view was that one could obtain strikingly different demand elasticities by regressing quantity on price, rather than price on quantity as Moore had done.

For example, using Moore's own data for corn in the 1914 study one finds:

$$\Delta Q/Q_{t-1} = 7.2 - 0.70\Delta P/P_{t-1}$$

$$R^2 = 0.61, \quad s = 14 \tag{1.5}$$

and, alternatively:

$$\Delta Q/Q_{t-1} = 0.8 - 0.67\Delta P/P + 0.02(\Delta P/P_{t-1})^2 - 0.0002(\Delta P/P_{t-1})^3$$

$$R^2 = 0.79, \quad s = 11. \tag{1.6}$$

so that elasticity appears to be about 30 percent less than the earlier estimates from (1.1). The ambiguity arising from this problem was a statistical phenomenon which varied inversely with the overall fit of the regression. For an R^2 on the order of 0.60, quite common in these studies, estimated coefficients could indicate both elastic and inelastic demand.

This suddenly appeared to be an endemic problem with Moore's approach. Schultz discovered this "choice of regression" puzzle in an even more drastic form in the course of his critique of Lehfeldt (1914), who for a time rivalled Moore for influence in estimating demand elasticities. Lehfeldt actually used procedures very similar to Moore's to transform his data but he computed his estimates simply as σ_Q/σ_P, which equalled .6 for his data on wheat. The reasoning was that elasticity should be approximated by the ratio of the two obvious measures of percentage variability. Schultz readily saw the connection between this method and an estimate based on a bivariate regression. For the quantity regression, the OLS estimate equalled $r\sigma_Q/\sigma_P$, where r was the sample correlation coefficient. Otherwise the estimate would be $1/r(\sigma_Q/\sigma_P)$, as with Moore. In either case Lehfeldt's procedure was tantamount to assuming an r of unity, which was very far from the sample value of 0.44. But then Schultz found elasticity estimates of -1.4 and -.26, based on the quantity and price regressions, respectively.

Schultz's strategy was simply to choose the regression with the better fit as determined by a Pearsonian chi-square test. He considered Lehfeldt's estimate to be invalid, although he did not seem to realize that it is an exact convex combination of his own estimate, with respective weights $1/(r+1)$ and $r/(r+1)$. He wrote, "It seems to me that Lehfeldt does not derive *any* line."[17] One could imagine, however, that the Lehfeldt results might even be superior for being an average of Schultz's divergent estimates. Schultz appealed to Moore for support of his position but he must have been startled by Moore's reply that he had "never read nor seen Professor Lehfeldt's paper."[18] Fortunately, a new generation of economists was emerging to create a larger research community concerned with the use of "higher statistics."

The comments on Lehfeldt led to a correspondence with Holbrook Working, an exceedingly acute economist at the University of Minnesota whose own thinking on "the interpretation of a coefficient of regression in cases where the correlation is not perfect" was first stimulated by a reading of the same paper.[19] Working is hardly remembered as an econometrician but he appears to be Schultz's equal in terms of the originality of his contributions to the subject.

It was Working who first made Schultz aware of the errors in variables regression model. He articulated the two basic results that observation errors in the independent variable lead to downward biases in the coefficient estimate, and that omitted variables do not cause bias provided they are not correlated with the included explanatory variables. He summarized his conclusions as follows:

> If the low correlation between quantity and price of wheat is chiefly the result of inaccuracy in production statistics, the line of regression of quantity on price gives the best indication of the true demand curve. On the other hand, if the low correlation results chiefly from the effects of other factors, the influence of which has not been removed from the data, it may be that the *best approximation* to the true

demand curve which [sic] *lies between the two lines of regression.* This much at least is clear—we can not at present state the elasticity of demand for wheat with any great degree of accuracy.[20]

It is remarkable that neither Moore nor Schultz was aware of the errors in variables literature although they prided themselves on their mastery of many other areas of statistics. Schultz replied to Working that "What you have to say about the effects of errors on the relationship found to exist between two variables is certainly interesting and most instructive. . . . I hope to find proofs of the conclusions stated in your letter."[21] Schultz immediately experimented with orthogonal regressions in his sugar study and wrote to Moore that "the 'best' demand curve is obtained by making the sum of the squares of the *normal* deviations a minimum." One might think that Moore made no use of the errors in variable model in his early work because the theory was not developed for the non-linear case and his interest was in fitting high order polynomials. But in fact the approach was so unknown to him that he misunderstood Schultz to mean deviation from a trend, i.e. the trend ratio, rather than perpendicular distance. Schultz subsequently sent him a number of references, undoubtedly suggested by Working.[22]

Working (1925) expanded on the themes in his letter to Schultz to produce one of the most thoughtful papers on econometric methodology by an American writer in the interwar period. Drawing on his intimate knowledge of futures markets as a professor at Minnesota, Working re-explained (or defended) the estimation of demand curves with a fine sense of the economic interpretation of such work and its limits. He, too, focused on agricultural goods for which supply could be regarded as given over some interval. At this stage in the history of econometrics, no one could deal with what Working called the "marketplace equilibrium" of the textbooks because all estimation methods presupposed zero elasticity of supply in each period. Many actual markets clearly were not bound by this assumption. In particular, Working was interested in the behavior of futures traders, each of whom was essentially free to buy or sell any quantity each day. Working could only concede that "the demand and supply of the marketplace are probably rarely if ever subject to satisfactory measurement." The major shortcoming of existing work in his view was the failure in all cases to model the demand for speculative inventories separately from consumption:

Will not the time come ultimately when the best forecasts will be obtained by calculating the probable carry-over into the next period and from that . . . determining the probable consumption during the period under consideration and the price necessary to give that rate of consumption? This method of procedure at least has the merit of encouraging a more rigorous analysis of the causal relationships involved.[23]

This point was never followed up by Moore or Schultz and the rigorous analysis sought by Working was not worked out until Muth (1961) presented rational expectations to the world.[24]

Errors in variables was one explanation for why estimated demand curves would not pass through all the observed points exactly. This was very reasonable given the nature of the data at that time but one could also wonder if such errors plausibly accounted for the magnitudes of the residual variances. As discussed earlier, Moore had presumed that the scatter about the regression line resulted from cyclical trends in the overall price level which could be viewed as *shifts* in the demand function along that dimension only. Working imaginatively extended his own argument to cover these broader possibilities:

> [Errors in variables] fails to answer the question which will be raised most often by economists. Suppose the scattering of the observations is due not to errors in the determination of either prices or quantity, but to a shifting of the demand curve during the period under consideration?

That is to say, prices and quantities observed with complete accuracy would not necessarily lie on the theoretical demand curve. Generalizing Moore's argument, he suggested additional economic examples which could cause shifts in the curve in either dimension. He found this affected the choice of the dependent variable in a multiple correlation analysis in the same way as pure errors in variables, assuming the demand curve was otherwise well determined by a suitably shifting supply schedule. The "shifts" would be statistically identical to errors in causing displacements of the observed curve from the "true" position after correcting for secular trends. Working concluded for simplicity that one should regress on the variable that was subject to the greater "disturbing factors," whether shifts or errors, although the orthogonal regression estimates were preferable and would lie between the OLS results.

1.2.3 *Elmer Working and the "Marketplace Equilibrium"*

Elmer Working, a brother of Holbrook Working also at Minnesota, became most famous chiefly for an article (1927) which broke new ground as a theoretical analysis of the problem of estimating the "marketplace equilibrium" that was earlier deemed intractable. The article in most respects summarized what had been recognized by insightful economists at least since Moore. He used the pig iron analysis as his starting point and indicated diagrammatically how the equilibrium in each period depended on the relative deviations from trend of both supply and demand.

The new and important part of his analysis was to treat the disturbance as a component of the model that was fully as important as elasticity or any other parameter. Working concentrated on the economic notion of shifts without regard for the presumably solvable problems of observation errors. These shifts were viewed as resulting from omitted variables or nonlinearities in the problem under study. As discussed earlier, Holbrook Working had emphasized omitted variables as a source of bias when they were correlated with the regressors of a single equation demand function. By focusing on the statistical properties of the disturbance terms, Elmer Working saw the possibility of bias even when no such correlation seemed to exist. He posed the question of the effect of allowing supply shifts to be be correlated with the demand disturbances, considering that the "market equilibrium" had to be interpreted as the joint result of all factors that influenced the position of the two curves. This was a major conceptual advance since it was the first time in econometrics that correlations were seen as a special property of an equation *system*. The implication was that in the "marketplace equilibrium" separate equations could no longer be studied in isolation. His point was deceptively simple. In particular, he never imagined that bias could result even with zero correlations of the shifts. Working's own analysis was suggestive but incomplete and years would pass before economists began to appreciate fully the problems that it entailed for estimation and statistical inference.

It was easy to show that an uncritical regression of price on quantity or the reverse could in fact yield an approximation to demand or supply if the shifts were uncorrelated. Standard textbook graphs readily demonstrated that great relative variability of supply implied a good approximation to the demand curve and vice versa. With equal variability, price and quantity showed zero correlation. It is not clear whether Working used diagrammatic arguments because of expositional simplicity or because he did not know how to make his points in terms of the algebra of the model. Econometricians in that era were already under pressure from the journals to avoid complicated mathematics. This is an instance, however, where the lack of an analytical model seriously hampered the interpretation of results.

Working is usually credited with the discovery of the "simultaneity problem," but he specifically asserted the *absence* of any bias in estimating the slope of the curve which had lower variability, provided the disturbances in the two equations were statistically independent. However, a graph with equal variability of the shifts would clearly suggest that OLS estimates would be biased towards zero and one might expect that the OLS bias would be a decreasing function of this ratio. But Working (1927) wrote that:

> If the shifting of the supply curve is greater than the shifting of the demand curve . . . we may fit a curve which will have the elasticity of the demand curve that we *originally assumed*. [emphasis added]

No method of fitting was described and, in particular, it was not proved that OLS estimates would have this property.

Perhaps like his brother, Elmer Working thought in terms of a regression with errors in all variables which would be parameterized by the relative variability. The setup would be slightly different in that each curve would have only one composite shift parameter (instead of a disturbance along each dimension as explained by Holbrook Working). This argument would go through and the comparison to OLS would be identical to the example of Lehfeldt that was discussed above. But Working never published an explicit estimation procedure. Moreover, irrespective of the particular method one might use, a satisfactory solution would still have to show the precise connection between all the underlying parameters and the observed scatter. Working's diagrammatic approach was not well suited to show, for example, how the underlying elasticities affected his results. Needless to say, this problem was far from simple and it continues to absorb the energies of highly technical econometricians.

Working's deepest concern lay elsewhere. In his graphical examples he discovered an intrinsic bias in the case of correlated shifts whose magnitude could be substantial. Furthermore, it constituted an estimation problem that could not be solved merely by assuming that supply had zero price elasticity or that the variability ratio was known. The futures market, the purest case of a "marketplace equilibrium," again provided an economic logic for correlated shifts:

> In the case of the wheat market, for example, the effect of news that wheat which is grown in Kansas has been damaged by rust will cause a shift in both supply and demand schedules of traders in the grain markets.

This seemed to be a pervasive source of bias which could not be ruled out in any of the earlier agricultural studies. Working's diagrams suggested, however, that the bias would not be so great as to change the sign of the estimated elasticity. That is to say, if supply were more variable than demand then one would always find a downward sloping curve. For this reason he distinguished between the "true" demand curve of economic theory and the "statistical" demand curve which could be biased but still useful for forecasting.

The lack of an analytical model, however, completely blocked further progress. The diagrams could not even decide the possibility of unbiased estimation, much less provide an estimation procedure. Moreover, Working greatly weakened his impact on other researchers by leaving the impression that the biases would be smaller than the underlying elasticities. As discussed below, the theoretical questions posed by the "marketplace equilibrium" appeared too remote compared to the other major problems that were surfacing in the course of applied work.

All of the foregoing issues are clearly seen in Schultz's (1928) early study of the sugar market, where demand and supply issues are discussed in great detail. The treatment of supply actually makes this book more interesting in many respects than the giant treatise on demand published by Schultz (1938) ten years later. The sugar studies are the 1924 papers mentioned before as revised after the correspondence with Holbrook Working. The sections on demand were completely redone in light of the errors in variable argument. The bivariate orthogonal demand regressions consistently showed greatest agreement with least squares regressions of quantity on price, contrary to Moore's specification. Schultz concluded that the trend ratios and link relatives were sufficient to eliminate secular shifts but that the consumption data were subject to far greater measurement error than prices.

Under the combined influences of Moore and Holbrook Working, Schultz was satisfied that the negative slope of his orthogonal regression was an unbiased estimate of the elasticity of the "true" demand curve. He was still thinking in terms of the original agricultural model. Schultz made no reference to Elmer Working's critique although the original stimulus for it in all probability was the same work presented by Schultz at a meeting in 1924. One surmises that the Working bias worried Schultz much less than other problems he had to face in formulating his models. He was not quite as confident compared to his Washington years and defended the inconclusive nature of some of his results by agreeing with Lehfeldt that "the roughest attempt to measure a coefficient of elasticity would be better than none."[25]

The analysis of supply presented great difficulties. Schultz used the lagged price model only as a starting point since there were compelling economic questions about its applicability to the sugar market. Unlike corn and most other crops, a sugar harvest could be postponed by up to several months if plantation owners were unhappy with prevailing prices. Hence one faced the problem of the "marketplace equilibrium" immediately. Sugar was also nonperishable and subject to extensive carry-over. In sum, he allowed that "for such a commodity it may well be that price follows production or that changes in price are synchronous with changes in production." He included a masterful discussion of the critical factors in the world sugar market that made it seem audacious to estimate any supply curve, given the complex economic relationships and data that were either limited (11 annual observations!), inaccurate, or even non-existent.

His strategy was to embark upon a basically heuristic search for positive correlations between price and production. For some markets he uncovered a synchronous correlation; for others the lagged price seemed best. Once a suitable correlation was found, the orthogonal regression was computed to find the supply elasticity. But the problem became much more confusing when Schultz specified multiple regressions to find partial elasticities of supply "holding everything else constant," adopting the approach of Moore (1926). This was particularly disturbing because these regressions were supposed to make the ceteris paribus clause operational to meet Edgeworth's objections. This is really the most interesting part of his book because it laid bare a number of additional problems of methodology which were also related to the choice of variables issue.

The basic approach was simple. In estimating the elasticity of supply for domestic production Schultz wanted to hold output constant in the rest of the world. This, of course, was the beauty of multiple correlation. Using data for 1903–1913 he found:

$$y_1 = 1.54 + .37x_3 - .89x_w \tag{1.7}$$

where y_1 is price, x_3 is domestic output, and x_w is other world production, with all variables measured as contemporaneous link-relatives. Schultz assumed that the signs for x_3 and x_w necessarily indicated supply and demand responses, respectively. He apparently felt that the lack of data and a strong a priori theory of the market structure made it impossible to say anything more about the estimated coefficients. Hence the work was essentially empirical.

Greater trouble came in estimating the elasticity. Solving equation (1.7) yielded a value of $1/.37$ or 2.70. But the direct regression of x_3 on y_1 and x_w yielded:

$$x_3 = .72 + .54y_1 - .19x_w \tag{1.8}$$

with an elasticity of 0.54. The orthogonal regression resulted in a value of 7.56. Although the term multicollinearity had not not yet been coined,

Schultz recognized that a high sample correlation between x_3 and x_w with only 11 observations was a recipe for unreliable coefficient estimates in (1.7). With his interest focused on the response of domestic production to price, he fitted ordinary bivariate regressions to find residuals of y_1 and x_3 that were not correlated with x_w. The orthogonal regression with these residuals then produced his final elasticity estimate of 0.68. Of course, the closeness of this value to .54 in equation (1.8) would be expected if the model really was driven by observation errors in x_3 (and OLS on the residuals would have yielded .54 exactly). Schultz's unstated motive in much of this work was to show that the bivariate errors in variable model was the main corrective required for Moore's type of demand or supply study. Since the results seldom differed from OLS with quantity as the dependent variable, simple regression in this form became rehabilitated for his later work.

The question remains how important the Elmer Working critique would be in such a context. Equation (1.8) suggests that, holding x_w constant, domestic demand had greater variability than domestic supply, if disturbances were uncorrelated. Schultz was satisfied by the a priori plausibility of his last estimate that an adequate approximation to the true domestic supply curve must have been found. It is not easy to reconcile his result with the demand side, however, since current domestic output amounted to nearly one half of current consumption and there the regression on price yielded a *negative* sign. At this level of analysis one cannot rule out the Working bias as a major influence on the empirical results, possibly one large enough even to change estimated signs. Schultz might have doubted the importance of cross equation correlations on institutional grounds but he had no strategy to estimate them in any case. Moreover, it is not clear that Schultz ever recognized the full force of Working's critique. His own personal loyalty to Moore was so enormous that he never developed any idea that could be construed as impugning him. He never thought it was urgent in this or later work to analyze demand and supply as a simultaneous system. Despite his own results for sugar that indicated such relations, Schultz did not publish further studies of supply. One may speculate that he found this sort of problem intractable given the data and the economic theory available to him.

1.2.4 *Sewall Wright and the End of the American Era*

The decisive breakthrough to the first analytical model of the marketplace equilibrium was made under circumstances that unfortunately nullified its impact on the econometrics profession. It came in the form of an extremely obscure appendix to another Brookings study of the tariff by Philip Wright (1928), the first economist to criticize Moore for confounding supply and demand curves. Wright himself had never been sympathetic to econometrics and he personally had no knowledge at all of "higher statistics." The appendix was written by his son Sewall Wright, a brilliant geneticist at the University of Chicago who some years earlier had seen that a market equilibrium could be analyzed using the same model he had independently developed to study certain problems in heredity.[26] The arguments went to the heart of many fundamental problems of econometrics. Its central achievement was to present an operational procedure for Elmer Working's conjecture that multiple correlation analysis could estimate demand and supply curves from the same data if the shifts were uncorrelated. Moreover, it could even be extended to handle the consistent estimation of a system with correlated disturbances, which Working himself had not thought possible.

The appendix reads as a final comment on Schultz's methods in the sugar study after the debates in 1923 and a critical review (1929) by the elder Wright, although it is doubtful that the father actually understood the technique. Philip Wright was nearing the end of a long life as a politically oriented institutionalist and in the face of the poor quality of the data and the many qualifications necessary for a sensible economic interpretation of them, one wonders whether he felt the results were particularly worthwhile. After this time he had no further contacts with the econometricians. Sewall Wright and Schultz soon became acquainted on the Chicago faculty and they discussed the approach on many occasions. Wright felt that Schultz simply did not comprehend his work and it does not seem that he tried to attract the attention of other economists.[27] Schultz apparently had lost interest in empirical studies of supply and no other econometrician followed up on Wright's example.

The younger Wright called his method "path analysis." At bottom, it was motivated by the question of whether a set of variables had a causal structure that could be determined from a matrix of simple correlation coefficients. Path analysis generalized the idea that simple correlations need not imply causality but could merely indicate the common effect of a third variable. The "path coefficients" that constituted a hypothesized causal model were essentially identical to what are now called beta coefficients, i.e. the coefficients in a regression such as:

$$Y/\sigma_Y = \beta_1(X/\sigma_X) + \beta_2(Z/\sigma_Z) \tag{1.9}$$

where each variable is scaled by its standard deviation. As is well known, such coefficients directly show the proportion of the explained variance due to each term in the equation. The network of paths that connected right hand side variables to left hand side variables in a large system clearly was not uniquely determined by the data but depended on prior notions about causal relations. On the other hand, once a structure of interest was been chosen, the estimation procedure would reveal the causal basis for the correlation matrix.

It is remarkable that Sewall Wright apparently was the first person to picture the market equilibrium in terms of what was later called the reduced form. Path analysis suggested this directly. In the appendix he simply wrote down two equations that represented the effects of demand and supply shifts on equilibrium price and output:

$$P = p_1 D\sigma_P/\sigma_D + p_2 S\sigma_P/\sigma_S \tag{1.10}$$

$$Q = q_1 D\sigma_Q/\sigma_D + q_2 S\sigma_Q/\sigma_S \tag{1.11}$$

The variables D and S stood for the shifts in the respective curves after transforming P and Q to trend ratios. Their existence was simply assumed as an economic fact stemming from the summation of a large number of omitted variables. Although Wright did not formally derive the path structure from the original demand and supply functions, he saw a clear correspondence heuristically.

It was straightforward to determine the two curves, provided one assumed constant elasticities. Demand elasticity was defined as Q/P with D equal to zero, i.e. it was the ratio of percentage changes with a hypothetically unshifting demand curve, which yielded $q_2/p_2\sigma_Q/\sigma_P$. Similarly, supply elasticity was found to be $q_1/p_1\sigma_Q/\sigma_P$. The path coefficients indicated the proportional responses of P and Q to the two kinds of shocks to the system.

The problem, of course, was that these regressions could not be estimated because D and S were not observable. Wright understood this setup as a system of two equations in the four unknown path coefficients p_1, p_2, q_1, and q_2 (the variances σ_Q^2 and σ_P^2 were directly estimable from the data). His key insight, like Elmer Working's, was to think of a model in purely statistical terms. To make the number of equations equal to the number of unknowns, Wright assumed he could find two "external variables" A and B with special properties. Variable A was assumed to be correlated with D but uncorrelated with S, while the reverse held true for B. D and S were assumed to be independently distributed, as were A and B. Hence in some sense A "caused" D and B "caused" S. It was clear that the assumptions that generated the solution were not themselves subject to test, but expert knowledge of the markets involved could at least suggest plausible structures and "external variables." The solution presented in the appendix followed directly:

> Now by the principles of path coefficients we have $r_{AP} = p_1 d$ and $r_{AQ} = q_1 d$ and hence $q_1/p_1 = r_{AQ}/r_{AP}$ and $\eta = r_{AQ}\sigma_Q/r_{AP}\sigma_P$. Similarly, $\gamma = r_{BQ}/r_{BP}\sigma_Q/\sigma_P$.

In his notation, "d" was the path coefficient between A and D, r was a sample correlation, η was the estimated elasticity of demand, and γ was the corresponding elasticity of supply.

Wright (1934) later refined the method to allow more general solutions. In particular, he found that the assumption r_{DS} equals zero meant the system could be completed with only one external variable.[28] The additional factor was needed only if shifts were correlated. He recommended the use of several factors of each type A and B when available, and experimented with different averaging procedures to combine the resulting range of estimates. But very commonly, in other examples drawn from outside economics, a complex model actually had *more* shifts than external factors so that no purely data based solution was possible. In such cases the investigator usually could obtain expressions to solve for the parameters by *assuming* plausible values for some of the unknowns. Hence Wright independently developed estimation procedures for what were later understood as overidentified and underidentified models.

It should be understood that questions of distribution theory for the different estimators were seldom raised in this early period of econometrics. The standard errors of coefficients were not often presented and the estimation procedures were justified at best by heuristic demonstrations of consistency. Analytical methods based on the study of sample likelihood functions were hardly known outside a small circle of mathematical statisticians at the time. Wright himself was not satisfied with econometrics because endemic small sample sizes made asymptotic significance tests questionable. He made a careful reading of Fisher (1925), the standard reference on maximum likelihood methods, and concluded that it was primarily a theory for inference in small samples, but one which was still not satisfactory for economics because the broader problem of evaluating many hypotheses with the same set of data was nearly intractable.[29]

Nonetheless, it is interesting to observe that an asymptotic view of path coefficients could also help to clarify the Lehfeldt "choice of regression" debate discussed earlier. Using (1.10) and (1.11) it is easy to show that:

$$p_2 = (r_{PS} - r_{SD}r_{DP}) / (1 - r_{DS}^2)$$
$$q_2 = (r_{QS} - r_{SD}r_{DP}) / (1 - r_{DS}^2) \qquad (1.12)$$

Now assume for simplicity that the shifts are uncorrelated so that r_{SD} equals zero. The elasticity of demand then is:

$$\eta = q_2/p_2 \sigma_Q/\sigma_P$$
$$= r_{QS}/r_{PS} \sigma_Q/\sigma_P \qquad (1.13)$$

Lehfeldt effectively assumed that r_{QS}/r_{PS} was unity so that a supply shock would affect P and Q equally. Schultz's regression of quantity on price set elasticity to:

$$\eta = r_{QP}\sigma_Q/\sigma_P \qquad (1.14)$$

which can be rewritten as:

$$(p_1q_1 + p_2q_2)\sigma_Q/\sigma_P$$

or

$$(r_{QD}r_{PD} + r_{QS}/r_{PS}r_{PS}^2)\sigma_Q/\sigma_P \qquad (1.15)$$

Compared to the path coefficients estimate, it follows that Schultz's method is biased towards zero if $r_{QD}r_{PD}$ has a positive sign, as seems reasonable.[30] Schultz's reverse regression would then be biased upwards in absolute value, and his empirical results cited earlier seem to support this deduction.

Wright's brief paper was a striking synthesis of econometric thought up to that time outside of the errors in variable school. Economists ever since Moore had wondered how to construct supply and demand curves from the same set of data. Moore had proposed the lagged price model but this entailed highly restrictive economic assumptions. Elmer Working was certain only that one curve could be estimated for the "marketplace equilibrium," leaving it unclear how to handle the curve which shifted more. Wright's procedure embodied the crucial idea that the unbiased estimation of a *system* of equations could be accomplished by combining information from all the constituent equations simultaneously. It prefigured the entire later development of instrumental variables methods that became standard practice for most applied researchers.[31]

Despite its conceptual appeal, Wright's work had no impact on econometrics. The examples presented in Wright (1934) were ingenious but almost anticlimactic. They only strengthed Moore's approach for the long-studied agricultural cases of hogs and potatoes.[32] Estimated demand elasticities were -0.944 and -0.815, respectively. Supply elasticities were very small, 0.133 and 0.034, confirming the standard view that current price was not critical in determining current output. Wright's work marked the culmination of almost two decades of progress in econometrics in the United States. Although his method was the most general formulation of the statistical problem first attacked by Moore, one may speculate that the impact of the depression and the vogue of monopolistic competition by 1930 had made most economists too sceptical of the neoclassical theory of supply to use it as a basis for much empirical work. Schultz, the leading American econometrician until his tragic death in an automobile accident in 1938, saw the real challenge as building the Hicks-Slutsky restrictions on consumer behavior into new empirical models of demand. Theoretical econometrics in America had reached a pause.

1.3 Stirrings in Europe

In the late 1920's a small group of young researchers in Europe highly trained in mathematics began to focus their energies on the econometric problems first analyzed in the United States. The leading figures among them were Jan Tinbergen in Holland and Ragnar Frisch in Norway, both men of tremendous energy and confidence. Each attracted a large following of students who no longer doubted the potential of econometrics to answer an extremely broad range of empirical economic questions. The empirical work was most important, however, for further emphasizing underlying questions of methodology. In the few years before World War II, the Europeans greatly clarified the peculiar nature of econometric inference that established it as a new intellectual endeavor between economics and mathematical statistics.

1.3.1 Jan Tinbergen

Tinbergen specialized in applied studies of Dutch overseas trade in such items as potato meal and ships, and of services such as ocean transport. In an interesting contrast to Moore, Tinbergen saw econometrics as the tool that would make possible effective intervention in the economy to carry out a Socialist program.[33] His interest was in determining the competitive position of Holland through an analysis of demand and supply elasticities, export propensities, and the cross elasticities of foreign goods. This early work led to a critique of Moore's model of supply because the simple cobweb generated unrealistic cyclical behavior. But it is also notable for the first formal, though extremely limited, discussion of the statistical identification of individual demand and supply equations.

Tinbergen (1930) appears to have been the first economist to derive a reduced form explicitly in terms of structural coefficients and what he called a "parameter with a known trend," i.e. a shift term. Unlike Elmer Working or Sewall Wright, Tinbergen did not see the shift as the result of numerous omitted variables. Instead, it represented the influence of a known outside force, an "exogenous variable" in later language, on the equilibrium of a system. In this, he was borrowing the model of a harmonic oscillator from physics as an alternative mechanism to explain observed cycles in the data. The implication was that supply and demand were exact relationships among the observables, with any lack of fit due to errors in variables or nonlinearities.

The potato meal model consisted of the following two equations, with all variables as deviations from mean:

$$Q = a_0 + a_1 P + a_2 A \qquad \textit{(supply)} \tag{1.16}$$

$$Q = n_0 + n_1 P + n_2 N \qquad \textit{(demand)} \tag{1.17}$$

where the shifts were N, the foreign potato harvest, and A, the lagged domestic meal production plus inventories. In view of the carry over, supply was interpreted as the amount sold, not produced. It was "easy to see," as Tinbergen put it, that the equilibrium was determined as:

$$P = (a_2 A - n_2 N)/(n_1 - a_1) \tag{1.18}$$

$$Q = n_0 + (n_1 a_2 A - n_2 a_1 N)/(n_1 - a_1) \tag{1.19}$$

and that the four structural parameters could be recovered from the four coefficients of this system.[34] It is doubtful that Tinbergen knew of the path coefficients model although he referred to at least one author, Hanau (1928), who cited Wright (1921).[35] His article in any case was the first demonstration that the marketplace equilibrium problem could in fact be solved by a combination of simple regressions that were not subject to the Elmer Working bias. It also revealed the necessary condition for the estimation of n_1, for example, that a_2 be non-zero and that A not appear in the demand equation. Of course, this was just a restatement of the fact that the supply curve had to shift in order to trace out the demand curve. This was the principle for the later concept of identification through exclusion restrictions.

The assumption of exact structural relationships, however, obscured a fundamental issue. After demonstrating the logic of estimating (1.18) and (1.19), Tinbergen went on to say:

> In this case one can also choose the direct way and attempt to model the fluctuations in q; once through those in P and A, whereby one finds a_1 and a_2; and again through those in P and N, to derive n_1 and n_2.[36]

That is, each equation that had a shift term allowed the other curve to be estimated by OLS after all!

Tinbergen did not explain his reasoning on this point. Both Elmer Working and Sewall Wright had specifically rejected the idea after suggesting that multiple correlation might still be used somehow to estimate the system correctly. It seems that by interpreting the shift as a single factor, instead of a host of omitted variables, Tinbergen thought that the regression (1.17) could measure the relationship between P and Q by holding the demand curve completely fixed by *controlling* for N. Uncontrolled changes in A would generate the P–Q demand correlation. The assumption of exact structural relationships meant that (1.17) and (1.19) should fit identically well and that both should be equivalent to:

$$Q = n_0 + n_1(n_0\text{-}a_0)/(a_1\text{-}n_1) + n_1n_2/(a_1\text{-}n_1)N + n_2N -$$

$$n_1a_2/(a_1\text{-}n_1)A \tag{1.20}$$

where (1.18) is substituted into (1.17). Only when a_2 was zero, implying the absence of a shift term for supply, would the direct regression (1.17) fail because (1.18) in this case shows perfect collinearity between P and N. The parallel argument could also be made for estimating a_1.

Algebra ultimately may have been the compelling factor that led Tinbergen to downplay the significance of the new approach. As soon as a model contained more than one external factor per equation, e.g. income, prices of substitutes, or factor input prices, the coefficients in (1.18) and (1.19) would comprise a system in more equations than unknowns, so that his method could not yield a unique solution.[37] The direct regressions avoided this problem. Tinbergen's major concern would then be to include all the relevant factors in each equation and to explore different functional forms. The alternative estimation procedure appeared to be either equivalent or non-computable, with no advantages of its own. This entire chain of reasoning, however, depended critically on the interpretation of the shift.

It was not at all clear that the same arguments would go through using the notion of a shift as a random variable. Tinbergen's original training in classical physics, where errors in variables was the basis for most statistical work, seems to have been a decisive influence. The self-evident nature of his analysis could not be challenged on its own terms. Moreover, its relevance was reinforced by the notorious inaccuracy of the published data and the use of obviously imperfect proxy variables for unobservable factors such as product quality, "intensity of demand," and, even at this early date, expectations. The Working critique was still ten years away from transforming how economists imagined their own data were generated.

The empirical results, though, appeared to confirm Tinbergen's direct approach. With the 6 available annual observations, the structural estimates derived from (1.18) and (1.19) were:

$$Q = 87 - 6.9P - .86 N \quad \textit{(demand)}$$

$$Q = 87 + 12.2P + 1.22A \quad \textit{(supply)} \qquad (1.21)$$

The direct regressions yielded:

$$Q = 87 - 6.2P - .85N \quad \textit{(demand)}$$

$$Q = 87 + 11.2P + 1.18A \quad \textit{(supply)} \qquad (1.22)$$

This close agreement perhaps should have been considered a puzzle but Tinbergen, always a pragmatist, averaged them without further comment.

But he, too, soon lost interest in this line of research. Complicated estimation procedures did not seem to yield significantly different results. Moreover, as the Depression wore on the great econometric question again came to be the nature of the business cycle, as it had once preoccupied Henry Moore. Tinbergen was convinced that he had the proper statistical tools to study this problem. It remained only to specify an economically believable model with tractable mathematical properties. This project lasted almost as long as the Depression itself but its greatest effect, almost paradoxically, was to provoke a revolution in econometric methodology.

1.3.2 *Ragnar Frisch*

Ragnar Frisch was drawn into econometrics not so much out of interest in policy or economic reform but a curiosity to test empirically the fundamental postulates of neoclassical utility theory. He had little patience with economists less mathematically trained than himself and he gloried in exposing the errors of his intellectual competitors. His keen insights into econometric problems were expressed in a brusque but inventive style that added many words to the modern economic vocabulary, including the term "econometrics" itself. Through the 1920's he was engaged in a variety of studies using cross sectional family budget data to derive actual estimates of the marginal utility of income. He became more and more interested in the pure theoretical statistical issues that arose in this work. The key problem for him was what he called "multicollinearity" or "confluent variables," and by the early 1930's it absorbed his attention almost completely.

In his first essay on the topic, Frisch (1933a) claimed that because of multicollinearity "much work that has been done in multiple correlation both on prices and otherwise is meaningless."[38] The essay is most significant as the conclusive mathematical treatment of Working (1927). Frisch started with the same model:

$$x = \alpha p + u \quad \text{(demand)}$$

$$x = \beta p + v \quad \text{(supply)} \tag{1.23}$$

where u and v were unobservable random shifts. As previously discussed, this setup implied a system of 2 equations in the four unknowns α, β, σ_u^2/σ_v^2, and r_{uv}.

Frisch merely solved for α and β in terms of the relative volatility, the shift correlation, and the observable moments of x and p (m_{xx}, m_{pp}, and m_{xp}). The algebra was extremely cumbersome but he obtained the key result that OLS was a biased estimator and that the bias existed even with *uncorrelated* disturbances in the equations. An unbiased solution was available if the variability ratio (σ_u/σ_v) was known but the presence of square roots led to nonunique estimates. This problem was exactly analogous, however, to the standard errors in variables setup where one solution maximized and the other minimized the sum of the squared deviations.[39]

While he greatly clarified the original market equilibrium question, Frisch was interested in simultaneity for reasons other than the potential estimation bias. Like Tinbergen and Schultz, he believed at bottom that econometric models were standard regression problems which could be estimated by the usual techniques of the day. Frisch recognized a general phenomenon in the market equilibrium, however, which set econometrics essentially apart from other areas of statistics. His major treatise (1934) argued that most economic variables were in fact simultaneously interconnected in "confluent systems." In such systems the independent variables in a particular equation might not be capable of independent variation as in an experimental laboratory design. His main concern was the resulting possibility of what he called "fictitious determinateness created by random errors," or in later language, the problem of (nearly) unidentified models. This was a fundamental critique which was to in different forms at many later stages in the history of econometrics. But unlike many later writers, Frisch was quite confident that "fictitious determinateness" stemmed from overfitting the equations and that, in principle, meaningful results could always be obtained from the data.[40]

His analysis returned to the assumption of exact linear relationships. A regression was considered properly specified if it was "complete," meaning that it contained *all* the relevant variables and so did not contain an error term. This was the standard framework that explained residual variance in terms of measurement errors in the variables. Frisch's innovation was to extend the framework to encompass what he termed the "complete system," i.e. the total of n equations that presumably were needed to determine the n variables appearing in the equation of interest. He took pains to avoid mentioning the market equilibrium problem in order to emphasize his notion of a system as a general feature of *any* econometric model.

Frisch was able to demonstrate a bewildering variety of outcomes when variables were connected by more than one equation, i.e. "multilinearly." In the simplest example, let a variable x_0 be determined by economic theory as:

$$x_0 + a_1 x_1 + a_2 x_2 = Xa = 0 \qquad (1.24)$$

The 3 variables are linearly dependent and the necessary condition for a unique solution is that the rank of X be 2. But suppose that, unknown to the econometrician, x_1 is exactly determined as:

$$b_0 x_0 + x_1 + b_2 x_2 = 0 \qquad (1.25)$$

It was obvious to Frisch that in such a case it would not be possible to distinguish convex combinations of (1.24) and (1.25) from (1.24) by itself. Alternatively, viewing (1.25) as a constraint implies that the rank of X in (1.24) would be at most 1, again ruling out a unique solution.

Although Frisch acknowledged special cases that yielded structural estimates despite this general problem, he did not approach the estimation problem by imposing any restrictions on the coefficients of the system. At the same time, he specifically did not think that every variable was necessarily a function of every other. He noted that this was an "extreme . . . [where] all the regression coefficients, independently of each other, may now be put equal to any values we please."[41] The root problem was that in a great many cases, particularly outside the market equilibrium context, existing economic theory simply did not provide much guidance in specifying the equations. He adopted an essentially empirical strategy which he called the "bunch map analysis" to find structural estimates under such circumstances.

The details of constructing the bunch map have been well described elsewhere.[42] It was an illuminating kind of data analysis but by requiring the regressions of all permutations of all combinations of a given set of variables it entailed a crushing burden of arithmetic. Although it never came into widespread use for this reason, the idea itself was simple. The bunch map was intended to find all the sets of the variables of interest such that the addition of one more would indicate a failure of the rank condition mentioned above. In practice this was determined by estimating all permutations for every possible set, solving each regression for the dependent variable of interest, and evaluating the "spread in the various determinations of a given regression coefficient."[43] A sudden and extreme increase in the spread was taken as good evidence for a multilinear relationship in the given combination.

The bunch map of course could not be used blindly. The typically small number of available observations tested the skill of the econometrician in judging the significance of the differences in the coefficients in a map with a wide spread. Frisch apparently rejected the use of any conventional confidence tests in this task because the underlying distribution theory presupposed correct model specification. His own emphasis was on the process of what could be called "model discovery" due precisely to the lack of a priori economic theory.[44] He argued that:

> It is on purpose that I have not attempted to give any formal and rigorous definition of the "probability" for a specified result obtained from the different minimalizations. Such a formal definition may indeed be obtained by starting from many *different* types of abstract schemes. Each scheme will lead to a particular definition of the probability in question. . . .
>
> It is indeed only in a very special meaning that any such probability can be said to measure the "significance" of the results. . . .
>
> One [should rely on] intuitive judgment of whether a given spread in the various determinations of a given regression coefficient is reasonable or not.[45]

His scepticism regarding significance tests was reinforced by a sampling experiment which, for 100 observations on four multilinear variates, actually showed very *high* t ratios for all the estimated coefficients when the regression ideally should have indicated zero precision. The decision whether to include a new variable in a relationship of interest was made

heuristically, depending on the improvement in the fit and on the interpretability of the signs and the magnitudes of the estimated coefficients.

Such results would inevitably have a tentative character, although
Frisch's examples could be quite plausible. It must be pointed out in this
connection that Tjalling Koopmans (1937), who studied with Tinbergen
and Frisch, showed that Frisch's objections to standard significance tests
were based on two misunderstandings of the underlying theory as developed by R. A. Fisher. First, Koopmans argued that the failure of the rank
condition meant that the model was not identified so that the t ratios were
not properly defined. Second, he proved that the usual formula for the
variance of an estimated coefficient was incorrect when observation errors
affected the independent variables. Koopmans, who was the most mathematically gifted of the early econometricians, also continually stressed the
importance of serially independent residuals in a properly specified equation but this warning often failed to register on generations of future practitioners.

As it turned out, Frisch's own study of the potato market included in
(1934) suffered from an extraordinary degree of intercorrelation in the variables so that the assumption of multilinearity was not unreasonable. He
related price to a variety of "quality" measures including size, color, shape,
bruises, cuts, and scale (quantity data was unavailable). The best regression explained price as a function of size and color. The addition of any
other variable indicated near "multilinearity," presumably due to a second
relationship between the non-price factors. With interest focused on price,
it could be ignored. It was understood, however, that the estimated coefficients had an important but imprecise margin of error. Frisch, and more
particularly Koopmans (1937), then argued that this bias was unimportant
for pure forecasting purposes if the underlying model was stable.

There was a deeper problem in the interpretation of "complete systems"
which the bunch maps could not solve when there were two or more variables of interest and prior theory was weak. If one had good evidence of
multilinearity in a system of 4 variates, for example, and it was desired to
find 2 "structural" equations, there were 4 very different possible regressions:

$$x_1 = \alpha_{11}x_2 + \alpha_{12}x_3$$

$$x_1 = \alpha_{21}x_2 + \alpha_{22}x_4$$

$$x_1 = \alpha_{31}x_3 + \alpha_{32}x_4$$

$$x_2 = \alpha_{41}x_3 + \alpha_{42}x_4 \tag{1.26}$$

which could account for the observed dependencies. In general, of course, these coefficients would be related by linear transformations (as in the case of Tinbergen's potato meal model). But, especially outside the market equilibrium context, their economic meaning was a disturbingly open question. Econometricians had grown accustomed to thinking that an estimated coefficient unambiguously measured the response of one variable to the stimulus of another. Frisch's analysis of (1.24) suggested on the contrary that such coefficients need be no more than a statistical artifact with no underlying interpretation.

The gravity of this problem grew in Frisch's mind as business cycle models started to be developed during the 1930's for purposes of directing economic policy. Such models were founded on the idea that econometrics could go beyond mere prediction and actually uncover the underlying "structural parameters" of an economy which could then be altered to meet any policy objective. The aspirations of econometricians had changed dramatically since Henry Moore first attributed cycles to the weather and his followers saw sufficient complexity in the individual stories of potatoes, melons, hogs, and other agricultural markets. It became an article of faith among the growing number of European econometricians that knowledge of structure would soon bring the entire cycle under control. Frisch shared this vision but continued to wonder how such knowledge could be obtained empirically. The problem of "structural estimation" became the overriding concern of these researchers which, as will be shown, developed into increasingly intimate connections with macroeconomics and the history of economic policy for the next thirty years.

NOTES TO CHAPTER 1

[1]See, for example, A. C. Pigou, *Econometric Science in Relation to Practice* (London: MacMillan, 1908).

[2]*Palgrave's Dictionary of Political Economy*, 1910 ed., s.v. "Demand Curves," by Francis Y. Edgeworth.

[3]From Moore (1911), p. 191ff. For related discussion on these points see section 3.4.1 below.

[4]These quotations are from Moore (1914), pp. 81-86.

[5]From Moore (1914), p. 1.

[6]Marshall to Edgeworth, 5 June 1912, Henry L. Moore Papers, Rare Book and Manuscript Library, Columbia University (emphasis added).

[7]The general problem of the proper statistical analysis of non-stationary time-series recurs throughout the history of econometrics and it continues to pose significant theoretical research problems. See below, especially sections 1.3.2, 4.4.1, 5.2, and 7.5.

[8]Elasticity was estimated by assuming first that at the sample means ΔP and ΔQ both equal zero. Then the derivative of $\Delta P/P_{t-1}$ with respect to $\Delta Q/Q_{t-1}$ is just the coefficient in the regression equation and by definition is the reciprocal of elasticity. The neglect of standard errors was typical in this era, possibly because sample sizes were small and applied workers were not yet familiar with the t distribution that had been derived some years earlier.

[9]Regressions would be of the form $y/a(t) = x/b(t)$, where Moore fit a separate trend, usually cubic, for each variable.

[10]Since Moore conveniently published his data in an appendix, a modern reader can experiment with his results. Including the price of oats in the corn equation, for example, has the correct positive sign but negligible significance.

[11]The significant positive slope does in fact disappear when the regressor set contains GNP.

[12]Marshall to Edgeworth, 5 June 1912, Henry L. Moore Papers.

[13]These episodes are recounted in Norman J. Kaye, "The Pioneer Econometrics of Henry L. Moore" (PhD dissertation, University of Wisconsin, 1956). For another analysis of Moore's work see Stigler (1962).

[14]For a recent description of these controls see Hugh Rockoff, *Drastic Measures: A History of Price Controls in the United States* (New York: Cambridge, 1985). Also see section 3.2 below.

[15]See, e.g., Ricci (1930) and Schultz (1938).

[16]Schultz to Moore, 12 August 1924, Henry L. Moore Papers.

[17]Schultz to Holbrook Working, 31 July 1923, Henry L. Moore Papers (emphasis in original).

[18]Moore to Schultz, 2 January 1924, Henry L. Moore Papers.

[19]Working to Schultz, 23 July 1924, Henry L. Moore Papers. Working had completed a PhD dissertation in 1921 that estimated demand curves for potatoes.

[20]Ibid., (emphasis added). Working may have been influenced here by a reading of Corrado Gini, "Sull'interpolazione di una retta quando i valori delle variabile indipendente sono affetti da errori accidentali," *Metron*, 1 (1921), pp. 63-82.

[21]Schultz to Working, 31 July 1923, Henry L. Moore Papers.

[22]Schultz to Moore, 2 January 1924 (emphasis in original); Moore to Schultz, 23 January 1924; Schultz to Moore, 25 February 1925, all from Henry L. Moore Papers.

[23]From Holbrook Working (1925), p. 526.

[24]See section 6.4 below.

[25]From Schultz (1928), p. 216.

[26]See Sewall Wright (1921). Wright had in fact already applied his methods to develop a rather elaborate model of corn and hog production while at the U. S. Department of Agriculture during World War I, later published as Wright (1925).

[27]Wright (1984) discusses the origins and uses of his statistical work. Goldberger (1972) offers some insightful comments on Wright's influence on his peers at Chicago and sees his work as the forerunner of the

latent variable models that proliferated in the 1960's. See section 5.3.4 below.

[28]Multiplying (1.10) and (1.11) to find σ_{PQ} yielded one more equation and one less unknown.

[29]Wright relied on extensive experimentation in his genetic work to dispense with maximum likelihood methods. The laboratory data was precise and numerous: Wright raised over 100,000 guinea pigs in the course of his research.

[30]Since $r_{QS}/r_{PS} < 0$ and $0 < r_{PS}^2 < 1$.

[31]See section 6.3.1 below.

[32]In each case he assumed that the structural disturbances were uncorrelated. Lagged price was an instrument for potato supply. Lagged corn crop was an instrument for hog supply.

[33]A most illuminating interview with Tinbergen has been published by Magnus and Morgan (1987).

[34]This method was rediscovered in 1945 by M. A. Girschick as an alternative to maximum likelihood estimation for exactly identified models. See section 2.2.2 below.

[35]Tinbergen's formulation was somewhat less restrictive by not requiring the two parameters to be uncorrelated.

[36]From Tinbergen (1930), p. 671.

[37]One of the major achievements of the Cowles Commission in the 1940's was to derive an estimation procedure for such "overidentified" models. See section 2.2.2 below.

[38]Frisch's essay was a very thorough refutation of a statistical method proposed by Wassily Leontief for the estimation of the market equilibrium.

[39]The present case is actually somewhat more complicated. Manipulation of Frisch's results shows the two possible solutions for α will have different signs if (in his notation) $k > \alpha/(\alpha-2\beta)$. See Frisch (1933a), p. 13. A priori information on a will determine the correct choice. Only if k is less than this critical value will the answer be inherently ambiguous, unless more precise prior information is available concerning the magnitude of the unknown coefficient. Such "multiple identification" was not investigated further until the work of the Cowles Commission,

described in chapter 2.

[40]There is a vital connection between Frisch's notion of the "confluent system" and the recent concept of "cointegrated systems." For important discussions of the latter see Granger and Engle (1985) and Phillips and Durlauf (1986).

[41]From Frisch (1934), p. 73.

[42]See Malinvaud (1966).

[43]From Frisch (1934), p. 88.

[44]The most complete recent discussion of modeling in this context is Leamer (1978).

[45]From Frisch (1934), p. 88 (emphasis in original).

CHAPTER 2

THE EMERGENCE OF STRUCTURAL ESTIMATION

2.1 Background: Macrodynamics and Complete Systems

The first econometric models of an entire economy were developed by Jan Tinbergen during the Great Depression as a grand experiment in the application of regression methods to the host of competing theories of the business cycle. His most ambitious project, completed for the League of Nations in 1939, was a dramatic sign that a new generation of economists had come to view the business cycle as the proper object of government action.[1] Earlier doctrine overwhelmingly viewed "panics" as brief, more or less inevitable, readjustments in wages and prices made necessary by the natural growth of the economy, or by unsound or ill-timed monetary policies. If the slump in 1929 had reversed itself within 12 to 18 months it would have fit well into a the American pattern, for example, where downswings in real per capita output had marked nearly half of the 40 preceding years.[2] Previous crises had also been comparable in severity and international scope. The further collapse in 1931–1933, however, aroused unprecedented fears about the long-run viability of capitalist economies.

Mathematically oriented economists in the 1930's were highly excited about the possibilities of using linear differential and difference equations to simulate trend and cyclical movements of time-series, e.g. Frisch (1933b), Kalecki (1935), and Samuelson (1939).[3] Consequently "macrodynamics" (the term is due to Ragnar Frisch) was catapulted into a major field of academic study in its own right. Tinbergen's models were attempts to formulate "dynamic" theories of investment and output through the use of discrete difference equations with exogenous variables. The essence of his method was the estimation of the "complete" system, based on Frisch's algebraic principle that for a solution of a system of equations the number of equations must equal the number of "endogenous" variables. After estimating all the coefficients and supplying values for the exogenous variables, i.e. the ones determined outside the system of interest, the values of the endogenous variables for each period could be calculated directly. The econometricians expected that the use of multiple correlation analysis, or ordinary least squares, would revolutionize government response to economic fluctuations by indicating the precise quantitative responses needed to minimize cyclical variations around a basic trend of growth.

Tinbergen made extremely confident claims for the methodological approach of his study:

> The coefficients [of a dynamic system represent] the structure of society . . . [where] the coefficients may also be changed as a consequence of policy, and the problem of finding the best stabilizing policy would consist in finding such values for the coefficients as would damp down the movements [of the endogenous variables] as much as possible. *The outstanding importance of the numerical values of the coefficients may be clear from these few considerations.*[4]

The difference equation model inspired great hopes for implementing "structural changes" that would eliminate the different cycles that had come to be accepted as characteristic for modern times.[5] Of course, Tinbergen was not alone in conceiving of a sweeping change in the economic structure of society. One does not have to look as far as the spread of communism and fascism to recognize that conventional economists in the years after the First World War were less and less sanguine about the relevance or even desirability of a purely laissez faire system. In the United States, certainly, many economists who opposed the politicized and often contradictory policies of the New Deal were attracted by the apparent precision and logical consistency of macrodynamic theories.[6] But the study of policy as the modification of the parameters of an equation system was much too abstract to gain automatic acceptance when few econometricians were persuaded that even simple demand functions had reliable interpretations.

It must also be said that, although the estimated equations in the model seemed to fit the data very well (the R^2 generally exceeded 0.98), Tinbergen did not often indicate operational means by which policy could alter them. For example, the annual investment in producer durables in the United States was explained as:

$$V_t = .33(Z_t - Z_{t-1}) - .47(M_t + M_{t-1}) - .015(Q_t + Q_{t-1})$$

$$+ .06(P_t - .5L_t + P_{t-1} - .5L_{t-1}) + .63t \tag{2.1}$$

where the unlagged right-hand side variables were profits, share yields, price index of investment goods, margin between price index for finished goods and price index for wages, and a trend.[7]

Tinbergen did not emphasize the danger of spurious correlations when fitting so many different equations to the same data, but his procedures suggest that he was as concerned as Moore and Schultz by this problem. Econometrics had advanced considerably since the days when Schultz complained that the Brookings staff "could not see why the existence of a pronounced trend might lead to spurious results [in a study of stock market prices and interest rates]. . . . My suggestions were dismissed as 'too theoretical' and of no 'practical importance.'"[8] Tinbergen was also highly attuned to measurement errors in the data, as discussed earlier. To compensate partially for these problems he constructed all his variables using a variety of transformations including differences from nine year moving averages, trend ratios, and percentage deviations from sample means. This variety and complexity of trend removal stands in remarkable contrast to almost all later econometric work, which assumed trends to be linear or sometimes, rather arbitrarily, quadratic.[9]

The idea of changing certain coefficients or even replacing some equations completely through "structural" policies was a basic theme in this early work. For example, Tinbergen suggested that increasing the elasticity of wages with respect to employment would be an effective stabilization policy.[10] But the precise, quantitative links between the actual measures to bring this about, such as possible restrictions on unemployment benefits or curbs on union activity or freer immigration laws, and the magnitude of the estimated coefficients were by no means clear.[11] Tinbergen noted a further complication that since the equations at best only represented a kind of simplified average behavior for the entire economy:

> It is not sure beforehand that a change in one coefficient will leave all other coefficients as they are; some coefficients may be linked to others by relations into which we did not enquire.[12]

The mathematical tractability of the macrodynamic models led Tinbergen, Frisch, and other early researchers to pass over such puzzling methodological questions rather quickly. Tinbergen's policy discussions actually placed only secondary emphasis on "structural" interventions. The above equation, for example, appeared intended for predicting private investment under unchanged structure in order to plan a level of compensatory public works.

Even as a forecasting tool, however, there was a serious question regarding the extent to which the equations described relations that would remain valid beyond the sample period. Tinbergen's original assignment from the League of Nations had been to determine which of the many business cycle theories was empirically most plausible.[13] This was an impossible task in that most of them did not specify a usable complete system or required data that were not available. The model he eventually presented was not derived from a prior economic theory but rather defined his own theory based on an extensive interrogation of the data.

Tinbergen's work created a sensation within the economics profession. Complete macrodynamic systems were much more controversial than any of the demand studies promoted a decade earlier. Discussion of his particular results proved to be insignificant compared to the hot debates that commenced immediately over the conceptual foundations of the econometric approach itself. These debates hardly ended in 1939. The objections to Tinbergen's methodology were serious and have a history that relates closely to more recent discontent within the econometrics profession over similar basic problems of modeling.

2.1.1 Early Reaction to Complete Systems

Keynes (1939a) subjected this work to stringent criticism, likening it to alchemy, but his arguments had scant influence on the new econometricians. He was not unmindful of Tinbergen's (1940) rejoinder but in his final comments (1940) he felt his key point had not been answered:

> It will be remembered that the seventy translators of the Septuagint were shut up in seventy separate rooms with the Hebrew text and brought out with them, when they emerged, seventy identical translations. Would the same miracle be vouchsafed if seventy multiple correlators were shut up with the same statistical material?

Less well known is a review of Tinbergen's second volume by Milton Friedman (1940). His criticism also focused on the method of model selection when the estimation procedure repeatedly used the same data to discriminate among plausible competing theories. As a statistician, he questioned the true size of tests that could not make use of controlled experiments, as in a laboratory, or many fresh observations, as in astronomy:

> Tinbergen's results cannot be judged by ordinary tests of statistical significance. The reason is that the variables with which he winds up . . . have been selected after an extensive process of trial and error because they yield high coefficients of correlation. . . . [They are] tautological reformulations of selected economic data.
>
> The methods do not and cannot provide an empirically tested explanation of business cycle movements. His methods are entirely appropriate, however, for deriving tentative hypotheses. . . .

Friedman was no stranger to this kind of work, as evidenced by his participation in the consumer demand studies of Schultz (1938). At the time of this review he was associated with the NBER: this position was frequently restated as econometrics later developed in Chicago at the Cowles Commission for Economic Research.[14]

The model selection problem had already emerged as a critical issue when Tinbergen's fellow econometricians reviewed his work at a special conference held by the League of Nations in Cambridge, England in July 1938. The key argument was presented by Frisch in an unpublished memorandum titled "Statistical versus Theoretical Relations in Economic Macrodynamics." This paper reworked the themes of complete systems, confluency, and identification but it stressed new aspects that were peculiar to the difference equation context. Even more clearly than Keynes or Friedman, he understood the danger of obtaining "fictitious" results in econometrics. At the same time, however, Frisch remained optimistic that useful "limits or other sorts of information concerning the structural coefficients" could in fact be found.

Frisch (1938), like Keynes and Friedman, also began by stating that he did *"not* think that it [Tinbergen's book] can be looked upon as 'A Test of Business Cycle Theories'" and, accordingly, he focused on the the question of *"what equations of this type really mean."* He specified the general structural linear difference equation model as:

$$\Sigma\Sigma\Sigma\alpha_{ki\theta}x_i(t-\theta) = 0, \quad (k = 1, 2, \ldots) \qquad (2.2)$$

where k indexed the equations and the summation iθ runs through the lags for each variable. His analysis centered on what he termed the "reducibility" of the individual structural equations. It was a brilliant generalization of the identification problem that was the basis for all later development of order and rank conditions and the role of a priori information.

Frisch's first point was the observation made in his 1934 work that no equation could be estimated free from "arbitrariness" if it possibly was comprised of, or could be reduced to, a linear combination of other structural relations in a complete system (cf. equation 1.24). This statement of the order condition seemed so evident as to require little further comment. The great interest in dynamic properties led to a quite different consideration. Frisch assumed that in the absence of this first type of "reducibility" the system (2.2) could be estimated directly by the usual methods and solved to express each variable as the solution to an ordinary homogeneous difference equation. His new argument was that such a solution need not indicate cyclical behavior as complicated as that suggested by the original system. In effect, for certain parameter values it was possible for the net influence of a given lag in a structural equation to be zero, and this reduction would make the equation itself unobservable. Frisch's memorandum summarized the issue as follows:

> In a big system of structural equations it would be quite exceptional if all the equations should be irreducible. . . . Think of a case where the initial conditions are such that only one single component [e.g. in (2.2)] is left with an amplitude different from zero, while many of the structural equations contain a large number of terms.

> An equation which is irreducible . . . we shall call a *coflux* equation. The others will be called *superflux* equations.

> The notion of coflux relations is fundamental when we ask what sorts of equations it is possible to determine from the knowledge of the time shapes that are actually produced. *The answer is obviously that all coflux equations and no other equations are discoverable from the knowledge of the time shapes of the functions that form the actual solution* [to the system of difference equations]. (emphasis in original)

Frisch's criticism of Tinbergen linked the notion of reducibility to the overall lack of theory behind the model. Certain structural equations were likely to be reducible simply because of the difficulty of capturing presumably elaborate lag schemes with only 14 annual observations. But Frisch also insisted that most of the equations in any case were arrived at "in an empirical way" and that one still had to doubt that an observed coflux relation represented a true equation of the complete system. Purely empirical methods could not distinguish an irreducible system from "an infinity" of other ones derived from it by a non-singular transformation.[14] This was a fatal objection to regressions chosen merely on the basis of fit and signs of coefficients when the purpose was to devise policies of "structural change." Frisch introduced the concept of "autonomy" and made it the essence of his definition of a structural system:

> [The question is what] features of our structure are *in fact* the most autonomous in the sense that they could *be maintained unaltered while other features of the structure were changed.* . . .

> The higher this degree of autonomy, the more *fundamental* is the equation, the deeper is the insight which it gives us into the way in which the system functions, in short, the nearer it comes to being a *real relationship.* Such relations form the essence of "theory." (emphasis in original)

It hardly made sense to discuss policies of structural change unless an underlying economic theory could give some basis for the autonomy of estimated structural coefficients. Here Frisch could only emphasize that such a theory was lacking from most of Tinbergen's work but he did not think that multiple correlation methods were thereby invalidated. They could always be used for forecasting purposes when structure did not change. But in so far as the economy was determined by the natural or induced evolution of a complete structural system, Frisch saw good theory simply as a prerequisite for tenable applied work in econometrics.

Keynes's prestige and literary powers unquestionably were influential in some quarters but Frisch's memorandum proved far more compelling for the circle of young European econometricians. A specific rejoinder to Keynes's critique came from Tjalling Koopmans (1941), then at Princeton but once a colleague of Tinbergen and Frisch. He succeeded Tinbergen at the League of Nations where, until the outbreak of the War, he had been planning similar studies of business cycles in Great Britain.[15] The essay initially defends econometrics as a tool to falsify hypotheses and the argument seems quite similar to the one elaborated by Popper for natural sciences.[16] Indeed, Tinbergen's project was to falsify as many business cycle theories as possible and neither Keynes nor Friedman took issue with this goal.

Koopmans appeared to concede the main point of the two critics by admitting that "the fluctuations in one given variable may be [plausibly] reconstructed in more than one way." The methodology of "disproof" was not able to yield very many positive conclusions for the economic hypotheses tested with Tinbergen's data. Of course, the data used in economics are seldom the outcome of an experiment specifically designed to discriminate among competing hypotheses. Frisch had already made clear that a set of data generated by a complete system in general will support quite different explanations of a phenomenon equally well. The dilemma for economic policy based on the need to choose a particular model under these conditions is clear.

The same problem confronts all inductive sciences but experimentation or the collection of new masses of data helps to restrict the inevitable uncertainty about the true model. The limited applicability of these procedures for econometric business cycle research threatened to make Tinbergen's work sterile.[17] Koopmans, like Frisch, argued that the only solution was to supplement the data with "a priori information," premises that in effect eliminate certain (or most) hypotheses from consideration.

The primary form of such information was zero restrictions to yield a system of irreducible structural equations. Koopmans also detailed the traditional heuristic specification procedures that defined the art of econometrics. For example, when estimated coefficients did not have the expected signs and magnitudes it was "quite sound" to include new variables and/or lags. If the data showed breaks or curvature, Koopmans

rationalized the adjustment of the sample period and the use of nonlinear
terms including time varying parameters. As in the days of Moore and
Schultz, the trend term played a crucial role as a catch-all when only a
handful of other variables were included. One might also think it more
reasonable to interpret zero restrictions as approximations for effects that
are considered a priori to be "small." Koopmans merely stressed that *any*
econometric inference depended on the validity of such premises, which
presumably did not contradict the data actually observed. As for their
source, he wrote:

> The choice is logically free and . . . derives from the desire to give a maximum of
> scientific value to the conditional conclusions obtained.

Koopmans seemed most hopeful that econometrics would be useful for
predicting the likely effects of a particular policy action, e.g. the change in
employment due to deficit spending. He did not express confidence, in the
1941 article or later work, in the possibility of forecasting the actual values
of future endogenous variables. He sought instead to quantify the influence of options directly available to a policymaker for stabilization purposes. For this reason the values of the structural parameters for the policy
variables had special importance. It seems that part of the "scientific value"
that Koopmans had in mind would be the near constancy of such parameters irrespective of the other variables included in the model.[18]

This emphasis on the role of prior information led Koopmans to interpret Tinbergen very differently than Friedman or Keynes had done. Economic data alone often supported too many plausible alternative hypotheses. Moreover, the key estimated policy coefficients were different in each
model. Koopmans believed the investigator should report all results in
such cases since there would be no empirical basis to prefer one to another.
Since Tinbergen apparently estimated many other equations than the ones
that appeared in his book, one could justifiably wonder about the variables
and coefficients which did *not* appear. Another econometrician starting out
with his initial collection of results could not, by reading his book, follow
the reasoning that led to the ones finally published. Indeed, in his last
published views on econometrics, Koopmans (1979) chose to emphasize
this continuing deficiency in the scientific documentation of many empirical studies.[19]

On one crucial point, however, Koopmans had more in common with
the critics than with Tinbergen or Frisch. Both Keynes and Friedman
appeared to think that realistically useful models of the business cycle
would need to incorporate a very large number of variables in each equation.[20] Tinbergen's reliance on annual observations obviously limited the

size of possible regressions. This is the basic problem in econometrics of inadequate data, as opposed to poor data, by which is meant those suffering from collinearity or serious measurement error.[22] Koopmans (1937) had already rejected the assumption of exact relations in econometrics and argued that the residual variance was an inevitable consequence of omitting many, hopefully minor, variables from the complete system. It was obvious that the model specification was ultimately a judgment as to which factors were expected to be most important. After Frisch's analysis of reducibility, Koopmans believed the major problem for econometrics was to explore more fully the *statistical* problems of inference in systems containing random shocks.

At this stage Koopmans was mainly concerned with reforming the usual estimation procedures by explicitly adapting the maximum likelihood approach of R. A. Fisher (1925), which was rapidly becoming a standard for workers in other fields of experimental science. He emphasized much more than Frisch, for example, the premise of "small" serially independent residuals in a properly specified model.[23] Koopmans thought that Fisher's concept of sampling error was generally much more important than pure measurement errors in models with few degrees of freedom. The information in the sampling error was essential for critical interpretation of different structural hypotheses but, as has been shown repeatedly, earlier econometricians almost always ignored it by assuming in effect that estimators were equal to their probability limits. In particular, Koopmans was interested in discovering the exact distribution of estimators in a difference equation to arrive at a more precise understanding of the dynamic behavior of Tinbergen's model. The point was that the likelihood framework made possible an entirely new battery of critical tests that could extract more information from the data in deciding among competing hypotheses. Koopmans could agree with Friedman that the significance levels of such tests were unknown. But he retained the faith of Tinbergen and Frisch that their methods would surely lead to the discovery of a true macrodynamic structure.

2.1.2 *The Discovery of Statistical Simultaneity*

Other researchers besides Koopmans became interested in the statistical properties of Tinbergen's equations, assuming that such specifications represented a real stochastic process. The use of lagged dependent variables placed his equations outside the domain of least squares distribution theory, in which all explanatory variables are regarded as fixed in repeated trials. While estimated coefficients were seen to be consistent in single equations with uncorrelated errors, attention was focused on whether they were biased in small samples and whether the usual significance tests and confidence intervals based on the normal distribution were justified.

Trygve Haavelmo (1943), another of Frisch's students who had made a careful study of the 1938 memorandum, was the first econometrician to rediscover the Working bias as a general phenomenon in any "complete" system view as a set of stochastic equations. Haavelmo's discovery added a shocking new level of complexity to Tinbergen's work since no one had previously seen any real kinship between market models and macrodynamic models. The issue was not just one of statistics. The notion of stochastic regressors threatened to rehabilitate Edgeworth's critique that multiple correlation could not *in principle* embody the ceteris paribus conditions of economic theory.

Haavelmo took his example of the simultaneous equations bias directly from Frisch (1933a). Clearly alluding to the uncritical OLS estimation of familiar demand and supply curves, Haavelmo demonstrated its inconsistency in the two variable model:

$$Y = \alpha X + u \; (demand)$$

$$X = \beta Y + v \; (supply) \tag{2.3}$$

where u and v were serially independent, orthogonal errors and all variables were measured as deviations from means. This is the simplest example of a stochastic complete system, of course, and it shows that the problem becomes endemic as soon as one postulates that economic data are jointly determined by more than one equation. Like Koopmans, Haavelmo thought it was imperative to analyze the short series of actual data with the maximum likelihood machinery. In this sense, the problem was even worse than what Frisch had found because the inconsistency would be compounded by the clearly very difficult problem of the finite sample behavior of the estimators.[24]

The "Haavelmo bias" appeared to be of enormous importance for statistical inference. It re-opened all the debates of the 1920's that Tinbergen, Frisch, and others had considered anachronistic. Unlike the bias arising from errors in variables, where an approximate bound could often be deduced, the asymptotic bias in OLS due to simultaneity had no known a priori limits. It was possible to construct examples in which the inconsistency ranged from zero to orders of magnitude greater than the true coefficient.[25] One could not expect the macrodynamic systems to bear much similarity to the agricultural markets where, as Sewall Wright had demonstrated, simultaneity was not a severe problem in practice. Haavelmo stressed that these problems were peculiar to data that were not generated by a controlled experiment, which by design allowed just one endogenous variable.

As a statistician, Haavelmo was also aware of the need to establish the logical estimability of a parameter before attempting actually to estimate it. His article went on to make the even more crucial point that, under the assumption of normal errors, the above model contained 4 unknowns (α, β, σ_u^2, σ_v^2) but could only provide information about 3 parameters ($E(Y_t^2)$, $E(X_t^2)$, $E(Y_t X_t)$). Although the data could provide information on higher order moments in the non-normal case, the usual assumption of normality implied that no method of estimation could succeed in this model without additional identifying information.

Haavelmo left Norway for the United States following the outbreak of World War II and in 1941 was working in New York at the Norwegian Shipping and Trade Mission. He had already conceived the basis for the article just mentioned in a thesis completed at Harvard in April of that year, later published as Haavelmo (1944). In New York he joined forces with Jacob Marschak, a Russian-born mathematical economist then at the New School, with whom he had been acquainted at least since the 1938 conference at Cambridge. Marschak formed an "econometrics seminar" with Haavelmo in the fall of 1941 that attracted interested graduate students and instructors from the New School, Columbia, the NBER, and the then existing Institute of Applied Econometrics. Haavelmo's ideas were so clearly compelling that the seminar soon agreed that least squares had to be replaced by some other method for econometric work.[26]

The econometrics seminar was attended by Abraham Wald, a brilliant theoretical statistician who had had a long-standing interest in economics. A mathematician by training, Wald had worked on economic theory in the early 1930's with Karl Menger, Oskar Morgenstern, and John von Neumann in Vienna.[27] Soon after receiving an appointment at Columbia University, Wald and his colleague Henry Mann undertook to solve the problem of estimation of stationary linear stochastic difference equations in the most general terms, reportedly aiming at a "systematic or 'codifying' treatise."[28]

In Mann and Wald (1943) they showed that using OLS on a single equation yielded asymptotically unbiased coefficient estimates that followed a multivariate normal distribution under plausible assumptions. The model considered was:

$$x_t = \alpha_1 x_{t-1} + \alpha_2 x_{t-2} + \ldots + \alpha_p x_{t-p} + \epsilon_t \qquad (2.4)$$

where ϵ was independently and identically distributed (i.i.d.) with mean zero and finite moments of all orders, and the autoregressive process was stable. Normality of ϵ was not necessary. In this case, they stated, significance tests and confidence regions could be constructed "in the usual manner," although in finite samples the results were only approximate.

Their article also treated treated the general structural equation system of G equations in G variables, where the explanatory variables were both current and lagged. The model was:

$$A^{(0)}x_t + A^{(1)}x_{t-1} + \ldots + A^{(p)}x_{t-p} = \epsilon_t \qquad (2.5)$$

where x and ϵ were G component vectors, $E(\epsilon\epsilon') = \Sigma$, a positive definite matrix, and all elements of ϵ were serially independent with mean zero with finite moments up to the eighth order. The approach was to maximize the joint "pseudo-likelihood" function of the endogenous variables, i.e. the likelihood function assuming normality of the errors. Mann and Wald distinguished several cases. (1) $A^{(0)}$ the identity matrix and Σ diagonal. Then maximum likelihood was equivalent to OLS performed on each equation separately. Consistency and asymptotic normality followed from the result for single equations. (2) $A^{(0)}$ the identity matrix, Σ arbitrary positive definite. Then maximum likelihood estimates were again equivalent to OLS on the individual equations and consistent and asymptotically normal. (3) The general case of arbitrary non-singular $A^{(0)}$, arbitrary positive definite Σ. For this case a more detailed analysis was needed.

Mann and Wald immediately proved that without additional a priori information, consistent estimation of the structural equations in case (3) was impossible. In later language, the system was not identified. All that could be estimated was what they termed the reduced form, borrowing the language of Frisch.[29] The reduced form could be estimated consistently on the strength of the result (2).

Mann and Wald acknowledged the economic crudity of this last model. In the first place, by making all lag lengths equal to p the model would ignore restrictions on the structural equations and so would not estimate the reduced form efficiently. If one is interested only in prediction then this condition may be acceptable because "we decrease the efficiency of our statistical procedure but we gain in simplicity." It is hardly necessary to add that the estimation of large systems in this way quickly becomes impossible, let alone inefficient, with the number of observations usually available in economic time-series.

The two investigators proceeded to consider the case where it was known a priori that certain coefficients and error covariances were zero. In particular, they assumed that this knowledge allowed the structural coefficients to be derived uniquely from the reduced form (in later language, the model was exactly identified). They concentrated on the use of restrictions to identify the system for a deeper reason than just statistical efficiency. Reflecting Haavelmo's and Tinbergen's insistence on the importance of the determination of structure they wrote:

> The coefficients [of the structural equations] have immediate meaning in economic theory, while the coefficients [of the reduced form] derive their significance merely from the fact that they are certain functions of the [structural] coefficients.

One might add that the assumption of stationarity in the model, implying invariant autocovariance sequences, was not likely to be true after a structural change and it would be desirable to estimate the structure in order to test for its stability over the sample period. They concluded by finding the maximum likelihood estimators for a structural system with exactly identifying restrictions, and proved their consistency and asymptotic normality as well.[30]

Haavelmo made it clear through the supply/demand model and a two equation Keynesian model that the consequences of simultaneity were widely relevant for the ordinary economist interested in estimates of elasticities and multipliers.[31] His examples, postulating exogenous investment for instance, were meant not as viable theoretical economic models but as simple illustrations of basic problems in the interpretation of economic data. The role of the structural equation was crucial, although observations could only be made of the reduced form. The structural equation system was the only means of incorporating into empirical analysis the a priori knowledge that certain variables were jointly determined. In addition, unlike the reduced form, structural equations represented definite hypotheses about economic behavior, e.g. downward sloping demand curves or positive marginal products. By constructing models with unambiguous hypotheses and observable implications that embodied as much a priori knowledge as possible "economists might get more useful and reliable information (and fewer spurious results) out of their data."[32] To the extent that "structural estimation" increased the power to refute hypotheses, the method promised major advances of economic science.

Haavelmo placed great stress on Frisch's concept of relative "degrees of autonomy" of structural vs. reduced form equations. The reduced form had less autonomy because a change in the coefficient of an endogenous variable in a single structural equation would ramify throughout the entire reduced form. If the reduced form coefficients were expected to change then it must be due to changes in "higher order" structural coefficients. Since the latter represented specific economic hypotheses it was important to trace the analysis back to them or else the phenomena would remain unexplained by theory. Haavelmo, like Tinbergen, considered the economic system subject to continual changes. The structural model, however, was held to be the key for properly interpreting them. Tinbergen's methodology attempted to fulfill the ceteris paribus clause when subjecting theories to empirical test only by inclusion of appropriate exogenous variables. Haavelmo showed that the problem was deeper and would likely require increasing the number of equations as well. How this was best accomplished was not always clear when models, such as Tinbergen's, did not have theoretical underpinnings as secure as the supply/demand example. Haavelmo (1944) concluded that the answer was not to be found in statistical theory but in economic analysis:

> To find a basic system of highly autonomous relations is not an analytical process — it is a task of making fruitful hypotheses about reality.

The two themes of structural change and simultaneity were ceaselessly repeated in these early years of econometrics.

2.2 The "Cowles Commission Method"

2.2.1 Background of the Commission

The Cowles Commission for Research in Economics, a non-profit corporation with close associations to the Econometric Society, enjoyed a growing reputation during the 1930's as a center for mathematical economics. It had been founded in Colorado Springs in 1932 by Alfred Cowles III, an investment advisor and member of a wealthy publishing family, in the hope that the application of mathematical methods to the study of economic issues would lead to better predictions of stock market behavior. Cowles attempted to recruit economists of high caliber—among them Irving Fisher, Harold Hotelling, and Ragnar Frisch. Although Cowles himself published several studies of common stock prices, with time he seemed not to expect directly usable results for his business affairs from the work of the Commission. Instead he became a patron of economic science in general. By 1934 the theoretical researches of the Commission were entrusted to a largely academic staff, although Cowles retained financial control.[33]

Their most valuable activities during this period were the annual summer seminars from 1935 to 1940. These attracted leading economists and statisticians from many parts of the world — such figures, for example, as R. A. Fisher, Joseph Schumpeter, Ragnar Frisch, and Jacob Marschak. The Commission provided an important forum for economics education in an era when mathematical economics was studied at only a few major universities. It is also appropriate to record Cowles's sponsorship of refugees from Nazism, in particular Abraham Wald and Horst Mendershausen. Perhaps owing to the liberal and internationalist outlook of the Cowles family, the Commission soon became a notable stopover point for many foreign economists visiting the United States.

The imposition of a state income tax in Colorado in 1937 persuaded Cowles to seek a new location for his activities.[34] He approached Yale, his alma mater, in July of that year. After initial enthusiasm on both sides, with the active support of Irving Fisher and James Harvey Rogers, Cowles suddenly backed away. A major consideration was probably the financing of the Commission, which came entirely from the Cowles family on a year to year basis and in 1937 amounted to over $50,000. Yale wanted a ten year guarantee of complete funding but evidently Alfred Cowles could not promise this. The question was settled by a move to Chicago in 1939 which Cowles explained as due to other business reasons.[35] At the University of Chicago, Cowles was able to work out an acceptable arrangement, and Chicago became the home of the Commission for the next 15 years.

After losing much of his staff to various wartime agencies during 1942, Alfred Cowles successfully induced Jacob Marschak to accept a joint position as professor at Chicago and research director of the Commission starting in January 1943. Marschak at once planned to devote all the resources of the Commission to develop the work of Tinbergen in the light of the works of Haavelmo and of Mann and Wald. He appeared absolutely certain of the necessity of this research, referring to it even as "the Gospel."[36] Earlier, discussing the use of economic research, he had written "I hope we can become 'social engineers'."[37] In spring 1943 he was finishing work on consumer demand carried over from the New School and started to think in larger terms. His first description of the future Cowles program stated:

> The basic principles of the statistical analysis of *systems* of relationships (such as supply and demand equations) have been revised. . . . The traditional method of least squares . . . must be replaced by certain other methods when the problem is one of "social engineering" (advice to firms, government agencies).[38]

The phrase "social engineering" was soon toned down to "economic policy," probably to avoid connotations of "central planning." But it remained a persistent image in their later writings. The new econometricians, under the spell of analogies between their methods and those of physics and thermodynamics, were not tempered by Keynes's suggestion that economists should strive to be "humble, capable, like dentists."[39] It was only natural, once the economy was conceived in terms of a system of equations, to think like Tinbergen of altering the system so as to drive the endogenous variables along any desired path. Within a year Marschak outlined a schedule for work on this idea that he called "Statistical Foundations of Rational Economic Policy":

> 1945-6: Work on method[ology] to be completed in the main.
> 1946-8: Final application of method to business cycle hypotheses and to (detailed)
>   single market problems.
> 1948-9: Discussion of policy. Extension to international economics.[40]

2.2.2 *The Theoretical Achievement*

Drawing on friendships made in Europe, Colorado Springs, and New York, Marschak built up a research staff of outstanding mathematical statisticians. Tjalling Koopmans joined the Cowles Commission in July 1944. The previous December he had given a lecture at Cowles on "Dynamic Economic Systems." Marschak had known him for some years already and seemed very pleased to be able to provide him with a secure position to pursue his research.[41] Leonid Hurwicz, a Polish statistician who had read Haavelmo's manuscript while at Harvard and MIT in 1941, had arrived at Cowles in January 1942 but was also on the faculty of the University's Institute of Meteorology. By late 1944 he was working full-time on theoretical econometric problems. Herman Rubin, another statistical theorist, was hired in July 1944. Lawrence Klein, primarily an empirical model builder, came that November to continue the work begun in his dissertation on the quantification of the Keynesian system. He, too, had already become familiar with Haavelmo's 1941 manuscript during his time at MIT. T. W. Anderson arrived in November 1945 as the last member of the original econometrics research staff. They were very young — Koopmans was senior at 35, Klein most junior at 24 — and immensely talented technically.[42] Their group developed the theoretical core of modern econometrics in remarkably short time.

The Commission called a small conference in January 1945 to expose the preliminary work to technical review.[43] The influence of the Mann and Wald article was very clear. Koopmans, assisted by Rubin, presented the longest paper that contained the results of his research into the identification problem.[44] It generalized the analysis of the estimability of parameters begun by Frisch in 1938 and began studying the statistical implications of overidentification restrictions. Moreover, it showed the practical steps involved in the maximization of the joint likelihood function (later known as the full-information method). This was obviously a very tedious calculation but it was the first way ever found to embody formally the overidentifying restrictions in an estimation procedure, thereby solving a problem that had frustrated Sewall Wright, Tinbergen, Frisch, and the other earlier econometricians. Hurwicz, analyzing the small sample rather than the asymptotic behavior of the estimators in a simple dynamic model, derived the exact first moment of the serial correlation coefficient for samples of 3 and 4 observations and found that the OLS estimator could be biased downwards by as much as 25 percent. Although his study was very limited, it indicated serious potential problems for inference whose complicated nature had already been indicated by Koopmans (1942).[45] Other papers by Hurwicz and Rubin introduced the idea of a random coefficients model.

The foundations were completed during the following eighteen months. Another paper by Koopmans suggested how the difference equation model might eventually be supplanted by a model formulated in continous time. His third contribution, to be discussed in chapter 6 of this book, explained the concept of an exogenous variable in the Mann and Wald model. The last major theoretical result was the derivation of the limited information estimator. It apparently had its origin in a suggestion by Girschick in December 1945 to dispense with overidentifying restrictions and to perform what has come to be called indirect least squares.[46] The idea was to sacrifice some efficiency in order to reduce the computational burden of FIML while preserving consistent estimation of the structure. This was another rediscovery of Tinbergen (1930) but Girschick, a gifted mathematical statistician himself, saw how to exploit the assumed normality of the errors to derive exact confidence limits for the structural estimates in finite samples. Anderson extended this idea along the lines of his doctoral dissertation and worked out the algebra of the LIML estimator in by March 1946.[47] An important by-product of his work was a test for the validity of the overidentifying restrictions for a single equation. Koopmans had already been aware that this information was subject to test but it appears that Anderson was the first to actually develop an operational procedure.[48]

Revised versions of these papers and contributions by the guests were finally published in 1950, after years of typographical problems with the printer. They constituted a brilliant synthesis and extension of the econometric research programs developed in the U. S. and Europe during the previous thirty years.[49] In many respects this volume continued to define much of the frontier of econometrics until the late 1960's.

2.3 Beginning Debate over Methodology of Structural Estimation

2.3.1 Measurement with Too Many Theories

The Cowles workers shared Haavelmo's view that empirical work in economics would best proceed scientifically by the specification of a model as a set of identified structural equations together with an assumed stochastic distribution of the error term. What soon came to be called the "Cowles Commission method" did not, however, enjoy automatic acceptance by the economics or even the statistics profession.[50] The famous debate with the NBER made public by Koopmans (1947) seems to have started with the "weekend seminar" in 1941. Referring to the problem of obtaining support from Joseph Willets at the Rockefeller Foundation, Marschak wrote of "a difference of opinions and sympathies between our approach here and that used by Mitchell and Kuznets at the National Bureau" and suspected that "Willets has been advised by representatives of the 'other school'." Willets had written of his confusion over the economic theory in Marschak's proposal in that it was not the kind found in textbooks and confessed, "I can't quite understand what Marschak really has in mind."[51]

It appears that Marschak did not think a satisfactory theory existed in the textbooks that could offer causal explanations of macroeconomic phenomena. Ideally, the Cowles method would improve upon Tinbergen's efforts to advance economic theory by classifying tentative theories as either consistent or inconsistent with observed data. For this reason they emphasized the need to develop new statistical theory, particularly for small sample testing of models with lagged dependent variables, to accompany the use of an economically appropriate estimation procedure. Marschak, perhaps influenced to some extent by Keynes and Friedman, took pains in early 1944 to concede the lack of certain knowledge of the structures they proposed to estimate:

> Any specification of *the* theory would, at present, mean merely setting one's mind on preconceived ideas affected by emotional preference, as in the case of the role of wage rigidity, monopolies, income distribution, and public spending.[52]

Marschak was offering a list here of extremely divisive questions that had preoccupied policy makers at least since the early 1930's. In the United States, the Temporary National Economic Committee, one of the last products of New Deal economic reform, had not been able to recommend politically feasible action to address them. But Marschak seemed to be suggesting that using the Cowles method for "social engineering" could eventually yield objective solutions to fundamental economic and social problems. This period marked the high point in their belief that the basic individual utility maximization framework of the textbooks could be extended to provide the basis for rational behavior by public policy makers.[53]

Marschak and Koopmans became the proselytizers for the econometrics "movement" in journal articles and professional meetings. *Econometrica* was little read outside of a small circle of "believers" so Koopmans (1945) first approached a possibly sympathetic audience with an expository piece in *JASA:*

> Any statistical method of estimation derives its meaning . . . from the concept of a well-defined probability model. . . . The identification problem in general arises from the fact that a given system of equations . . . can be written in many ways. . . . But there is only one (possibly unknown) way of writing the system such that a specified economic meaning attaches to each equation.

These themes were repeated in the opening sections of his January 1945 conference paper:

> The study of an equation system derives its sense from the postulate that there exists one and only one representation in which each equation corresponds to a specific law of behavior (attributed to a specified group of economic agents). . . . Any discussion of the effects of changes in economic structure, whether brought about by trends or policies, is best put in terms of changes in structural equations. For these are the elements that can, at least in theory, be changed one by one, independently. For this reason it is important that the system be recognizable as structural equations. ⟩

Economics naturally is the study of the interactions of rational decision makers: demanders and suppliers, workers and employers, consumers and investors. The Cowles group saw econometrics as the statistical study of the behavior of such actors. Economic theory defined their existence and was supposed to describe their separate motivations and goals. These differences in behavior, derived from an underlying theory, are the source of the additional maintained restrictions on the equation system. The tradition of classical economic theory assumed that it was possible to aggregate at some level over individuals to identify distinct classes of actors for purposes of analysis. It was then natural to posit behavioral laws for each class (the structural equations) and to observe the outcome of their interactions (the reduced form).

The Cowles position on econometric modeling was most forcefully put by Koopmans in an unpublished first draft of his now famous polemic (1947). This paper merits quoting *in extenso:*

> Economic agents (consumers, workers, entrepreneurs, dealers) . . . are the ultimate determinants of economic variables, as well as their fluctuations. . . . [Burns and Mitchell] instead study "behavior" (in a more mechanical sense) of certain measurable effects of those actions and responses. This shift of attention from ultimate causes to measurable effects is a DECISIVE step. It eliminates all benefits that might be received from a causal theory of the aggregative effects of the economic behavior of many individuals.

> One may ask: why should measurement of the behavior equations of consumers, workers, entrepreneurs be necessary? If observed regularities are due to the simultaneous validity of several behavior equations, these regularities will persist as long as each of the underlying behavior patterns persists. . . .

> While one particular behavior pattern may be deemed fairly stable over a certain period, a much greater risk is involved in assuming that a whole system of structural equations is stable over time. An observed regularity not traced to underlying behavior patterns, institutional rules, and laws of production is therefore an instrument of unknown reliability. The predictions it yields cannot be qualified with the help of even known trends in behavior or technology. It is of no help whatever in assessing the probable effects of stated economic policies or institutional changes.

> Measurable effects of economic actions are scrutinized in complete detachment from any knowledge we may have of the motives of such actions. The movements of economic variables are studied as if they were the eruptions of a mysterious volcano. . . .[54]

Koopmans questioned the value of studying business cycles per se, saying "it is not clear why cyclical forms of movement should receive such exclusive attention." Economists had known since the research in time series by Yule (1927) and Slutsky (1937) that univariate stochastic autoregressive and moving average processes could generate paths much like those of cyclical economic variables. The economic basis of such movements, however, is beyond analysis without some structural model.[55] Koopmans thought it conceptually preferable to identify causal economic factors whose past outcomes may happen to have been cyclical. Then through testable hypotheses, if such could be framed, one could specify precisely "in what manner randomness enters into the formation of economic variables." In sum, "each structural equation should be analyzed to the point where at least a conceptual isolation of the random influences at work is attained." By this Koopmans seemed to mean analyzing a model to determine the extent to which fluctuations might be controlled through policy. Only if the estimated residuals were serially correlated regardless of the chosen specification would one have to grant an inherently cyclical form of movement.

Marschak was not a statistical theorist but wrote many papers to introduce the Cowles work to a general audience of economists. Seeking to portray econometrics as the field which would enable the realization of the rising hopes for welfare economics after World War II, he characteristically wrote:

> The knowledge of structure means greater flexibility with regard to policies. Hence interest in economic theory. . . . Equations of the model must describe plausible behavior of specified economic agents, thus making full use of our a priori knowledge. Otherwise we have "anonymous" relations. Welfare changes due to human, institutional, or technical factors cannot be evaluated unless these factors are explicitly stated.[56]

Marschak saw the policy problem as really consisting of two parts. First would be the estimation of various equations of interest. Then the econometrician would combine these results with a "social welfare function" and discover the mathematical route to attain a "social optimum." This step would yield the policy actions: setting the paths of exogenous variables under the policy maker's control and choosing optimal values of parameters in the structural equations. Maximization of a chosen welfare function would seem to define rational behavior on the part of the policy maker.

This formulation was derived from the utility maximization paradigm. Marschak conceived of a welfare function in terms of an index number computed from observable endogenous variables. While offering a certain plausibility, it is certainly problematic to assume that optimal policy decisions can be deduced in this way. The maximization problem involves major behavioral assumptions. Realistically, if policy makers must take on a variety of roles simultaneously and reconcile possibly competing objectives, the problem is likely to require additional side constraints to lead to an institutionally feasible outcome.[57] Furthermore, if policy makers revise their goals in the light of experience it is not clear that a fixed form of a "social utility function" is relevant for most real policy problems. The one Cowles seminar that treated applied policy problems in detail revealed major dissatisfaction with the approach outlined by Marschak.[58] Indeed, although it was a short step to connect his approach to the newly emerging field of optimal control theory, that step was not taken within Cowles. It had to await the growth of a new generation of econometricians who came into the subject from formal engineering backgrounds. "Social engineering" in this framework was for them a straightforward technical challenge.[59] But their models have seldom found application in the actual development or administration of economic policy.

Koopmans's suggestion that one structural equation could be changed independently of all the others in the system would require a very carefully specified model. An economic example can be found in international trade where a tariff on imports by a small country can shift its demand curve without affecting the world supply curve. Similar independence between the investment schedule and exogenous government expenditure would be harder to justify. For example, New Deal programs financed by taxation in an era before fiscal policy was widely accepted arguably had negative effects on business confidence, regardless of the level of interest rates.[60] In addition, if the original system had a non-diagonal covariance matrix then it would be necessary to explain how changing the generating process for the first equation would not affect the process for the second.[61] This problem was demonstrably acute for Marschak's model of price control discussed in section 3.2 below.

2.3.2 *Limitations of Aggregate Linear Difference Equations*

There are other interpretive problems as well. The autoregressive "dynamic" model seemed derived more from patterns found in aggregate data than from any specific laws of individual economic behavior. Schumpeter had already lectured at the 1937 Cowles Commission summer conference that such models were "likely to be either empty or misleading," in that a causal variable "practically never directly acts on other aggregates but only through, say, prices and quantities of individual commodities." He concluded that they were theoretically unsatisfactory because they were "compatible with almost any view about the nature and causes of business cycles."[62] Marschak, who attended this conference, still believed that simple lag schemes were essential to interpreting macro phenomena but recognized important limitations to their usefulness:

> The abruptness of many economic fluctuations does not fit well with the description of damped harmonic oscillations and may make a revision imperative. . . . [Linearity is] a very crude approximation to economic facts if only because it neglects the fact of capacity limitation.[63]

When Marschak wrote this in 1944, capacity limitations had taken the place of Depression-era "deficient demand" as a focus of policy discussion, dramatized most by civilian employment that stood at 50 million out of a labor force of 51 million and steel production that at times exceeded theoretical capacity.[64] But Schumpeter seemed to be suggesting a different source of non-linearity that was not as tractable theoretically as a vertical supply curve for labor. From a neo-classical perspective, the coefficients in the autoregressive model could themselves be conceived as functions of other variables, particularly prices, that would connect the usual sort of Keynesian model to other theories of the business cycle, such as those of Aftalion and Spiethoff.[65] From this point of view, the structural coefficients could have one component varying with price and another based on more autonomous behavior patterns, institutional rules, and laws of production.

In this connection it is interesting to note that Lawrence Klein's favorite example of the need for structural estimation would seemingly imply inherently non-linear equations for designing counter-cyclical policies. To cite one instance, he wrote to Alvin Hansen in late 1946 that "there are policies which are designed to change the [structural] function as well as change the exogenous variables. An example is the influence of social security programs in altering the marginal propensity to save."[66] In the simplest possible set-up one could postulate:

$$w_t = k(Y_t - Y_{t-1}), \quad k > 0$$
$$C_t = a + c(1 - w_t)Y_t \tag{2.6}$$

where w_t is the withholding tax rate in a given period that depends on the increase in income in the preceding period. It then follows that consumption is a markedly non-linear function of present and past incomes. The models that Klein actually estimated assumed a fixed MPC with at most a linear distributed lag on income.[67] While the dynamic behavior of the tax rate proposal would not be easy to analyze, the potential equation misspecification implied by ignoring the frequent income tax rate changes over the 1921–1940 period could help to explain the prevalence of serially correlated errors in his empirical work that is discussed in section 4.2.2.

Marschak was anxious to claim a special epistemological status for simultaneous equations estimation. He described it as the "'rational empirical' approach: the only possible way of using past experience for current rational action (policy as distinct from passive prediction)."[68] This is certainly accurate provided the correct model is known. It does presuppose, however, that the available aggregate data actually represent homogeneous underlying behavior. The individual events in a national economy which constitute the reported aggregate figures take place within a host of determining factors that are admittedly left out of the analysis. The error terms in the aggregate regressions do contain past experience that is relevant for rational action. But to elucidate these factors, even to judge whether the data were valid as claimed, would require an analysis that would become more the province of the historian.

One has to be impressed by the enormous pioneer confidence displayed by the Cowles researchers in these early years. They believed they had found the tool that promised an end to the wild swings of the business cycle which earlier writers had largely considered to be endemic in the capitalist process. Coming onstage after the worst depression in history and the great economic transformations wrought by the New Deal reforms and World War II, Marschak could easily declare that "we do not believe in past or future stability of structure."[69] But unlike the piecemeal and largely politically determined policies of the preceding fifteen years, the Cowles group held out the vision of systematic government that could even dare to claim to "optimize" for society as a whole. Structural estimation was expected to achieve what in counterfactual histories could only remain speculation.

NOTES TO CHAPTER 2

[1]See Tinbergen (1939). Prototype models in which he developed most of his approach were published as Tinbergen (1937).

[2]U.S. Bureau of the Census, *Historical Statistics of the United States*, Part I, Series F-4, p. 224. Recovery in these terms did not begin until 1934 and took until 1937 to reach pre-Depression real per capita output levels.

[3]An early warning that economic data often displayed serious dynamic non-linearities was given in Tjalling Koopmans, *Tanker Freight Rates and Tankship Building* (Haarlem, 1939), p. 163.

[4]From Tinbergen (1939), 2:18, emphasis in original.

[5]See Joseph Schumpeter, *The Theory of Capitalist Development* (Cambridge: Harvard University Press, 1934), pp. 214-23.

[6]Henry Schultz's diary, for example, contains many deprecating references to the National Recovery Administration made during his European tour in 1934 to visit Frisch, Jacob Marschak, Colin Clark, and other mathematical economists. An unpublished mimeographed copy is in the Cowles Foundation Library, Yale University.

[7]The sum of a current and lagged value for a particular variable was meant to approximate a lag of a half period. Appropriately weighted sums were also used as proxies for unavailable quarterly data.

[8]Schultz to Moore, 12 August 1924, Henry L. Moore Papers, Rare Book and Manuscript Library, Columbia University.

[9]Frisch and Waugh (1933) had shown that removal of a linear trend from each variable prior to estimation was equivalent to using the original data with a separate trend term in the regression. This discovery is often ascribed to Lovell (1963) although he referenced the earlier work. Most later econometricians paid much less attention to these issues but the misleading inferences caused by the use of trending and non-stationary variables motivated much theoretical econometric research in England. See section 5.1 below.

[10]From Tinbergen (1939), 2:164. Wage deflation policies were of particular

interest to economists in open economies such as Holland and Sweden.

[11]In the U.S., Herbert Hoover argued that the unemployment problem was better attacked through *restricting* immigration because "a most important part of recovery . . . rested on maintenance of wages." See his *Memoirs of Herbert Hoover*, 3 vols. (New York: MacMillan, 1952), 3:43-47.

[12]From Tinbergen (1939), 2:167.

[13]Gottfried Haberler, *Prosperity and Depression* (Geneva: League of Nations, 1937) had cataloged the theories which Tinbergen was supposed to deal with.

[14]Friedman's interpretation is mirrored, though not referenced, in the latest work of European researchers who now evaluate econometric models as "tentatively adequate conditional data characterizations." See Hendry and Richard (1982) and Hendry (1983) for a presentation and further references. More comments on their approach are offered in section 4.2.2.1 below. The thrust of Vining's (1949) critique of "the choice of variables to be studied," originally put forward as a defense of NBER research methods, has recently been sympathetically discussed by Malinvaud (1983).

[15]Frisch's non-probabilistic thinking precluded the discovery of statistical tests such as the validity of overidentifying restrictions. See section 4.1 below.

[16]See Jacob Marschak, "Research Plans for two years beginning 7/1/44," CCA, Rockefeller Foundation notebook (hereafter cited as RFN).

[17]Karl Popper, *Logik der Forschung* [The Logic of Scientific Discovery] (Vienna: J. Springer, 1935). This kind of thinking also became extremely influential among a number of historians and philosophers who sought to place the writing of history on similar epistemological foundations. The seminal article is Carl Hempel, "The Function of General Laws in History," *Journal of Philosophy* 39 (1942), 35-48. For critical reaction by philosophers to these attempts see William Dray, *Laws and Explanation in History* (London: Oxford, 1957) and Louis Mink, "The Autonomy of Historical Understanding," *History and Theory* 5 (1966), 24-47. The parallel between econometrics and historiography has occurred to several econometricians; see, e.g., Fisher (1966b, p. 12). The simultaneous rise of "structuralist" schools in many intellectual fields besides economics

during this period deserves analysis in a separate study.

[18]Koopmans here and in (1949b) reported that the crude multiplier-accelerator model appeared convincingly disproved but many other investigators reached the same conclusion without using extensive multiple correlation analysis.

[19]This notion, related to the bunch map analysis, has received a great deal of attention recently in Leamer (1982). See also section 4.2.2.1.

[20]A modern example of the problem is the consumption function work reported by Davidson, Hendry, et. al (1978), which Deaton and Muellbauer (1980, p. 334) diplomatically called "a remarkable piece of econometric detective work."

[21]See sections 4.2.3 and 5.1.2 below.

[22]For remarks on the implicit issue of correct hypothesis tests for small samples see section 4.2 below. For remarks on a recent alternative methodology for modeling large numbers of variables see section 5.3 below.

[23]The proper course to follow is not always clear when this premise is violated. Tinbergen and Lawrence Klein, whose work is discussed below in section 4.2.2, thought inclusion of additional explanatory variables was justified until the residuals appeared serially random. Koopmans was doubtful of the statistical rationale for this procedure but a critique with the alternative of an "autoregressive transformation," discussed below in section 5.1.3.1, was not put forward until Cochrane and Orcutt (1949a). See Minutes of Staff Meeting, 25 January 1946, CCA.

[24]The extension of Haavelmo's (1947) asymptotic results only commenced with the work of Bergstrom (1962).

[25]This was a common exercise at the outset of the Cowles Commission work in structural estimation, viz. Koopmans (1945). Leonid Hurwicz made up even more extreme cases. See Minutes of Staff Meeting, 28 January 1946, CCA. The magnitude of the bias in the general case was not clarified until the work surveyed in Phillips (1984).

[26]Jacob Marschak, "Report to the Rockefeller Foundation, 20 May 1943," CCA, RFN.

[27]His early studies concerned general equilibrium and seasonal adjustment. After arriving in the United States Wald became affiliated with

the Cowles Commission and attended its 1939 and 1940 summer programs. Haavelmo (1944) wrote he "had drawn very heavily" on Wald in
the course of his own work.

[28]Marschak, "Report to the Rockefeller Foundation."

[29]The VAR (vector autoregressive model) of the type presented by Sims
(1980a) is seen to be formally identical to this system.

[30]This article and Haavelmo (1944) were once intended to appear together
in book form under the title *Contributions to the Theory of Economic Measurements*. From Marschak, "Economic Behavior and Business Fluctuations," Memorandum to the Rockefeller Foundation, December 1943,
CCA, RFN. It is not known whether the book would have contained
any additional material or results. The analysis of overidentified systems commenced with Koopmans at the Cowles Commission (see
below, section 2.2.2).

[31]Marschak and Andrews (1944) applied the analysis to production functions.

[32]From Haavelmo (1944), p. 144.

[33]This information is from Carl Christ, *Economic Theory and Measurement: a
twenty year research report of the Cowles Commission* (Chicago: Cowles
Commission, 1952), p. 12 ff.

[34]James Harvey Rogers to Dean Edward S. Furniss, 21 July 1937, Box 34,
James Harvey Rogers Papers, Yale University Library. Christ, loc. cit.,
states that the remoteness of Colorado Springs from major universities
was the reason.

[35]Alfred Cowles to Rogers, 25 March 1939, Box 39, Rogers Papers.

[36]Marschak to Joseph Willets, 17 June 1946, CCA, RFN.

[37]From Marschak (1941).

[38]Marschak, "Report to the Rockefeller Foundation." This document
reported that M. A. Girschick was already using the new methods at the
Department of Agriculture. Haavelmo soon became his collaborator.

[39]But as such they could be crucial in avoiding the kinds of "disastrous
mistakes we have made" in economic policy after the First World War.
See his "Economic Possibilities for our Grandchildren," in *The Collected
Writings of John Maynard Keynes*, ed. Malcolm Moggridge, 28 vols.

(Cambridge: University Press), 9:321-332. Tinbergen, Frisch, and Koopmans — as well as Samuelson and others — had all been trained initially in physics. See, e.g., Tinbergen, *Minimumproblemen in de Naturkunde en de Economie* (Amsterdam: J. H. Paris, 1929) and Koopmans, "Ueber die Zuordnung von Wellenfunktionen und Eigenwerten zu den einzelnen Elektronen eines Atoms [1934]," reprinted in *Scientific Papers of Tjalling Koopmans*, ed. Martin Beckmann (Berlin: Springer, 1970), pp. 1-10.

[40]Jacob Marschak, Memorandum to Social Science Research Committee [SSRC], 9 October 1944, cited in Marschak, Memorandum to SSRC re Cowles Commission Plans, 6 February 1946, CCA, University Advisory Committee Notebook (hereafter cited as ACN).

[41]They had met at Oxford in 1938 when Marschak was director of its Institute of Statistics. Marschak wrote "I have often discussed with Koopmans the plans which he had conceived during his work on business cycles." Marschak to Joseph Willets, "Research Plans for Two Years beginning July 1, 1944," CCA, RFN.

[42]Counting Kenneth Arrow, who joined the Commission in 1947, Marschak had assembled three future Nobel laureates.

[43]Their guests were Robert Anderson, Trygve Haavelmo, Harold Hotelling, William Madow, Henry Mann, and Abraham Wald.

[44]This work was not significantly extended until Wegge (1965) and Fisher (1966a).

[45]Small sample bias in dynamic models was important in two ways. First was the error in estimating the effect of policy variables. Second was the incorrect inference regarding the period of oscillation in the solution of the difference equations. The Cowles group, particularly Marschak and Koopmans, always emphasized the need to develop a small sample distribution theory for econometric estimators but they made little headway. Further research by econometricians in this important area languished for a generation. Phillips (1977, 1983) renewed study of the finite sample distribution using various methods of approximation that promise eventually to make small sample significance tests routine in applied work.

[46]See Tjalling Koopmans and Herman Rubin, "Remarks on Girschick's Letter of 24 December 1945," 10 January 1946, CCA, folder: statistics.

[47]See T. W. Anderson and Herman Rubin, "A Generalization of Girschick's Method," Manuscript dated "Feb. or March 1946," CCA, folder: statistics. Of course, this work culminated in Anderson and Rubin (1949).

[48]See Minutes of Staff Meeting, 1 February 1946, CCA. The vital question of how much information would be lost by disregarding the overidentifying restrictions was not made transparent until much later work by Anderson et al. (1983). The important result is that consistent estimation methods are not likely to differ very much from OLS when the degree of overidentification is low.

[49]*Statistical Inference in Dynamic Economic Models*, Cowles Commission Monograph 10, ed. Tjalling Koopmans (New York: Wiley, 1950). Anderson and Rubin were also at work on identification and estimation of combined "shock-error" models but they never felt their results warranted publication. Draft copies of these papers are in the Cowles archive.

[50]For the view of a statistician see R. M. Frechet, "Degager les possibilites et les limites de l'application des sciences mathematiques (et en particulier du calcul des probabilites) a l'etude des phenomenes economiques," *Revue de l'Institut International de Statistique* 14 (1946) pp. 16-51 with reply *inter alia* by Marschak. Frechet was on the editorial board of *Econometrica*.

[51]Marschak to Louis Wirth, 8 February 1944; Willets to Robert Redfield, 25 January 1944, CCA, RFN. Ames (1948) stressed the level of aggregation as a principal difference between regression analyses of the business cycle and the NBER approach to the same problem.

[52]Marschak to Robert Redfield, 15 February 1944, CCA, RFN.

[53]Section 2.3.2 discusses Marschak's views on the nature of policy in more detail.

[54]Draft dated 14 April 1947, CCA, Cowles Commission Staff Papers (hereafter cited as CCSP) Folder O37/C83S.

[55]See Zellner and Palm (1974) for a modern synthesis of these two approaches.

[56]From Marschak (1950).

[57]Cf. the eventual views of Frisch and Tinbergen, discussed in sections

4.4.1 and 5.2, that these were overriding factors that diminished the policy relevance of many macroeconomic models.

[58]See P. J. Bjerve, "What Kind of Economic Research is Necessary for Economic Policy," April 1949, CCA, Cowles Commission Discussion Paper (hereafter cited as CCDP), Econ. 259. Bjerve objected in particular to the use of highly aggregated equations.

[59]Attempts in this area have grown steadily more sophisticated from Phillips (1954) to Chow (1981). Vehement opposition to econometrics by a systems engineer has come from Kalman (1982), who called structural estimation a "delusion."

[60]See, e.g., Statement of Winthrop W. Aldrich, Chairman of Chase National Bank, in U.S., Congress, Senate, *Hearings before a Special Committee to Investigate Unemployment and Relief*, 75th Cong., 3rd sess., 1937, pp. 521-538. Aldrich also feared that federal spending on utilities and public works like the TVA would initiate the socialization of private industry.

[61]Cf. the discussion of rational expectations and econometric models in section 6.4.1 below.

[62]Joseph Schumpeter, "Suggestions for Quantitative Studies of the Business Cycle," in Cowles Commission, *Reports of the Annual Research Conferences 1935-40*, CCA.

[63]Marschak to Robert Redfield, 15 February 1944. Cf. Koopmans, *Tanker Freight Rates*.

[64]See *Survey of Current Business* (1944) and American Iron and Steel Institute, *Annual Statistical Report for 1944* (New York: AISI, 1944).

[65]See Albert Aftalion, *Les Crises Periodiques de Surproduction* (Paris: Riviere, 1913) and Arthur Spiethoff, *Beiträge zur Analyse und Theorie der allgemeinen Wirtschaftscrisen* (Leipzig: Duncker und Humblot, 1905).

[66]Klein to Hansen, 10 October 1946, CCA, CCSP notebook O37 C83s. During 1942 Keynes was enthusiastically endorsing tax schemes by James Meade aimed at "reducing future slumps by varying employers' and employees' contributions to social insurance." From Roy Harrod, *Life of Keynes* (London: MacMillan, 1951), p. 535.

[67]Keynes was not alone in opposing this assumption for short run analysis. Bertil Ohlin insisted very early that the marginal propensity to con-

sume did not remain constant over the course of the business cycle. See
his *The Problem of Employment Stabilization* (New York: Columbia University Press, 1949), pp. 147-150. Keynes's belief that multiple correlation analysis of time series was generally specious is discussed in section 5.1.2.1.

[68]Marschak to Joseph Willets, 7 October 1944, CCA, RFN.

[69]Minutes of 12th Meeting of U. of Chicago Advisory Committee, 24 March
1947, CCA, ACN.

CHAPTER 3

THE HISTORICAL CONTEXT OF STRUCTURAL
ESTIMATION

3.1 The Full Employment Act and Post-War Policies

Don Patinkin shocked no one at Cowles in December 1946 when he proposed that the federal government closely watch GNP every month and increase expenditures whenever it fell below some desired level.[1] When contrasted to Alvin Hansen's lonely propagandizing in 1938-39, it is apparent that Keynesian ideas had been accepted by liberal academics with remarkable speed.[2] Patinkin's comment was made at a significant point in modern history when most western governments were making formal pledges to undertake regular and massive peacetime interventions in their economies for unemployment stabilization and other purposes. Economists suddenly found themselves in great demand to give advice on major policy problems for which they had few precedents as a guide. This was perhaps the kind of professional opportunity that econometricians such as Tinbergen and Schultz could only dream of a decade earlier. The developers of structural estimation had many arenas in which they could compete with other schools of economists to advise on the organization of the post-War world.

In the United States, for example, the Congress debated a bill throughout much of 1945 that would oblige the federal government to "assure the existence at all times of sufficient employment" for all those "able to work and seeking to work." The President was to appoint a "Council of Economic Advisors" which would forecast trends in output and employment, appraise economic consequences of federal programs, and recommend a National Production and Employment Budget to accomplish the purposes of the act.

The proposed bill had originated in the widespread belief that World War II would be followed by an inflation and collapse much like the one from 1918 to 1921. Many policy makers feared the potential upheaval of twelve million discharged soldiers returning home to find conditions as they had been even in 1941, when unemployment had still averaged almost 10 percent.[3] The first political expression of this concern in the United States was President Roosevelt's "Economic Bill of Rights" in his 1944 State of the Union Address, which proclaimed "the right to a useful and remunerative job." He made a direct connection between restoring mass faith in the ability of the American economy to provide full employment and preserving the free enterprise system against collectivist philosophies, both fascist and communist. A diverse coalition of labor groups and progressive business organizations, notably the Committee for Economic Development, gathered support for the legislation.

In part this bill was also an attempt by Robert Wagner and other liberal political leaders to revive the pro-labor sentiment of the New Deal, which had been dissipated by the Memorial Day massacre of marchers in the "Little Steel" strike of 1937 when Roosevelt had wished "a plague on both your houses." Opposition to the bill centered almost entirely on the meaning of the word "assure." Conservatives feared a permanent WPA or even a nationalization of private industry. They frequently referred to England, where in 1944 the Beveridge plan for "cradle to grave" social security was nearing passage and the Labor Party was preparing the take-over of the coal and steel producers.[4] The bill eventually passed as the Employment Act of 1946 but the word "assure" was stricken from the preamble, which was reworded to read "afford useful employment in the spirit of free enterprise." Similar measures were enacted in many other countries from Norway to New Zealand. The bill lost its teeth in this change: nevertheless, its passage marked the real beginning of compensatory fiscal policy in the United States.[5]

In addition to these domestic concerns, the post-War world appeared to require new policies of every description. In a clear effort to avoid the errors of economic nationalism that followed the First World War, a proliferation of new international agencies enjoyed far broader mandates for economic assistance and intervention than were entrusted to any committee within the League of Nations. Moreover, western opposition to the expansion of Soviet influence took the new form of promoting economic growth in war devastated or former colonial areas. The United States, starting with the Marshall Plan, and organizations like the International Monetary Fund undertook responsibility for the economic reconstruction and development of entire countries in the non-Communist world. For example, foreign grants by the U.S. reached 3948 million dollars in 1948, compared to a total private merchandise export of under 13,000 million. Initial U.S. subscriptions to the International Bank for Reconstruction and

Development and to the IMF totaled 3175 million and 2750 million, respectively.[6] In such an environment the restructuring of entire economies, viz. Japan and Germany, was a further invitation to theorists who wished to assist the policymakers.[7] Never before had there been such a demand for technical economic expertise in nearly every branch of government activity.

An extraordinary paper by Marschak, Klein, and Edward Teller indicated a special new domain of policy opened to economists after 1945.[8] To minimize the effects of an atomic attack on the U.S., they advocated the relocation of all metropolitan areas with over 50,000 residents into "ribbon cities," so-called because of their proposed layout. This was to involve the "almost complete replacement of our dwellings, industrial plants, other buildings, and a considerable part of our transportation system." Their calculations suggested that the expenditure of 20 billion dollars per year over a span of fifteen years would place the program "easily within our reach." They added that "in order to live in ribbon cities we shall have to abandon many of the habits which the people of our big cities have acquired in the course of the last century," but described the alternative only as "suburban" and based on "fast transportation." While not based on any sort of structural economic model this paper is significant as one of the rare occasions on which the Cowles staff made relatively specific policy recommendations. It was an echo of Army defense ideas of the period, to be sure, but the development of grand economic and military strategy soon became the specialized preoccupation of new government sponsored research bodies such as the RAND corporation.[9]

As a general rule, however, Cowles workers did not comment on contemporary economic policy problems in their writings. Neither did they appear before any of the numerous post-War House and Senate hearings concerning such questions as the future of the price control program, the level of corporate profits, the passage of the Employment Act, and the passage of the Taft-Hartley Act. No doubt they believed that really valuable statements on these kinds of issues would have to await empirical verification of relevant simultaneous equations models. But in the spring of 1947 Marschak, like many other economists, received a questionnaire from Senator Robert A. Taft of the newly created Joint Economic Committee soliciting his analysis of current policy problems. He responded to it without consulting the rest of the Cowles staff but his answers perhaps spoke for all of them.[10]

In answer to the question "What conditions are most important to attainment of the objectives of the Full Employment Act?" he specified (1) adequate total demand, (2) high factor mobilities, and (3) no monopoly

elements. He stressed that (1) was most important due to "lack of understanding of required policies." For the second item on the questionnaire,
whether there was a relation between inequality of income and economic
instability, Marschak asserted that "variation in the degree of inequality of
incomes can hardly affect employment." To a question on the danger, if
any, of a large national debt he wrote "debt [should] not stop expenditures
when they are required by the goals of national prosperity or security."
One of the most important questions was aimed at the proponents of
Keynesian countercyclical policies by asking, "Is there any way to make
analyses of current economic data which deserve sufficient confidence to
form the basis of government action . . . e.g. so-called barometers."[11]
Marschak answered with unqualified optimism. He restated Frisch's 1938
critique that the Harvard barometer, based on correlations among three
leading indicators, presupposed unchanging underlying economic relationships and that "this is a serious limitation [for the analysis of] e.g. rent
control or changes in government expenditure." He closed his reply by
stating that the Cowles method, instead, "can be used to evaluate the effect
of any intended policy or change in policy, or any other given impact from
outside of the economic system." Although he did not specify any model to
buttress his arguments, it appears that the role of the income distribution,
earlier left as an unsettled question of emotional preference, had since been
determined to be of little significance for economic stability.[12] This would
certainly have been a relevant finding for the turbulent debates over the
burden of the post-War tax structure but there is no evidence in the Cowles
archive of further correspondence on the subject. The tone of Marschak's
reply, which also repeated the "ribbon city" idea, accorded with the conventional American Keynesianism of the time that embraced foreign aid,
large public works such as highways and urban construction, and military
expenditures as appropriate government actions to maintain full employment.

3.2 Wartime Price Controls and the Cowles Commission

Marschak frequently used the two examples of changing tax rates and
imposition of price controls as instances requiring structural estimation to
devise optimal policy. Price control was explained with a two equation
model:

$$Q = f(P,Y) \quad \text{(demand)}$$
$$Q = f(P) \quad \text{(supply)}$$

With this structure the supply curve is identified. If the government set an exogenous demand for the commodity, the supply curve would then reveal the appropriate equilibrium price, which presumably would be a useful fact for planning purposes. Knowledge of only the reduced form, which explained P on the basis of Y, could not predict the price in the new situation. Marschak's tax rate example was similar and discussed optimal response by a monopolist to various sales and income taxes. By offering solutions to two of the most controversial policy problems in the history of the New Deal and wartime economies he seemed to be intimating a spectacular demonstration of the power of econometrics.[13]

The price control program during World War II was part of an unprecedented effort to make total war economically sustainable. It was so far-reaching that by 1944 over 80 percent of the U.S. economy was subject to the pricing and rationing decisions of the Office of Price Administration (OPA).[14] Controls were imposed very early in the War, starting in April 1942, in order to avoid labor unrest in the face of a general freeze on wages and an official no-strike pledge taken by union leadership. The OPA became the largest civilian office in the government with more than 500,000 employees and volunteers at its peak. Needless to say, such control over industry by a government agency was anathema to most of the business world. The attacks on the agency's authority by hostile Senators and Congressmen during the War and afterwards (controls lasted officially until November 1946) were among the most ferocious legislative battles ever waged in the U.S.

In addition to the political resistance and a frequently imperfect understanding of the industries involved, the many professional economists who were charged with developing workable price and rationing policies faced formidable technical challenges.[15] Although the OPA tried to hold all prices at variously defined freeze levels (generally based on averages for 1941 or as of a particular date), it was constantly necessary to estimate industry cost curves when the historical prices did not equilibrate new demands. Prices were actually kept below equilibrium in many instances to reduce producer surplus, while the required extra production was obtained from a marginal supplier by means of subsidies based on estimated costs. Cost curves were also needed for new products that were continually appearing on the market with no prior price history. Many products were invented during the War, of course, but many "improved" ones were obvious attempts to evade the price regulations.

In this connection it is important to note that Marschak's illustration would frequently be inappropriate if it assumed that a supply curve based on historical time-series was correct for the war years. Pricing formulas had to take into consideration the new market structure where selling costs were often negligible and firms were granted large tax and depreciation advantages for constructing new facilities. The difficulty of fixing a price structure was so great that by 1944 individual prices were no longer the main focus of attention. Petitions for price increases were not evaluated on the basis of profit and loss on the particular item but instead on the overall rate of the firm's return compared to its average for the 1936-39 period.[16]

In addition, it was often necessary to make estimates of the elasticity of demand for various items, notably food, in order to set ration point prices to allocate available supplies. The War Labor Board also implicitly derived labor supply schedules as it became necessary to adjust wage rates to eliminate shortages in various regions and job classifications. The overall program succeeded in holding measured inflation to under 2 percent from Roosevelt's emergency "Hold the Line" executive order in April 1943 until the end of the War while output, employment, and profits reached record levels.

At the time of Marschak's arrival from the New School for Social Research in January 1943, a price control study was already underway at Cowles. Marschak appears to have thoroughly opposed this research. Joseph Willets of the Rockefeller Foundation, which was then becoming a regular financial sponsor of the Cowles Commission, wrote to Simeon Leland of the Chicago Economics department that he had "made the point to Marschak that . . . I didn't think that this study [of price control] should be put last on the list of priorities." In a request for funding from the Rockefeller Foundation made in early 1944 Marschak wrote "it is now planned to revert the facilities of the Cowles Commission to its original and proper field of quantitative economic research." He appeared quite indifferent to the results of the price control study, published as Katona (1945), and referred to its author somewhat cooly as "an enthusiast of the interviewing method." In contrast to the extreme vigor with which he propounded simultaneous equations estimation, his letter of transmittal to Rockefeller merely suggested that they judge the value of the price control work themselves.[17]

The project consisted of field questionnaires on the pricing procedures of distributors and retailers around Chicago and explored several specific and widely recognized problems with the program of controls. Among these were illegal price increases, quality deterioration, reduction in number and size of markdowns, and unavailability of cheaper grades of merchandise. In addition, the study discussed relative effectiveness of different kinds of price regulations, e.g. freeze as of a certain date or price by formula, in different market structures, e.g. wholesale vs. retail and large vs. small firms. Examples of survey questions were "What considerations govern your discontinuing old merchandise or old styles, grades, patterns?"; "Can you satisfy the demand of your customers? If not . . . in what way do you allocate your merchandise?"; and "Why did price and quality remain unchanged in some articles; price go up or quality deteriorate in others? Because of differences in regulation . . . compliance . . . one commodity more controllable than another?"[18]

Katona presented interim reports to the NBER's Conference on Price Research, whose chairman reported that "representatives of the Office of Price Administration and the BLS were impressed by the usefulness of these studies."[19] The BLS was convulsed at this time over charges that the CPI grossly understated the increases in wartime living costs, with vital implications for labor stability under the wage freeze.[20] Frederick Mills of the BLS wrote Marschak that "what you and Katona have told us throws light on a number of puzzling matters in regard to the cost of living controversy." Marschak reported to Willets that they supplied material on quality deterioration and shifts of consumer purchases.[21]

Katona ended his monograph with a passage that seems aimed at the budding econometrics movement and the extreme simplicity of its models. Like many of his counterparts at the NBER he was concerned that the statistical technique was out of proportion with the underlying economic content. In particular, he doubted the validity of highly aggregated "behavioral" equations:

> It is sometimes possible to ascertain the presence or absence of causal connections by analysing correlations among various statistical data. [But] we found that individual businessmen belonging to the same field and operating under the same price regulations often acted very differently. . . . [Without interviews] our knowledge of economic motivations . . . must otherwise remain mere guesswork, individual opinions - often contradictory - or even wishful thinking.

These reservations had no effect on the Cowles program at the time. Former Cowles staff in wartime posts included Joel Dean, director of gasoline rationing at OPA, and Jacob Mosak, chief of the OPA Statistical Trends and Forecasting Branch. There is no record in the Cowles archive of their reaction to the new econometric approach. Following Katona's departure in 1944, Marschak's staff worked on structural estimation with undiminished faith that it would eventually dominate all of applied economics.

3.3 **Fiscal Policy and Debates over Taxation**

This study can only suggest the political intensity of the almost continual debates over taxation in the United States in the years following the election of Franklin Roosevelt. Throughout the Depression Roosevelt, along with his Treasury Secretary Henry Morgenthau, had to face the constant problem of financing New Deal programs. Roosevelt remained philosophically opposed, at least until after the 1937 economic collapse, to running an annual budget deficit. His administration nearly doubled the federal debt over the 1929 level during its first term but doubted that the trend could be sustained in a peacetime economy. New tariffs were considered to be ruled out by political factors and the depressed state of international trade. The need for more revenue marked a distinct change from Republican policies during the 1920's which had generally reduced federal taxes.

As the New Deal moved politically to the left in 1935-36 the function of taxation itself became an independent economic issue. Robert Jackson, Morgenthau's assistant general counsel, testified before the Senate Finance Committee on the importance of increased revenue from the proposed tax program for fiscal 1935 but he stressed the administration's goals of adjusting the tax structure so that it would bear most heavily on those best able to pay. He argued also for using taxes to break up large private fortunes and concentrations of corporate power, to redistribute wealth, and equalize business competition. This program against those termed "economic royalists" by Roosevelt naturally encountered stiff opposition. Raymond Moley, a former "brains truster" who by 1936 was denouncing the course of the New Deal, attacked the whole concept of "reform through taxation" and said it would "force the guiltless rich into rags and tatters." Concerning the undistributed corporate profits tax proposal of 1936, the Republican minority of the House Ways and Means Committee asserted that the bill had Communist approval, that it would lead to instability, regimentation, further waste of public money, and continuing depressions. Little of this tax program was enacted. Still, in the judgment of Morgenthau's biographer, the President and the Secretary "took pride in the frankly redistributive impact of New Deal taxation."[22]

With the coming of World War II taxes were no longer considered as a means to economic recovery or social reform but as a technical tool to avoid inflation.[23] The personal income tax, originally aimed at the upper income class, was gradually extended to affect nearly every wage earner by 1945. During 1925-31 married individuals filing a joint return were required to file if net income exceeded 3500 dollars. From 1932-39 the minimum taxable net income was 2500 dollars. In 1942 it dropped to 1200 dollars and for 1943 it was set at 642 dollars gross income. The need for increased taxation and personal savings during a war was understood by many policy makers besides Keynes (1939b), but specific proposals quickly became mired in sharp debates between the White House, the Congress, and the Federal Reserve Board. They considered increased personal and business taxes, a consumption tax, excess profits taxes, voluntary savings drives, and compulsory savings of the sort advocated by Keynes in Britain. While the various parties could agree on an approximate "inflationary gap" that had to be neutralized, battles raged for months over the distributive aspects of the different plans. For example, the influential tax forgiveness proposal of Beardsley Ruml, ostensibly an idea to put income tax collections on a more current basis, was denounced by Roosevelt as an "unjust and discriminatory enrichment of thousands of taxpayers in the upper income groups." For fiscal 1943, a low point for the entire anti-inflation program of taxes and price controls, delays in passing a tax bill required the federal governement to finance 72 percent of its expenditures with borrowing and concomitant increases in the money supply.

The fierce debates after the War over a huge variety of corporate and personal taxes were less important than the general fact that broad based taxation was becoming the accepted foundation of the welfare state. Total IRS collections from the income tax, for example, rose from 2300 million dollars in 1929 to 29,000 million in 1947.[24] The major fiscal tools of American Keynesianism were in place by the end of the war. The "new economics" was well established in the thinking of a great many political leaders and their academic counselors. Their conclusion regarding the Depression and World War II was that such tools were able to do the job of maintaining steady prosperity. Koopmans, Klein, and Marschak were anxious to take part in making this dream a reality.

3.4 Structural Estimation and American Institutionalism

In this context one can understand the conceptual appeal of policy oriented structural models. Cowles researchers considered their development of a theory for estimation of simultaneous equations models to be a fundamental advance for scientific resolution of economic debates. They presented their few empirical results as very tentative first steps in a wholesale redirection of applied work in economics. These included Girschick and

Haavelmo (1947), originally a wartime project on food demand at the Department of Agriculture, and Klein (1950), the pioneering Keynesian macro-model.

No one on the Cowles staff by this time had direct experience in the actual formulation or administration of economic policy. Previous associates of the Commission had been involved with the NRA as well as the war effort, and after 1945 joined such organizations as the Committee for Economic Development and the United Nations. As social scientists, Marschak's group represented the ascendancy of the technical expert who sought solutions to economic and social problems outside of the political arena.

Koopmans (1949c) seems to have had the clearest sense of the role of government economic policies in the wake of the Full Employment Act. His arguments for studying econometrics undoubtedly help to explain the level of financial support for this purpose that was eventually made available after the creation of the National Science Foundation in 1947, in addition to funding from the various research offices of the armed forces:

> If we do not learn how to introduce greater stability in the economy by the indirect inducements of money supply, tax schedules, and other general incentives . . . political processes and social necessities will make us move more to the method of direct administrative prescription of individual behavior.

This theme was very common among liberals in the early Cold War years.[25] It dated at least from Keynes, who in the *General Theory* saw counter-cyclical policy as the means to preserve the social basis of capitalism.[26] A similar belief had also motivated Tinbergen and Frisch in the 1930's, although after the War they placed greater hopes in direct central planning as a means to change the economic structure of society.

The motivation behind structural estimation suggested here offers important similarities and contrasts to the earlier spirit of economic reform represented by the American Institutionalist school of economics of the period 1910-1940. These economists — Veblen, Commons, and others — and the original members of the NBER were concerned that the classical liberal state often displayed conflicts of interest rather than harmony.[27] The Institutionalist outlook was most clearly expressed in John Commons's phrase "trying to save capitalism by making it good."[28] Not mathematically inclined, they nevertheless emphasized a close first-hand study of economic life to establish themselves as authoritative spokesmen for the neutral "public" of Progressive era thought, caught in the struggle between labor and capital.

3.4.1 *The National Bureau of Economic Research*

It is somewhat ironic that the Cowles Commission found the NBER its arch-methodological rival in the 1940's. At bottom they adopted very similar approaches to business cycle policy. The differences lay more in matters of emphasis and choice of analytic technique.

The NBER was first conceived in August 1914 as an "Institute of Economic Research" by the newly established Rockefeller Foundation. The proposal was "actuated by the desire to study the causes of social and industrial unrest."[29] It was a response to the national public outcry after the April 1914 massacre of thirteen wives and children of strikers by the Rockefeller-controlled Colorado Fuel and Iron Company.[30] The unpublished report that emerged from this special investigation by William Lyons MacKenzie King, former Labor Minister and future Prime Minister of Canada, was among the more important economic studies performed in that era. It proposed one of the first employer sponsored "employee representation plans" in the United States. These were to become very common throughout industry in the 1920's as part of the American Plan that is discussed in the next subsection. The Foundation found that the plan successfully "lessened many of the occasions for misunderstandings, has proved a means for adjusting grievances, and has created a degree of goodwill," where formerly there had been open warfare in the Colorado mines.[31] The idea for the Institute was put aside after King's report but the additional labor turmoil plus the severe crisis of inflation and depression after World War I led to the formal incorporation of the NBER in 1920.

The NBER's first research attempted to measure the size of the national income and its distribution by social class.[32] This work was considered important at the time because it documented the fact that labor's share was no less than 70 percent (although the top 1 percent of receivers accounted for 14 percent of all income). Business cycle investigations dominated subsequent activity but the original basis for the Bureau remained clear for at least another decade:

> Men differ, often violently, in their philosophy of life, in their views as to the means best adapted to those ends. . . . It will ultimately be possible by the gradual extension of the field of exact knowledge, to narrow the contentious field and to enlarge the basis upon which useful social action may rest.[33]

In 1921 the Bureau was prominent in advocating counter-cyclical public works to relieve unemployment.[34] Macroeconomic policy prescription was then de-emphasized in favor of raw data collection and detailed studies of particular phenomena such as the income distribution and inventory investment processes. This kind of information was utilized in the design of tax legislation, for example. The national accounts system proved its independent value as a planning tool during the administration of the economy during World War II.[35]

1.4.2 *The John R. Commons School: Non-Market Policy*

The Institutionalists outside the NBER did not merely collect data, which they recognized as indispensable for intelligent action, but saw their broader mission as the introduction of key structural changes in a laissez faire society. John R. Commons is best known as a leader of those "progressive" economists who believed that completely unregulated markets were the source of many social and economic problems. Although the members of this school did not subscribe to an identical platform, they all displayed a particular interest in trade unionism and government action as a counterbalance to the power of trusts and large corporations. Economic "factfinding" was a most important activity that often merged attempts at economic, legal, and social reforms.[36] One part of their program dealt with "maxima and minima" in labor markets, e.g. for hours and wages and limits to child labor, for developing what they called "common standards of right and justice."[37] They were also interested in state operated unemployment insurance, workman's compensation, and pension plans. The experience gained from designing such programs on a limited scale in states like Wisconsin and New York considerably influenced the form of later New Deal social security legislation. In this respect the Institutionalists could experiment with actual structural changes and profit from experience in ways that were closed to the econometricians.

The central interest of Commons and his followers after the decade of intense industrial strife between 1909 and 1919 was the cultivation of collective bargaining.[38] Few Institutionalists wished to see the continued free use of lockouts, blacklists, and private armies by employers or walkouts, sympathy strikes, and boycotts by workers. They had hoped earlier that state mandated maxima and minima and welfare measures would keep disputes within relatively narrow bounds. With these controls, market forces were expected to determine the outcome of most situations. As many industries became less competitive after World War I, another approach to the labor question was formulated.

The Institutionalists' industrial government model envisaged management-labor councils whose fairness in devising "working rules of collective action" would be the means of maintaining peace and order on the shop floor. The Colorado Fuel and Iron plan was a pioneer in this area. Moreover, the industrial government movement promised to promote maximum economic growth through the encouragement of maximum rationalization and efficiency of production. It was the academic expression of what was known in the 1920's as the American Plan, the business program to implement the basic principles of scientific management in a shop environment free of traditional unions.[39] While Commons and his colleagues supported the "business unionism" espoused by Samuel Gompers and the craft-oriented American Federation of Labor, they had no ready program for the large number of unorganized and often militant industrial workers. Industrial government was one solution to this problem that was predicated on the assumed latent goodwill of employers, and on the belief that their drive for maximum efficiency represented labor's interests better than historical craft union demands, e.g. craft prerogatives and preservation of standard wage rates.[40] It was profoundly a reaction to Bolshevik rule and the international spread of "workers' control" ideologies among workers who were not necessarily even members of any union.[41] The advocates of industrial government claimed that worker aspirations were instead sufficiently described as "wages, hours, and security without financial responsibility but with power enough to command respect."[42] If irreconcilable differences did arise in the individual plant council or in a traditional collective bargaining process, the Institutionalists looked to compulsory arbitration supervised by representatives from "the public," and use of the court imposed injunction as the appropriate instruments of industrial justice.

1.4.3 *Comparison to the Cowles Commission Research*

The New Deal codified a startling number of these ideas at the national level. Many of them formed the backbone of what were later called the "automatic stabilizers." The National Labor Relations Act of 1935 also marked an astounding change in public policy by declaring "it to be the policy of the United States to eliminate the causes of certain substantial obstructions to the free flow of commerce . . . by encourag[ing] the practice and procedures of collective bargaining." It is not at all clear how Koopmans and Marschak would relate these changes to their list of factor immobility, wage rigidity, and monopoly as key problems for business cycle analysis.

It is a curious omission that their descriptions of the institutional rules embodied in econometric models could dwell upon tax rates and yet never mention such fundamental rules as the National Labor Relations Act or the Taft-Hartley Act. In several respects the Institutionalist program would seem to have directly altered economic structure in ways they would be inclined to oppose. But as will be seen in the next chapter, the interest of the Cowles workers in changing structure disappeared by late 1946. Their attention focused on the "indirect inducements" and public investment, including military expenditure and foreign aid, that are under the control of centralized policy makers.

Keynesian theory must have proved attractive precisely because of its seeming independence from the broader institutional environment. Fluctuations of whatever origin could be counteracted by aggregate measures regardless of the individual nature of particular labor and product markets. For example, to explain the severe post-War housing shortage Marschak blamed union work rules and rent controls for the slow pace of new construction.[43] He alluded to the "resistance of private building interests" to a government housing program but recommended no course of action.

Another approach came from OPA Administrator Chester Bowles who wrote the War Mobilization and Conversion Board in December 1945, "urging the immediate use of shipyard and aircraft plants for the production of two million homes a year." Bowles was trying to provide continued useful employment in these expanded industries along the lines of the Full Employment Act. Walter Reuther, who in 1940 had proposed the enormously successful conversion of automobile plants to aircraft production, outlined a similar plan for "utilization of idle aircraft facilities for the mass production of high-quality, low-cost housing."[44] Although Bowles, too, attributed failure to act at the national level to "the real estate lobby finally [taking] over," he was able to institute an effective publicly financed housing program after a major legislative effort when he became governor of Connecticut in 1948.

It is paradoxical that the econometric advocates of structural change seemed virtually unprepared to indicate the mechanisms by which policy can bring it about. Perhaps they wished to avoid the political confrontations that many structural changes would necessarily entail. On the basis of the admittedly small number of their writings on policy, the tone of the Cowles researchers certainly suggests a preference for measures that could be considered above political debate. Klein (1947), in a reflection on the famous post-War forecasting debacles, even asserted that:

Econometric models . . . eventually should lead all investigators to the same conclusions. The usual experience in the field of economic policy is that there are about as many types of advice as there are advisors.

The early econometricians seem to have shared a hope that their science could in time produce consensus in place of controversy in economic discussion. But, compared to the Institutionalists, they had limitless faith in the power of pure economic and statistical theory to uncover the secret for achieving it.

NOTES TO CHAPTER 3

[1]Minutes of Staff Meeting, 6 December 1946, CCA, Minutes.

[2]Had Keynes lived beyond 1946 he might well have followed Marx in renouncing the visions of his followers. He wrote to James Meade in May 1943 that "it is quite true that a fluctuating volume of public works at short notice is clumsy . . . and not likely to be completely successful. [With] a *stable* long term programme serious fluctuations are enormously less likely." From Keynes, *Collected Writings*, 27:326, emphasis added.

[3]In England, writing of the popular mood during government efforts to obtain post-War American loans, Roy Harrod feared "violence of a kind unknown in this fair island for many generations" in the event of another depression. See his *Life of Keynes*, p. 600.

[4]See U.S. Senate, Committee on Banking and Currency, *Full Employment Act of 1945, Hearings*, 79th Cong., 1st sess., 1945.

[5]Fiscal policy was the main tool available to the Keynesians until the early 1950's because the Treasury and the Federal Reserve felt it necessary to stabilize interest rates at a low level both to reduce the cost of borrowing and to preserve the value of the enormous amount of outstanding federal debt, which had mushroomed during the War to 60 percent of the privately held debt in the country. They believed that any weakening of confidence in the value of these bonds would lead to a calamitous selling wave that could destroy the major private financial institutions. See, e.g., the memoirs of Mariner Eccles, *Beckoning Frontiers* (New York: Knopf, 1951). Although rates were fixed until the 1951 Treasure Accord, bond portfolios necessarily depreciated with the severe inflation of 1946-48. It would be worthwhile to study whether the confidence of bondholders reacts asymmetrically to these two sources of risk.

[6]Data from *Statistical Abstract of the United States 1949*.

[7]See, e.g., U.S. Tax Mission to Japan [Carl Shoup], *Report on Japanese Taxation* (Tokyo: Supreme Allied Commander Headquarters, 1949) which successfully proposed a completely new system based on neoclassical principles that "avoids double taxation of corporate income . . . [and exempts] large capital gains that are due merely to a change in the value

of money."

[8]"Dispersal of Cities and Industries," *Bulletin of the Atomic Scientists*, April 15, 1946. This article originally had been solicited for a book by weapons scientists who sought to halt further development of a nuclear arsenal but it was not included in the eventual volume published as *One World or None*, ed. Dexter Masters (New York: McGraw Hill, 1946), with the backing of the Federation of American Atomic Scientists. The earliest issues of the *Bulletin of the Atomic Scientists* make astonishing reading now as one recalls the scope of the first nuclear freeze campaign. Marschak and Klein also presented a paper at the 1946 meeting of the Econometric Society that discussed moving to underground cities.

[9]In January 1949, shortly after RAND's founding, Cowles received a contract for a project called "Theory of Resources Allocation." RAND hoped to develop Koopmans's work on linear programming models of transportation systems to plan "dispersal [of industry], logistics, bombing of railway nets" but the project was eventually terminated as "too long run and too speculative." George Dantzig to Charles Hitch, Memo re Cowles Commission Subcontract, 11 August 1952, CCA, folder: Resources Allocation; Charles Hitch to Koopmans, 21 January 1954, CCA, folder: Resources Allocation.

[10]Marschak, "Answers to Questionnaire Addressed to Economists, 20 June 1947," CCA, CCDP Ec. 203.

[11]A thoughtful answer in the negative was given by John Williams of Harvard. See U.S., Congress, Joint Committee on the Economic Report, *Current Price Developments, Hearings*, 80th Cong., 1st sess., 1947, pp. 188-206. Williams probably introduced the Committee to the term "econometrics."

[12]Taft himself wrote "I have always felt that the 1929 depression was caused in part by the fact that savings became so excessive that money was directed into investment and speculation instead of being spent for consumer's goods." Robert A. Taft to Walter Lippmann, 15 February 1947, Box 105, Folder 2043, Lippmann Papers, Yale University Library.

[13]Marschak wrote that "objective studies of food price control--one of the most passionately discussed problems of home front policy--are most urgently needed." See his "Report for the Period Ending June 30, 1943," 8 June 1943, CCA, RFN.

[14]Office of Price Administration, *20th Quarterly Report for Period ended 12/31/46* (Washington D.C: Gov. Printing Office, 1947), pp. 13-19.

[15]The classic analysis is John Kenneth Galbraith, *A Theory of Price Control* (Cambridge: Harvard U. Press, 1951). A diplomatic account of the conflict between professors, lawyers, and businessmen within the OPA is contained in the memoirs of OPA Administrator Chester Bowles, *Promises to Keep* (New York: Harper and Row, 1971). For a detailed record of the evolution of rationing policies for the case of gasoline see Maxwell (1946).

[16]The problems from the regulator's point of view are well presented in U.S. Office of Temporary Controls, *Historical Reports on War Administration*, ed. Harvey Mansfield, 8 vols. (Washington D.C.: Gov. Printing Office, 1947). See also Office of Price Administration, *A Manual of Price Control: lecture series delivered at the training program* (Washington D.C.: Gov. Printing Office, 1943).

[17]Joseph Willets to Simeon Leland, 17 November 1942, CCA, RFN. Marschak, "Research Plans for Two Years beginning July 1, 1944." Marschak to Willets, 12 January 1945, CCA, RFN. In this letter Marschak also stressed the relative costliness of field studies and added he had never been enthusiastic about the method he described as "non-quantitative interviews with businessmen."

[18]From Katona (1945), p. 227.

[19]Edward S. Mason to Joseph Willets, 4 May 1943, CCA, RFN.

[20]For arguments against the accuracy of the price index see Phillip Murray, *Living Costs in World War II* (Washington D.C.: CIO, 1944).

[21]Mills to Marschak, 11 June 1943; Marschak to Willets, 21 May 1943; CCA, RFN.

[22]This paragraph is based upon John Morton Blum, *From the Morgenthau Diaries*, 3 vols. (Boston: Houghton Mifflin, 1959), 1:305-337.

[23]Cf. the unsuccessful proposals in *The CIO's Tax Program: tax wealth not wages* (Washington D.C.: CIO, June 1941).

[24]Tax rate and revenue data from *Statistical Abstract of the United States.*

[25]Typical of many books that appeared just after the War was *Saving American Capitalism*, ed. Seymour Harris (New York: Knopf, 1948), con-

taining essays by founders of the new Americans for Democratic Action.

[26]John Maynard Keynes, *The General Theory of Employment, Interest, and Money* (New York: Harcourt Brace, 1936), pp. 379-382.

[27]They retained the concept of "class" in their critiques of conventional economic theory but opposed Marxist analysis. See, e.g., Thorstein Veblen, *The Theory of Business Enterprise* (New York: Scribners, 1904).

[28]John Commons, *Myself* (New York: MacMillan, 1934), p. 97.

[29]*President's Review and Annual Report for 1913-14* (New York: Rockefeller Foundation, 1915), p. 18.

[30]Cf. George P. West, *Report on the Colorado Strike* Washington D.C.: Gov. Printing Office, 1915) and Rockefeller Foundation, *Information furnished by the Rockefeller Foundation in response to questionnaires submitted by the United States Commission on Industrial Relations* (New York: Rockefeller Foundation, 1915).

[31]*President's Review and Annual Report for 1915* (New York: Rockefeller Foundation, 1915), p. 25.

[32]Wesley C. Mitchell et al., *Income in the United States, its amount and distribution*, NBER Publication nos. 1 and 2 (New York: Harcourt Brace, 1921-22).

[33]*For Social Disarmament: the story of the NBER* (New York: NBER, 1927), p. 7.

[34]*Business Cycles and Unemployment: report and recommendations of a Committee of the President's Conference on Unemployment* [1921], NBER Publication no. 4 (New York: McGraw-Hill, 1923).

[35]Cf. the British experience discussed in chapter 5.

[36]The remarkable scope of Institutionalist concerns is made clear in the detailed investigations published as *The Pittsburgh Survey*, ed. Paul U. Kellog (New York: Charities Publication Committee, 1910).

[37]Robert Hoxie, *Trade Unionism in the United States*, 2nd ed. (New York: Appleton, 1923), pp. 368-375.

[38]See John R. Commons, *Industrial Goodwill* (New York: McGraw-Hill, 1919) and John R. Commons et al., *Industrial Government* (New York: MacMillan, 1921).

[39]Veblen's "soviet of engineers" to control the major industries shared the efficiency ideal but was too far removed from the established interests of capital and labor to become reality. See his *The Engineers and the Price System* (New York: B. Huebsch, 1921).

[40]The "industrial democracy" school in England was similar but placed even greater emphasis on efficiency as an alternative to the shop steward movement there. Cf. Sidney Webb and Beatrice Webb, *Industrial Democracy* (London: Longmans and Green, 1926) to James Hinton, *The First Shop Stewards Movement* (London: Allen and Unwin, 1973).

[41]For a penetrating analysis of this phenomenon in the United States see David Montgomery, *Workers' Control in America* (New York: Cambridge, 1979).

[42]Commons, *Industrial Government*, p. 267. A study that was more critical of "welfare capitalism" and seems closer to Commons's pre-1914 outlook is Selig Perlman, *A Theory of the Labor Movement* (New York: MacMillan, 1928), pp. 207-219.

[43]Marschak, "Questionnaire to Economists," but no model was given.

[44]Chester Bowles to Walter Reuther, 26 July 1949, Box 44, Folder 410, Chester Bowles Papers, Yale University Library; Walter Reuther to Chester Bowles, 5 May 1949, Box 44, Folder 410, Bowles Papers.

CHAPTER 4

PROMISES AND PROBLEMS OF STRUCTURAL
ESTIMATION

4.1 Attempts to Recruit Mathematical Statisticians

The Cowles group journeyed to Ithaca, N. Y., in August 1946 to present their methods to a meeting of the Institute for Mathematical Statistics. The theoretical statisticians had had spectacular successes in solving problems related to the war effort (e.g. sequential sampling and the theory of time series) and were clearly ready to tackle many new areas that were suggested by this experience. Their reaction to the Cowles work, however, was markedly critical of the idea that the estimation techniques, despite their ingenuity, were likely to uncover meaningful parameters. Abraham Wald was most sympathetic and observed that as a purely theoretical matter the methods could be extended to use a priori knowledge of non-normal errors to identify structural equations.[1] Drawing on his research in decision theory, he also suggested that "we attach too much importance to unbiased estimates" and advanced the idea that biased estimators could sometimes be better than the best unbiased ones.[2] W. Cochrane seemed sceptical of the utility of simultaneous methods in so far as the finite sample bias involved was of the same order as the sampling error in the available data.[3]

Several participants, including M. A. Girschick, concluded that the greatest problem in applying the methods would arise from unavailability of data relevant for testing the economic theories under examination.[4] The audience well knew the enormous computational problems of maximum likelihood but they expected ultimately to surmount them with new computing techniques and the recently invented electronic calculating machines. Their major concern was the prior stage of analysis where the raw data are collected. In one sense, the simultaneous equations approach was intended precisely to make economic data "relevant" for inference. The recurrent argument at the conference, however, was that such correctives were of second-order importance compared to improving the concepts and methods of measuring the national accounts.

The Cowles researchers adopted a cautious manner at Ithaca. Koopmans, in particular, stressed the incomplete development of their estimation theory. Their empirical results showed few differences with OLS. The broader purpose of the trip seems to have been to attract more mathematical statisticians to the theoretical study of simultaneous equations. This synthesis did not happen, probably to the lasting detriment of econometric theory in the United States. Wald consistently offered insightful criticisms and suggestions to the Cowles group but was preoccupied with other statistical problems after 1943. The most detailed, and possibly representative, reaction to the Cowles presentation at the conference was offered by John Tukey:

> I distrust MLE [maximum likelihood estimators] in small samples because (i) we know little of their properties, (ii) we understand little of their behavior, and (iii) we are likely to work to too much accuracy. . . .

> To predict the effects of structural change you must have structure. But I have yet to see evidence as to how strong a "must" this is. If we postulate the same change in structure occurring within two different structures [of a given model] how much difference will there be between the two modified values [of the reduced form coefficients]? Need we know structure at all accurately in order to predict the effect of structural change? This seems to be a key question. . . .[5]

Tukey was also sceptical of what he termed "data as bad as economic data" to make fine distinctions between rival economic theories. The Cowles workers certainly knew the shortcomings of the data, although their estimation procedure did not account for measurement error. Of course, they hoped that further development of statistical test procedures, particularly for small samples, would make more informative use of the short time-series that were available.

As mentioned in section 2.2.2, by February 1946 Anderson had already developed a test for the statistical validity of the overidentifying restrictions and the rank condition for identification.[6] These tests were clearly discussed in Koopmans and Hood (1953) but it remains one of the mysteries of the evolution of econometrics that they are seldom reported in practice. Of course, as Koopmans and Hood also pointed out, estimation when the rank condition was not satisfied would lead to a nearly singular covariance matrix for the structural errors so that this particular problem would be likely to be revealed in any case. As for the overidentifying restrictions, Koopmans (1949a) expressed the hope that while the exactly identifying restrictions could not be subjected to statistical test, one's faith in their correctness would be enhanced if the overidentifying restrictions were supported. But the published tests have very commonly rejected them.[7] This result would seem to reduce one's faith in the untestable hypotheses as well since, as Koopmans and Hood (1953) remarked, it is to some extent arbitrary which of the two roles a given restriction is made to play.

The statisticians did not share, or perhaps simply did not understand, the economists' faith in the prior restrictions, without which structural estimation was pointless.[8] Tukey's interest was aroused enough to propose an alternative estimation procedure to FIML which was asymptotically equivalent but allowed the overidentifying restrictions to be checked more readily. His suggestion was to minimize the generalized variance of the reduced form after linearizing it in the structural parameters. Overidentifying restrictions could be introduced one by one to constrain the minimization. Invalid restrictions would be pinpointed as causing large increases in the variance.[9] Characteristically for Tukey, this method sacrificed "optimal" accuracy to gain more familiarity with the data at hand. With his great empirical intuition, however, he concluded his remarks by declaring that "the hope of getting directly useful facts from this [time-series] data lies in detouring the details of identification."[10] This scepticism regarding the prospects for identification (including the problem of "multiple hypotheses" discussed in section 4.2.2.1 below), combined with the familiar and severe problems of poor data, serially correlated errors, and the interpretability of aggregate equations offered the statisticians abundant reason at that time not to take greater interest in the efforts of the Cowles workers.

4.2 Empirical Work at Cowles

4.2.1 *Introduction*

The experience of constructing actual models soon revealed the relative weakness of existing economic theory compared to the new body of statistical knowledge. It was becoming evident that the data still supported too many different structures that were equally plausible a priori. For example, Marschak wrote in summer 1946 in regard to their Keynesian macro-model:

> Discussions in 1945-6 have helped to locate the economic sectors where causation is particularly difficult to unravel: especially the theory of investment and inventories. If possible, the clarification of the behavior motives by well prepared interviews with a small number of businessmen will be attempted.[11]

There is some irony here after Marschak's earlier condemnation of Katona's survey research methods. His comments were tantamount to confessing no confidence in the econometric models in the light of the crucial role of inventories and investment in any business cycle theory. These interviews were never conducted at Cowles but Klein later joined Katona at the Michigan Survey Research Center to explore the use of survey data in studies of consumer behavior.

Marschak had arrived at the same conclusion for the study of investment behavior as Theodore Yntema, his predecessor as the Cowles director of research. In a clear reference to the work of Tinbergen, Yntema had written "since attempts to study business cycle phenomena in the aggregate by statistical techniques have not yielded very encouraging results . . . we shall use all available techniques — close observation of relevant case material, correlation analysis, formal logic . . . and that congeries of processes called judgment."[12] Yntema was also interested in tax policy and proposed a detailed analysis of the effects of taxation on private investment. Where the econometric models presumed to model tax policy through a single aggregate measure of total collections, Yntema emphasized the differential effects of "capital loss and gain provisions; tax-free investments, [and] other taxes." Not even mentioning correlation analysis in this context, he wrote that this problem would involve "considerable personal interviewing and case study to appraise the effects of these factors."[13] This proposal apparently did not receive funding before he left for the War Shipping Administration. In his post-War position as research director of the Committee for Economic Development he designed major tax legislation but it does not appear that he maintained any contacts with the Cowles Commission.

The problem of model specification was the most vexing theoretical economic issue the Cowles group had to face in their efforts to "sell" their methods to other economists. Schumpeter still opposed the use of aggregate difference equations, as he wrote to Marschak in late 1946:

> I cannot rest content with this [use of linear difference equations] and consider it futile to try to explain the sequence of economic situations merely in terms of these effects. . . . The insertion of some quantity that expresses some repercussions on output and employment of additions to Plant and Equipment does not present great difficulties . . . except for the fact that these additions, or their products, compete with pre-existing Plant and Equipment also in other ways than by merely adding to it. It is this which I, for one, am unable to formulate and so long as this is so there cannot be an exact model that will realistically describe the capitalist process as a whole. Sad state of things for my General Theory . . . yet the vision of a sequence that proceeds by alternating cumulative processes is quite simple. . . .

Schumpeter was referring to his central idea that "swarmlike" technological innovations in capitalist development caused waves of "creative destruction" of the existing capital stock. He appears not to have altered the views he expressed at the Cowles summer seminars in 1937 that were discussed in section 2.3.2. Marschak's reply seemed aimed at defending a simple Keynesian macro-approach in the absence of accepted microeconomic underpinnings:

> You have put your finger on two of the main problems that bother us here . . .
> [On aggregation] we are trying to formulate . . . index numbers such that their use
> . . . will involve minimum loss. [This] "pragmatic" approach is an application of a
> general principle recently emphasized by some statisticians (especially A. Wald).
> . . . Nothing but the formulation is available so far.[14]

There is evidence Schumpeter was not convinced of the utility of this approach. He wrote at the close of his life that effective analysis of the business cycle would require study of the "rise and fall" of individual firms.[15]

Irving Fisher, who was not a Keynesian, wrote to Alfred Cowles upon receiving his report of the Commission's empirical work:

> In regard to the studies of fluctuations, my chief comment is that there is practically no reference to the chief factor involved in the *big* fluctuations . . . namely, changes in the volume of deposits subject to check.[16]

Fisher took an even dimmer view in a letter to his collaborator on his studies of monetary velocity:

> I have seen in my long life a lot of people burn their fingers over discoveries of cycles. The discoverer "sees things" almost as bizarre as drunkards. Once we were satisfied that "the" cycle was ten years in length and since that was smashed, we have had almost every other conceivable discovery.[17]

Although Fisher had been one of the founders of the Econometric Society, it does not appear that he was sympathetic to structural equation modeling. His opposition could have been related in part to the treatment of expectations in the early models. The mechanical use of a distributed lag (i.e. a difference equation), the technique Fisher himself had introduced into econometrics,[18] by no means automatically corresponded to rational behavior. In his view, the logical basis for forecasting the trends of post-War economic activity would not be the years immediately prior to 1945 but rather the history of earlier demobilizations. Fisher's macroeconomic theories stressed the role of money and the price level and, accordingly, the real interest rate and investment. This analysis led to the conclusion that inflation followed by collapse was the outstanding characteristic of the end of every major American war since the Revolution, which, he recalled, spawned the phrase "not worth a continental [dollar]." His concern over this danger was revealed by the strong language quoted above. But the real basis for Fisher's opposition was the detailed monetarist view of the business cycle he had developed over many years. The Commission's model offered only the weakest test of his theory, the negative result of which had little import in view of the uncertainty surrounding the specification of the Keynesian alternative.

Since he had strong views on economic policy as well, he was advocating an emergency measure whereby the government would freeze a large fraction of the existing demand deposits and issue interest bearing bonds against them. Without some action to reduce the enormous liquidity of the private sector created by the War he feared that price stabilization would prove impossible before full reconversion to a peacetime economy.[19] His parallels seemed justified as the price control program was being scrapped during 1946. The consumer price level rose 35 percent in five months and the year surpassed 1919 as the greatest strike wave in American history. The difference was that the downturn of 1948-49 bore little resemblance to the very severe 1920-21 depression. Unfortunately Fisher did not live long enough to witness the first of the "recessions," so we do not know how he would have explained this remarkable damping of the extremes of the business cycle.

4.2.2 Model Specification: Klein's Models I-III and Others

The Cowles Commission soon turned away from empirical econometric work but its archive contains numerous memoranda on the specification of various models by Klein, Haavelmo, and many guests from England and elsewhere. It is a testimonial to the seriousness with which the Commission approached its work that it kept official minutes of each research seminar. This material offers a revealing view of the process of model building as carried out under the founders of structural estimation. The following series of excerpts are from typical weekly meetings. It will be noted that most of the discussion is concerned with the work that culminated in Klein's (1950) groundbreaking monograph:

> Klein's equations of consumption were discussed [including] a long list of trial equations which were not included in the memorandum because they showed non-random residuals (but high correlation). . . .
>
> Hurwicz urged interest rate in consumption function of rich. Klein: This belongs in cash demand equation.
>
> Marschak declared use of [aggregate] W/Y economically meaningless, it cannot be derived by aggregating family consumptions.

Koopmans and Marschak: The last equation [in the memo] was obtained after rejecting others but the trials were not exhaustive. For example, lagged income was used in one of the rejected equations: why not try again its effect in the last equation?

T. Anderson's suggestion that both Y and C might be lagged was rejected by Koopmans as economically meaningless.[20]

* * *

Koopmans and K. Arrow: Cited Tukey on whether we need to know whole structure or only part for prediction. Try out policies to see how much we need.
Hurwicz: Better to get whole structure.
Koopmans: Specify policies for which we don't need to know structure.
Klein: If policy changes exogenous variables (budget, taxes) we don't need structure; if policy changes behavior we need structure.[21]

* * *

Haavelmo: When first developed reduced form thought it important only as way to get back to structure. But really much more important since predictions are made through reduced form.[22]

* * *

re Haavelmo's food demand model: The question was raised whether the least squares bias in this particular case was important for most of the uses to which the model would be put. No answer was given.[23]

It is remarkable to observe the downplaying of structure in the comments of Koopmans and Klein as early as 1946. Marschak, too, did not wish to claim much for Klein's early efforts:

The present admittedly very crude and preliminary results were tentatively applied to measuring the effects of policies; though it may have been wiser not to include the discussion even in a privately circulated monograph.[24]

Koopmans, perhaps conceding the unsatisfactory state of economic theory, suggested using policies for which structural knowledge was unnecessary. Klein, now differing from his letter to Hansen that was discussed in section 2.3.2, wanted to view taxes as another exogenous variable. This is certainly possible if rates or yields have varied enough in the past but it undermines the original idea that structural estimation was for making predictions when there was no historical experience with the proposed policy. Even Haavelmo's comments seem to imply that structural information was mainly useful for more efficient estimation of the reduced form. No longer was he emphasizing the role of this knowledge in designing structural changes or critically testing economic theories.

One is also struck by the large degree of uncertainty concerning Klein's equations, particularly with regard to lag lengths and the interpretation of serially correlated errors, with important consequences for the cyclical behavior of the estimated models. This state of affairs was hardly an improvement over Tinbergen's work, whose "results, as given by damping ratio and period of the main typical movement and the 'policy-guiding' derivatives of these quantities . . . is somewhat disappointing."[25] Indeed, the work of Kendall (1946) in England made it appear most unlikely that regression analysis using asymptotic distribution theory could accurately determine periods of economic cycles with fewer than 200 observations.

4.2.2.1 Multiple Hypotheses

This profusion of competing models, of course, has continued to be the bane of empirical macroeconomics. In contradistinction to Koopmans's (1941) treatment of the selection problem, discussed above in section 2.1.1, Haavelmo (1944) had written:

> Frequently our greatest difficulty in economic research does not lie in establishing simple relations between actual observation series but rather . . . [that they] appear to be still simpler than we expect them to be from theory. . . .

However, the actual experience of model specification at Cowles inspired a staff skit in 1946, in which Klein was put on trial for secretly breaking into the building and "finagling" with his data sources.[26] Nonetheless, their early papers were commendable for the frank recognition of the problem of statistical confidence in results from models which lacked firm roots in a priori knowledge. For example, Don Patinkin ended a study of U.S. manufacturing with the proviso:

> I have no idea of the magnitudes of the confidence intervals for the parameters estimated. The basic estimating procedure leads me to believe that they are very large, for the basic procedure consisted of adding and subtracting variables until "reasonable" results were obtained. To handle this type of problem we must have a much further developed theory of multiple hypotheses.[27]

"Multiple hypotheses" was the problem that has since been renamed "model selection." In 1946 Marschak called it "the still remaining core of current criticisms against the application of statistics to economics."[28] He properly distinguished between the algebraic problem of computing parameter estimates and the statistical problem of determining the true size of significance tests when many different models were tried with the same data. Koopmans (1949a) saw it as requiring a new theory of inference to make progress on the dilemmas he had outlined in his 1941 essay. One of Kenneth Arrow's first papers at Cowles after his arrival in 1947 dealt with this topic using Wald's decision theory framework. It was discussed at a staff meeting with Jimmie Savage, Charles Stein, W. A. Wallis, and Milton Friedman and apparently was not judged to be a satisfactory answer to the problem.[29]

Friedman attended many of the Cowles Commission seminars during 1946-8 and continued to make the same criticism he had earlier leveled at Tinbergen. His question was: How does one choose a model, given that numerous possible models exist for the same period? Marschak once replied to him simply that more data would eventually reveal the true hypothesis.[30] This argument assumes that the true model would be revealed by the accumulation of more data because the coefficients of the false models must asymptotically approach zero. Friedman was not content with this and, not unlike Koopmans, made a plea for more published information on methods and models that proved had to be unsatisfactory. He understood the problem of multiple hypotheses but never suggested any theoretical approach to its solution. He instead constantly intimated in the seminars that the estimation results discussed there merely reflected the prejudices of the investigator, prompting Koopmans to exclaim at one point, "But what if the investigator is honest?"[31]

This problem creates profound difficulties, as Marschak acknowledged. Even if all of the proposed models save one were completely false, the fact remains that they could all receive significant confirmation from the one sample of data. If one is strongly committed to a particular specification, then one might ascribe the "success" of the competing models purely to chance—disregarding any arguments for *their* validity—but such a choice seems to imply a degree of prior confidence that is seldom applicable.

The answer given by Marschak to Friedman is not entirely satisfactory for other reasons as well. Using Marschak's own reasoning on other occasions, one should expect structural changes in any long period of time that would be necessary to provide the additional observations for asymptotically powerful hypothesis tests. It is surprising that the record of these debates does not indicate Marschak's previous emphasis on the need for small sample distribution theory to test the different hypotheses more accurately. Phillips (1984) has presented an argument that would seem to reconcile this view with Friedman's critique:

> As the size and the coverage of the sample increase, there is a natural tendency to model an always more complex phenomena in increasing degrees of sophistication. . . .When a model grows in complexity with increases in the available data, traditional asymptotic methods of statistical analysis become self-defeating.

Moreover, it can still be true that all the competing models are valid for the original sample period but for different agents whose identities were lost in the aggregation of the data. The fact that the different models are often estimated by the same researcher is prima facie evidence of belief in their economic plausibility. If a unique model is selected under these circumstances then it would seem economically more sound to admit specification error, explaining how the omitted variables should have comparatively "small" coefficients.[32] It seems equally plausible, however, that the data are actually more informative than is commonly thought. The plethora of statistically significant models could indicate a more complex reality than the investigator expected to find.

Koopmans took stock of the Cowles theoretical work in a memorandum in early 1947.[33] In a slight change of language from the 1945 papers he referred to "a priori notions" of the plausibility of alternative hypotheses and acknowledged "this may be quite a subjective matter."[34] Using a somewhat different approach from his 1941 essay, he suggested that a particular model should be chosen on the basis of the "cost" of the error if the model was in fact misspecified. In this vein he mentioned the possible construction of "multi-model estimates, i.e. estimates based on a priori degrees of confidence in alternative models, without being committed to any particular single model." Presumably these estimates would be functions of the different estimates of the coefficient for a variable of interest.

This idea attests to the growing influence of Abraham Wald's decision theoretic approach to statistical inference. It is also similar in spirit to a problem posed to Koopmans by Meyer Girschick. Girschick had apparently lost interest in structural estimation by 1947 and instead experimented briefly with ways to combine independent judgments of experts to guide policy.[35] The "multi-model" idea was not developed further, however, in the work of the Cowles Commission.[36]

4.2.3 The Friedman Counterattack

Milton Friedman apparently felt quite strongly that the problem of multiple hypotheses made structural estimation a blind alley for empirical research.[37] He also believed the Keynesian models were fundamentally mistaken and he strove to prevent the use of deliberate countercyclical policies, particularly any policies in accordance with the terms of the Full Employment Act of 1946.[38] His manifesto (1948) did not oppose large government economic activities per se but it demanded that they be democratically determined and fully funded by appropriate taxation or debt issue. After attending the Cowles seminars he introduced the idea of the naive model to compete with structural models and even claimed a structural interpretation for it:

> The naive model . . . can simply assert that a proposed change in policy or in an exogenous variable will have no effect.

He went on to predict that models such as Klein's will "in due time be judged failures." In his view:

> [A workable theory] will have to be concerned very largely with leads and lags, with intertemporal relations among phenomena, with the mechanisms of transmission of impulses. . . .[39]

Like many other economists associated with the NBER in those years, Friedman understood the economy in terms radically different from Haavelmo and the early Keynesian econometricians. It is worth repeating his description of the working of the investment multiplier from an essay that outlined a proposal for wartime tax policy:

> The increase in income that will accompany expanded outlays on armaments · depends on a complex of interrelated factors, many of which cannot be observed before the event: who receives the increased outlays, how much of it they decide to save, . . . the reactions of consumers to price changes, the anticipations of consumers about future price movements and availability of supplies, the extent to which entrepreneurs try to expand their capital equipment, the costs that entrepreneurs must incur to expand output, their anticipations about future price movements and hence their inventory policy, the flexibility of wage rates and prices of other factors of production, the demand for credit, the policies adopted by the banking community. . . . The expansion in output depends on the quantity and kind of unused resources, the mobility and transferability of these resources, the rapidity with which output can be increased, [and] the degree of competition.[40]

Indeed, this fleshing out of the Keynesian skeleton should have cast doubt on the "significance" of the tiny residual variances almost invariably reported in the Tinbergen-style empirical work on the multiplier. Friedman concluded:

> Despairing of their abilities to reach quantitative answers by a direct analysis of these complex interrelationships most investigators have sought refuge in empiricism and have based their estimates on historical relationships that have appeared fairly stable.

Here, as in his 1951 comments, Friedman accurately summed up the problems of finding autonomous structural equations and associated policies of structural change. Koopmans's suggestion, cited earlier, to concentrate on relationships that were immune to "structural" interventions did seem to bring him rather close to Friedman's notion of stable lags, leads, and transmission mechanisms.

Of course, for Friedman the one steady, though hardly perfect, relationship was between income and the money stock (while Keynesians soon held fast to Okun's Law and the Phillips Curve). It is important to note the emphasis on diverse disaggregate behaviors, expectations (both of prices and future government and private banking policies), and the state of individual labor and commodity markets. The complexity of this passage contrasts rather strongly with the naive model and with Friedman's retort to Koopmans that "Ockam's razor is a helpful principle" in dealing with aggregate data and multiple hypotheses.[41] Indeed, it can be read as an amplification of his view, cited above in section 2.1.1, that the "complete" systems of Tinbergen could at best offer only a highly selective description of the economic process. Perhaps the experience of having to insist in a Cowles Commission seminar that "producer behavior [was] not separable from prices" helped lead Friedman (1948) to dismiss the ambition of using structural econometric models for control of the business cycle.[42]

4.3 Retreat from Structure

Econometrics started to become a secondary interest of the Cowles staff as the 1940's ended. Marschak wrote to Evsey Domar in April 1947 that their intent was "to move gradually into the field of long-run economics, while bringing to completion our attempts in the field of business cycle theory."[43] These attempts apparently did not yield the fruit they originally expected. Two years earlier he had written that by 1949 they planned "to make possible discussions of specific issues of economic policy (e.g. fiscal measures, means to influence savings habits, price and wage policies, effect of monopolies)."[44] The optimism for resolution of such questions in the context of the Full Employment Act has been discussed in the preceding chapter. One senses, however, that the empirical work was an exhausting disappointment, both for the tedium of computation and the lack of professional acceptance.

The aggregation problem, in particular, was proving less generally solvable than Marschak's letter to Schumpeter had indicated. Koopmans (1949c), in his rejoinder to Vining (1949), already cited Arrow as believing that econometrics should dispense with aggregate relations. The policy problem, however, would become more difficult in so far as the different behavioral groups could have conflicting goals to be mediated by the policymaker. But questions of this kind were not easily addressable within the structural equation framework.[45]

The Cowles staff attended the NBER Conference on Business Cycles in late 1949 hoping to stimulate practical use of their methods. They apparently received substantial criticism beyond that finally published in Burns (1951). Koopmans noted afterwards in a memo that the conference "showed differences in expectation regarding possible results of our work." Their critics included Samuelson, who stressed identification difficulties caused by serial correlation and lagged dependent variables; Leontief, who even at that argued that many data do not need "hyper-refined" methods; and Metzler, who reproved the theory in Klein's work for not being sufficiently systematic. The pride of the staff was obviously stung. In their discussion of a response Koopmans wanted to include mention of the potential value of deriving a distribution theory for medium sized samples but finally counseled, "Let's not fight too much."[46]

Few new theoretical econometric results were derived at Cowles after the 1947 memo on the remaining statistical problems. A major proposal to study continuous time stochastic processes apparently did not attract the necessary personnel or funding.[47] In Koopmans and Reiersøl (1950), the last contribution by Koopmans to the theoretical econometrics literature, there is a marked restraint compared to his earlier papers:

> Scientific honesty demands that the specification of a model be based on prior knowledge of the phenomenon studied, and possibly on criteria of simplicity, but not on the desire for identification of characteristics in which the researcher happens to be interested.

As Tukey, Girschick, and others had suspected, the available data were not allowing clear determination of structure. Marschak (1953) no longer discussed macro policy issues and suggested instead that the random disturbances to investment "may well be so large as to make even the full knowledge of the old structure . . . useless for practical decisions." But he did not venture a suggestion as to how "rational" policy might otherwise be constructed. And in another memorandum Koopmans wrote:

> Can we meet the Friedman critique: that [Carl] Christ's experiments have shown that the information contained in the data so far processed have been insufficient for good forecasting?[48]

Christ (1951) had performed out of sample tests on the Klein III model and called the predictions for the price level and disposable income for 1941 "absurd." These results were especially discouraging in that no structural changes were presumed to have taken place and the within sample fits were extremely close.

The appearance in 1950 of the volume containing the papers from the 1945 Cowles Commission conference was a long awaited event in the econometrics world. The many reviews in the technical journals, generally written by fellow practitioners, warned other economists of its high mathematical level and took the view that time would prove the value of the methods. Herman Wold (1951), however, continued to question the logical status of causality in the simultaneous model.[49] Robert Solow (1951) wanted an explanation for why simultaneous equations estimators and OLS estimators seemed to yield similar results in practice.[50] Solow was also of the opinion that "when they differ, good sense often favors least squares." In an obscure review written in German, Tinbergen was most critical of himself for "command[ing] only a small part of the mathematics" and largely confined the essay to a simple description of the contents of the monograph. But, as the discussion in section 5.2 will make clear, his comments read as a most diplomatic refusal to endorse the new methodology.[51]

Guy Orcutt (1952a) reviewed the book somewhat differently. In a disparaging image, he likened structural estimation to an attempt to discover the internal circuitry of a radio through manipulation of the dials. He stressed the crucial role of prior information in the theory as comprising "most of the big problems of inference." Orcutt called the crucial assumption of orthogonal errors between exogenous and endogenous variables "not operational," and he was clearly unwilling to let it rest as one of Haavelmo's "fruitful hypotheses." He admired the lucidity of the analysis of identification but pronounced that working with existing macroeconomic data was an "intractable problem" with the "way out" not clear.

Orcutt (1952b, c) argued that econometrics could develop as an experimental science and thereby escape the identification snare. By collecting data at the individual level one could hope to exploit better the process that was the source of the a priori knowledge in the first place. This kind of detail would let econometrics serve as a better "wind tunnel," to use Marschak's (1950) metaphor. One can add the advantage that the econometrician might also become more familiar with the data: especially outliers, non-linearities, and observation errors. Orcutt wrote in a very pragmatic vein, emphasizing the practical problems of a policy maker and not at all looking to further development of statistical theory as a solution.[52]

The Cowles Commission did not completely ignore the theory of structural estimation after relocating at Yale University in 1954. Tobin's (1958) estimator provided an important demonstration that adherence to the "probability approach" can also exploit special distributional properties of the cross section data recommended by Orcutt. After the move, however, the Commission focused much more on pure mathematical economics. The staff members involved with macroeconomic policy tended not to rely on large structural models for their conclusions.

The development of activity analysis at Cowles after 1947, under the direction of Koopmans, stood in remarkable contrast to the work in structural estimation in that it did not involve problems of statistical inference or hypothesis testing. A basic difficulty with structural estimation, as Friedman delighted in emphasizing, was that the choice of a model was often not independent of unwitting "psychological needs," i.e. ideological preconceptions, on the part of the investigator.[53] Activity analysis seemed to have some appeal as an economic model based on uncontroversial technical processes that could avoid the puzzles of multiple hypotheses and aggregation.[54] Structural estimation had always been exposited by the Cowles researchers as a problem in mathematical statistics, with few convincing examples drawn from actual economic experience. Consider, for example, Koopmans's lecture notes for his econometrics course:

> [One] raises the question of the meaning of a structural equation defined in terms of aggregates and/or index numbers. . . . Structural equations are formally defined by specifications derived from "theory." It is a problem of theory to explore how good these specifications are and whether they imply the postulated autonomy [and] the possibility for one relation to remain the same when structural changes occur in other equations of the model.[55]

Although it is not the purpose of this study to discuss activity analysis in detail, the method seemed to hold out the possibility of solving concrete economic planning problems. The suggestion here is that the Cowles group in the late 1940's saw it as a new methodology to realize many of the frustrated hopes for structural estimation.

Koopmans (1957) offered a last view of the state of econometrics as a science.[56] There he carefully stated the problems and prospects of the field, referring to themes he had reiterated since 1945. Now apparently more in agreement with some of the persistent criticisms of the existing models, he wrote:

> [There are] three avenues of possible improvement . . . more observations, better use of a priori knowledge, and better control of observations . . . all three avenues point towards further disaggregation.

In one brief paper in 1956 he revealed the feeling that the apparent superiority of the Klein-Goldberger model to a very naive GNP forecast for 1954 "constitutes the first ray of hope for structural estimation in a long time."[57] Such a small success after so many years was not enough to draw the Commission back into fundamental research in econometric theory. This tradition would not be revived until a new group of comparably skilled mathematical statisticians arrived on their staff in the late 1970's.

4.4 Structural Estimation after Cowles

A new generation of empirical research workers during the 1950's expected their work to reveal the value of the new estimation techniques, which soon included two-stage least squares (2SLS) — developed by Theil (1953) and Basmann (1957) as a computationally simpler alternative to LIML. In this context Bergstrom (1955) ventured the summary view that:

> Such empirical results as have been published provide little or no evidence that
> the estimates obtained by these methods, from small samples, are likely to be
> better than the asymptotically biased estimates obtained by least squares . . .

To explore this question further, Bergstrom constructed a model of export demand for New Zealand along neoclassical lines and estimated it using both OLS and LIML. He felt there was "little doubt" that LIML yielded preferable results and attributed it in part to specifying a "much larger number of equations" than was usually done in such work. His model for just three commodities (lamb, mutton, dairy) actually required eighteen endogenous variables. The resulting heavy degree of overidenti-fication for the demand equations might be expected to demonstrate the advantages of a systems estimator better than the miniscule differences with OLS reported, for example, in the very simple model of Haavelmo (1947).

This work is interesting as support for Koopmans, who wanted future econometric models to depend more, like linear programming models, on prices and technological details to incorporate microeconomic knowledge about the production side. Bergstrom's model also made good use of prior knowledge of the very competitive nature of the world markets under study, so that traditional economic theory could account satisfactorily for the consumer side. Production in his post-sample period was carried on under a novel system of guaranteed producer prices, precisely the kind of changed circumstance that theoretically requires structural estimation for effective prediction. In this instance the LIML results predicted as well or better than OLS in 13 out of 15 cases.

4.4.1 *The Klein-Goldberger Model and Its Critics*

The most influential work in simultaneous equations modeling, how-ever, continued to be the large Keynesian models developed under the aegis of Lawrence Klein. In his time at the Cowles Commission he had become painfully aware of specification problems and the poor quality of national income data. Experience had also shown that the "Haavelmo bias" was often hardly detectable. Moreover, nothwithstanding work such as Bergstrom's, macroeconomic applications placed less and less emphasis on the idea of structural interventions. Klein viewed the simultaneous equations methodology mainly as a technique to increase statistical efficiency through the prior restrictions. But even the very limited forecasting experience with models I-III revealed the doubtful validity of this information. The gross failure to predict the post-War surge in inflation and consumer demand compelled model revisions that were so major as to make efficient parameter estimation a matter of distinctly secondary importance. Klein framed his own research program after leaving the Cowles Commission in 1947, which constituted still another effort to meet the basic criticisms against Tinbergen-style models leveled by Friedman, Keynes, and others.

With his young assistant Arthur Goldberger, Klein restructured his earlier work into a form that proved immensely successful in popularizing the econometric analysis of macroeconomic policy. Their model was economically much more sophisticated than the Cowles project. It embodied many features, such as a production function, that Marschak had always argued were essential for a serious microeconomic approach to the Keynesian system.[58] The consumption function was also radically extended to include factors other than current income in an attempt to build in wealth effects, behavioral lags, and taxes. These improvements, which received good empirical support, no doubt led Klein to believe that the attacks by Friedman had been premature.

The Klein-Goldberger monograph (1955) made no direct reference to the great debates over methodology that had raged in Chicago a few years before. Its strengthened Keynesian foundations were accompanied by a broader theoretical eclecticism that usually dispensed with deduction of the structural equations from any rigorous model of behavior. Klein never directly discussed the implicit question of multiple hypotheses and it seems that he adopted Marshack's position, mentioned above in section 4.2.2.1, that the "true" model would eventually reveal itself given sufficient observations. He described his modeling strategy as follows:

> The task is not being viewed as a "once and for all" job. The research described here is part of a more continuous program in that new data, reformulations, and extrapolations are constantly being studied. As new observations or revised observations become available, the parameters of the model are re-estimated. As a result of forecasting experience and the acquisition of other a priori information, the equations are restructured. . . .[59]

This passage clearly indicates a degree of uncertainty in the model at any given moment that had little connection with computed measures such as R^2 or t ratios on particular coefficients. R.A. Fisher's "axiom of correct specification" stressed by Koopmans (1937) and Friedman (1940) continued to bedevil the interpretation of within sample significance tests in econometrics. Perhaps inevitably, Klein turned to out of sample forecasting as the most revealing test of a chosen structure, for the simple reason that it was not contaminated by the "statistical forcing towards conformity" which pervaded the estimation phase.

Klein had never been greatly interested in the formal small sample distribution problems that were studied in detail by other members of the Cowles Commission. The Klein-Goldberger model was estimated by LIML using 16 predetermined variables in a reduced form with only 18 observations but as to the statistical properties of the estimates Klein merely noted that "we do not introduce [asymptotic] bias." Exact confidence intervals were not urgent when coefficients of interest would be retained even if they were not "two or three time as large as their sampling error." The major inference problem arose instead from multicollinearity and the interpretation of different structures with "empirically unstable coefficients due to the presence of certain particular variables."[60] There was not much reason to expect that the sample information as embodied in asymptotic t ratios and the von Neumann ratio test for serially correlated residuals would be capable of determining a unique hypothesis. These difficulties lent a common-sense appeal to Klein's approach but it is fair to note that validation through forecasting under unchanged structure still did not justify a neglect of the available test for the overidentifying restrictions, which was particularly easy to carry out once the LIML calculations had been made. At the same time, one is struck by the virtual absence of the data based techniques used by earlier econometricians to reduce the danger of spurious inferences. It will be recalled that Tinbergen, in particular, used a great variety of trend and moving average corrections to filter the data prior to estimation. The Klein-Goldberger model used all variables in level form, presumably to maintain linearity of the structure, and used an occasional linear trend only to capture secular growth in population, inflation, or productivity.

The book did make one lasting innovation in technique that unfortunately became greatly abused in later years. A sequence of residuals from a structural equation, with the same sign and magnitude at the very end of the sample period, was taken as a sign of a structural change *if* it could be corroborated by other evidence, e.g. from survey data. In such cases the last residual would be added to the constant term of the equation in question as a rough correction for the forecasts until the structure could be revised more carefully. The "constant adjustment" was applied all too soon by many practitioners as a kind of patent medicine for cranky models when there was no other way to generate a plausible forecast. The adjustment never had a firm statistical basis and the original requirement to obtain outside evidence before its use was seldom respected by later generations of model builders.

As mentioned earlier, the Klein-Goldberger model made an auspicious debut with its forecasts for 1954. The 15 equation system was noticeably more accurate than the naive model and correctly predicted a turning point in GNP. The most important issues, however, pertained to the economic meaning of the estimated structure. Controversies that were not dispelled by forecasting successes again arose.

Klein himself was greatly puzzled by the continuing extremely weak relationship between interest rates and investment despite his best efforts to build it into the model.[61] The estimated investment function was driven almost entirely by non-wage income with a one year lag as a proxy for expected profits. This was of course the textbook extreme Keynesian case where the implied IS curve was vertical. Investment was still endogenous since expected profits were presumably correlated with a distributed lag on income, incidentally even strengthening the multiplier since the propensity to spend would exceed the simple MPC. Without an interest rate effect, however, the model left unanswered how one was to assess the liquidity preference theory. This linkage between the nominal and real sides of the economy was a vital feature of Keynes's break with classical doctrine.

The sample period in the earlier study covered the years 1921–1941. Klein-Goldberger, using revised data, was estimated over 1929–1952 while omitting 1942–1945. The new estimated long run marginal propensity to consume, when averaged over the three income categories, was slightly larger than the simple MPC from model III and also suggested a higher value for the multiplier. One of the major findings of the Klein-Goldberger project, however, was that the long run government spending multiplier was not likely to exceed 1.6 — compared to estimates of 1.9 and 3.37 in Klein (1950). The results might have been taken as evidence that the multiplier was unstable. Klein's view seemed to be that the lower values incorporated the effects of taxes and other automatic stabilizers. On this interpretation a falling multiplier for data sets with more observations after about 1940 (when income and social security taxes became more broad-based) would be capturing a genuine structural change in the economy. This question of stability was clearly important for policy analysis but it was not analysed further in the monograph. Since the importance of the stabilizers would bulk even larger with future data, it appears that Klein decided that the new model was simply more correct as the latest "reformulation."

No estimate was offered of the money supply multiplier but there was little reason to expect an effect much larger than the puny .19 reported in model II in 1950. The role of monetary policy was restricted to influencing excess reserves in the banking system and, in turn, the short term interest rate. Statistically, this relationship was also very weak. The long term rate was determined by the short rate with lags of 3 and 5 years but the authors themselves seemed sceptical about this equation. The household money demand function was notable for including a liquidity trap. In general, however, the monetary side of the model had minimal basis in prior theory and stood as an empirical add-on to the rest of the structure.[62]

4.4.1.1 The Econometrica Symposium

The number of simultaneous equations models grew swiftly after the appearance of the Klein-Goldberger work. More and more applied researchers were being trained in the techniques and the first programmable computers were coming on line to lower the real cost of estimating and simulating complicated systems. Microeconomic models were being developed, e.g. Hildreth and Jarrett (1955), and some work on sampling properties of different estimators was being conducted through now feasible Monte Carlo studies.

This high level of activity inspired the editors of *Econometrica* to sponsor a symposium in 1958 titled "Simultaneous equations estimation: Any verdict yet?" This was to be the first large public forum to evaluate the Cowles method since the tumultuous seminars in Chicago and Ithaca. Four papers were commissioned from some of the most experienced applied workers in the field. Remarkably, none of them expressed a clearly affirmative point of view.

Carl Christ (1960) and Clifford Hildreth (1960), former staff members of the Cowles Commission, expressed very cautious optimism. Christ's paper began with a footnote, however, that stated "the position taken here is somewhat more favorable than . . . that taken in the paper [as] presented in 1958." He cited favorable Monte Carlo evidence for simultaneous methods but stressed that OLS seemed to perform better in the presence of incorrect identifying restrictions, a very likely case in his view.[63]

Early in his paper Christ commented that the restrictions in empirical studies often lacked a compelling rationale and he was led to conclude that OLS as a practical matter was "by no means dead." The comparatively slow development of basic econometric theory during the 1950's is indicated by the almost identical statement made by Christ ten years earlier:

> Until it is shown in what cases least squares errors (i.e. bias plus sampling error) in small samples is in fact so large as to make least squares a poorer method than limited information for small samples, it may be just as well to use both methods.[64]

Christ based his comments on his review (1955) of the Klein-Goldberger model. They were more subdued than his very negative evaluation of models I-III at the NBER conference in 1949 but they left the impression that a prudent economist should be wary of the claims of the large model builders.

Hildreth wrote that current knowledge did not allow a verdict. He distinguished the roles of the "empirical researcher" and the "theoretical statistician" in econometrics. The first would always have to consider many problems besides simultaneity in judging a model. Hildreth at this time stressed serial correlation, non-normal disturbances, and time-varying parameters. The solution to any of them of course would require some use of theory so the job of the theorist would be to expand the repertoire of techniques and to determine their mathematical properties. Hildreth believed that the simultaneous model was conceptually inescapable in certain contexts and he reserved judgment on the various possible estimation methods until their small sample properties were better understood.

Lawrence Klein (1960) finally appeared to dispense with simultaneous methods on pragmatic grounds:

> The building of institutional reality into a priori formulations of economic relationships and the refinement of basic data collection have contributed much more to the improvement of empirical econometric results than have more elaborate methods of statistical inference.

Klein expected these factors to yield fifty percent gains in accuracy compared to at most ten percent from "more elaborate methods." He made less and less use of systems estimators and eventually chose to use only OLS, without correcting for serially correlated errors, to estimate the hundreds of equations in the Wharton quarterly model of the United States as late as 1979.

It appears that Klein was comparing the performance of 2SLS to OLS in large models, where the reduced forms necessarily have few degrees of freedom. A small number of degrees of freedom for the reduced form equations, of course, will tend to make the two procedures yield the same results: the small sample bias of 2SLS will approximate that of least squares. By the early 1960's applied workers were experimenting with a few principle components of the exogenous variables for large systems because the reduced forms could not even be estimated with all of them. This period marked the low point of concern with the true sampling properties of different econometric estimators in realistic sample sizes. Klein did not argue, as did Christ, that OLS may actually be preferable to 2SLS because of likely misspecification. However, to the extent that greater institutional realism was attained by imposing more overidentifying restrictions, failure to use a systems estimator passes up an opportunity to test some of the theory represented by the model.[65] Perhaps Klein was suggesting that the variations in parameter estimates from competing models dwarfed those found using different estimation procedures for the same model. This seems a likely possibility but econometrics had entered a period in which "multiple hypotheses" and related problems of hypothesis testing were no longer stressed as outstanding problems.[66]

Ta-Chung Liu (1960) became famous among econometricians for his contribution to the symposium. He believed that the typical identifying restriction in macroeconomic models was spurious, with little theoretical justification and not seriously believed even by the researcher who imposed it. He wrote:

> Statistical difficulties . . . rather than economic theory or a priori information are probably responsible for the tendency towards oversimplification. . . . [L]east squares reduced forms are likely to be better forecasting equations than the [solved] reduced form.

Since solved reduced forms were believed to generate more efficient forecasts, Liu took the frequently poor predictions as evidence of invalid restrictions.[67] He thought the only honest course would be to specify structural equations on the basis of available theory, without regard to their identifiablity. If the resulting system turned out to be identified then structural estimation would be justified. If not, the investigator would have to remain content with estimation of the reduced form until a theory could be developed to suggest more identifying variables or restrictions. Liu did not believe identification was a hopeless undertaking and, like Frisch, he specifically rejected "the foolish extreme of specifying that every variable is a function of all other variables." Since, however, macroeconomic theory usually did not provide sufficient restrictions, Liu advocated "freeing ourselves from the pretension of estimating structure." And in a specific rejection of the putative advantage of structural methods he used Klein's argument from 1946:

> Most of the structural changes we have in mind are changes in public policy variables (e.g. tax rates). These variables can be included in the structure as exogenous variables if we have past experience with them.[68]

Liu's severe comments on identification are thus part of a continuous current of thought in the history of econometrics. Of course, the usefulness of the estimated equations after the policy intervention, such as an unusual sequence of tax rate changes, would largely depend on the assumed structural model. For example, if the tax altered the marginal propensity to consume then a change in the tax might affect every parameter in the reduced form forecasting equation. Alternatively, a structural change could arise from factors not under the control of the policy maker (e.g. decreased transaction demand for cash due to technical advances in electronic banking technology) and an effective model might have to account for this trend explicitly. Liu seemed to doubt the feasibility of tracing behavior back to underlying tastes, institutions, and technology, at least in the context of aggregate macroeconomic models. The Cowles Commission thought this was best done if a structural parameter were used to represent a behavioral, institutional, or technical constraint. But by arguing that the "true" structure contains many variables in each equation, Liu described behaviors possibly too complex to understand with the available quantity of data.[69]

The seminar can only be described as inconclusive but the general view seemed to be that large macro models had become necessary tools even if their properties were not well understood. No policy debate would be complete from this time forward without some kind of econometric evidence. These pressures led to an emphasis on sheer estimation of the parameters of the different models with ever diminishing interest in the formal problems of statistical theory and multiple hypotheses. This would have been benign if the models did not imply contradictory policies and so could coexist peacefully. Reality, however, was different.

4.4.1.2 Monetarist Econometrics I: Friedman-Becker

The methodological war between Friedman and the Keynesian econometricians heated up publicly with a brief article published by Friedman and Becker (1957). Their argument focused on the sensitivity of the multiplier to different specifications of the consumption function. Friedman doubtless relished the steadily shrinking value of the spending multiplier reported in applied work, from approximately 5.0 in Ezekiel (1942) to a short run value of unity in the Klein-Goldberger model. The underlying question in Friedman-Becker was whether changes in investment due to Keynesian animal spirits could plausibly explain the business cycle, given that investment was on the order of only 10 percent of GNP. A small multiplier would seem to require extreme fluctuations for appreciable effects on total demand. Such instability could not be ruled out, as proved by the extraordinary collapse of investment in the early years of the Depression. Moreover, if consumer durables spending was more akin to investment than consumption, a relatively small multiplier working through their sum could still be an important economic mechanism. Nevertheless, the stage was being set for an alternative, monetary theory of the cycle.

Klein, of course, had already abandoned the basic textbook multiplier long before. Its obvious deficiencies led him to consumption functions of near Ptolomaic complexity. In contrast, Friedman and Becker explored the range of outcomes from a variety of simple models, each of which had at most two parameters. Their test at bottom consisted of the reduced form predictions of income using (1) the textbook $C_t = a + cY_t$, (2) the naive $C = C_{t-1}$, and (3) the textbook function modified to use a geometrically declining lag on income. Cases (2) and (3) had surprisingly small forecast errors that seemed comparable to the best results of Klein and others. But the naive model implied a multiplier of unity. Case (3) was very similar mathematically to the Klein-Goldberger formulation and its estimated parameters yielded a one year multiplier of about 1.4 directly.

Much has been written about the role of prediction in Friedman's (1953) notion of "positive economics." His argument should not be interpreted to mean that good forecasts necessarily validate a theory regardless of its assumptions. Friedman's insistence that assumptions not be judged by their a priori "realism" of course would be moot if they could be tested empirically. In so far as they were untestable, they were formally in the same category as the exactly identifying restrictions of a simultaneous equations model. Here Friedman had to face the same issue he had brought up in the Cowles seminars. The various consumption functions could not be significantly differentiated on the basis of R^2 or residual correlations. As posed, the naive model contained no economic hypothesis at all. By forecasting about as well as the Keynesian models, Friedman perhaps meant to suggest that both approaches were equally *unrealistic* in the sense that neither represented an autonomous economic structure. The key issue for model selection then was whether the particular a priori assumptions employed by a given theory generated fruitful insights for additional theoretical or applied work.

In this context the distributed lag function was of interest not merely because it forecast well but because it represented Friedman's new "permanent income" theory of consumption.[70] The "unrealism" of the theory was literally that permanent income could not be observed. This problem was seen to be a special case of the long neglected errors in variables regression model, which now could be interpreted as an *economic* hypothesis for the first time since Holbrook Working (1925). The distributed lag in essence used lags on measured income as instruments for the unmeasured ,factor in the estimation procedure. The more detailed theoretical and empirical work that followed in Friedman (1957) stood in the most remarkable contrast to the work in structural estimation that has been discussed up to this point. The hypothesis motivated a greatly simplified consumption function that had a clear basis in economic theory, received excellent empirical support, and resolved paradoxes in the data much more satisfactorily than. a great variety of ad hoc explanations that had been advanced elsewhere.

Friedman as usual knew how to nettle his opponents and accused them of accepting an empirical model that led to "a specification of the character of the economic system that our data do not support."[71] The lowered multiplier and the smoothing of consumption suggested that unstable private investment was not a general explanation of cycles. One might think that other econometricians would have been interested in the permanent income hypothesis, with the low weight it attached to current period income, as an explanation for the virtual absence of observed simultaneity bias in most macro-models. Such, however, was not the case. The initial reaction to the Friedman-Becker piece was obsessed with its use of the simplistic Keynesian consumption function, although more elaborate possibilities seemed only to lead back to Friedman's substantive conclusion.[72] Klein (1958), in particular, responded with a volley of new functions that, regardless of their other merits, implied multipliers of 1.3 or less.

The rebuttals might have done better to object to the two equation income-expenditure model as a test of Keynesian theory but this, of course, would have raised the deep question of the proper form of *the* model that was to be defended. Friedman was trying to win over the greatest number of economists by starting with simple hypotheses that, a la Marschak, could be checked over the longest possible time span (deflated income and savings data were available over the period 1905–1951). The implications over the choice of model were so momentous, however, that this bit of evidence limiting the multiplier was hardly enough to redirect the research program of either side in the debate. The Friedman-Becker article was only an opening skirmish in the long battle over the econometric interpretation of fiscal and monetary policy.

4.4.1.3 Monetarist Econometrics II: Freidman-Meiselman

By the end of the 1950's Friedman felt prepared to attempt a full scale assault on Keynesian economics. The alternative structure of the modern quantity theory had already received impressive empirical support in the unusual circumstances of a hyperinflation.[73] It was not specifically a theory of cycles and the question remained whether it could also dominate the "income-expenditure" approach as an explanation for deviations of real output from trend. The multiplier concept per se was not at issue: it also entered the quantity theory in the form of income velocity. Friedman was interested in elucidating a far more complex monetary mechanism than was recognized in the standard theory of liquidity preference. His real purpose was to argue that Keynesianism was properly treated as at best a special case of his revised classical theory (although his antagonists claimed exactly the reverse).

The small values of the spending multiplier found in nearly all applied work implied that household consumption had a large autonomous component that probably exceeded autonomous investment. As noted above, one of the principal devices used by Klein and others to explain swings in autonomous consumption was to specify dynamic, but ad hoc, "adjustment lags" in spending behavior. The other main innovation was to specify disaggregated consumption and investment demand equations that contained a liquid assets term (defined as holdings of currency and checking deposits) to capture wealth effects, as in Suits (1962). Liquidity preference theory was supposed to determine the stock of liquid assets. In Klein-Goldberger and many other Keynesian models this was the only way for interest rates to affect investment and consumption. The striking result was that the interest rate (measured as a corporate or government bond yield) had very doubtful significance when entered directly into any of these equations. The stock of liquid assets, however, appeared to be an extremely robust variable in explaining household and firm demand.

Hence by a process of trial and error the Keynesians seemed slowly to be acknowledging a critical role for the money supply also. Unlike Friedman, however, they argued that this had little policy relevance because the money supply was endogenous and not directly controllable. Open market operations might well be subsidiary to unpredictable borrowing at the discount window, changes in the currency ratio, or movements from demand deposits to near monies. Keynesians still insisted on fiscal policies for stabilization purposes.

The empirical strategy which Friedman chose to test the two approaches was nearly the same as the one he had described in 1943.[74] Given that both models probably contained a grain of truth, it would be crucial to explore (1) whether one systematically predicted better, and (2) whether one had significantly more *stable* estimated parameters regardless of its forecasting ability. Neither property is implied by the other. The emphasis on stability was uncannily reminiscent of one of the original questions stressed by the Cowles Commission. It was dropped there presumably because the size of the models left too few degrees of freedom in the data to make very meaningful inferences about possible structural changes. Friedman kept his competing models extremely simple to allow testing over the few years of each cycle since 1897. Of course he had to assume that the differences between them were so gross that they would be clearly discernable even with the misspecification inherent in three-parameter equations estimated often with fewer than 10 observations.

The empirical results were published by Friedman and Meiselman (1963) as a contribution to a research volume sponsored by the Commission on Money and Credit. This organization was created by the Committee for Economic Development, the group referred to in section 4.2.1 above. The blue-chip composition of the Commission suggested it might actually have the influence to change "the structure, operations, regulation, and control of our monetary and credit system," as their preface to the volume proclaimed. Perhaps this accounts for the uncompromising tone of the article. In addition, it was completed as the Keynesians were celebrating their attainment of power in Washington after the election of John Kennedy. One assumes that Friedman now decided he had to take his case before a wider audience.

Their conclusion instantly became famous, even notorious:

> The empirical results are remarkably consistent and unambiguous. The evidence is so one-sided that its import is clear *without* the nice balancing of conflicting bits of evidence, the *sophisticated examination of statistical tests of significance,* and the *introduction of supplementary information.* The income velocity of circulation of money is consistently and decidedly stabler than the investment multiplier except only during the early years of the Great Depression. . . .[75]

This was intended as a first round knockout punch. The allusion to Cowles Commission style models suggested that their major weakness was to overgeneralize from a limited, and possibly exceptional, post-1929 sample period. Friedman sidestepped the simultaneity issue by estimating very simple reduced forms (similar to Klein's Model II) where consumption C was explained as a function of either autonomous spending A (measured as private net investment plus the government deficit), money M (liquid assets plus time deposits), or both. The major statistical problem was still consistency of the estimates but this arose from the old problem of errors in variables, not simultaneity. Variables A and M were theoretical constructs that were not necessarily correctly represented by the measures used by Friedman and Meiselman. First differences were used extensively to remove common trends in the variables. The flavor of their many results is conveyed by their finding that the sample partial correlation $r_{CA.M}$ over 1897-1958 was a *negative* value of -.222 while $r_{CM.A}$ equalled .967. Moreover, $r_{CA.M}$ varied wildly over the subperiods while $r_{CM.A}$ remained quite steady.[76]

The most important implication was that money was a better predictor of nominal income (and real income in the short run). The case for the k percent growth rule of the money supply seemed established, whereas fiscal policy appeared to act as a dangerously unpredictable drug. From Friedman's point of view, his monetary theory was a little David that succeeded against the Goliath of Keynesian multi-equation systems. His results were all the more disturbing to Keynesians who, as mentioned before, were positing structures of greatly increased complexity. The quantity theory rested on the microeconomic premise of a stable demand function for real money balances. Like the permanent income hypothesis, it had a simplicity that seemed almost incredible for the scale of the phenomena it was supposed to explain. But Friedman could argue that his theory was truly structural and that the apparent richness of the empirical Keynesian alternatives was a hodgepodge of correlations that either were spurious or had little "autonomy" in Frisch's sense.

As might be expected, the Friedman-Meiselman study generated a vigorous counterliterature. The most cogent criticisms focused on the role of particular definitions of autonomous spending and the money supply and the possibility that the money supply in fact had a significant *endogenous* component, thereby necessitating a simultaneous model after all. For example, by counting only government spending rather than the budget deficit as part of autonomous spending, DePrano and Mayer (1965) reversed the negative correlation with consumption and were able to draw much more favorable inferences for the "income-expenditure" approach. They did not examine stability over subperiods, however, and it also was not clear if different concepts of spending were relevant for short and long run analysis. Ando and Modigliani (1965) argued that money had autonomous and induced components which could not be correctly modeled with a single equation.

Friedman and Meiselman (1965) yielded ground partially on the autonomous spending issue. Empirically, however, they doubted the importance of the induced component of the money supply. Two other problems with the quantity theory were of greater policy interest. First, even perfect control of nominal money and nominal income (via the velocity multiplier) did not imply the same control over real income. Neither Friedman nor the Keynesians had a well developed theory to predict the magnitude of inflation in this context. Only in a hyperinflation could one argue that price changes act swiftly to keep the real money supply independent of money creation. The second difficulty was that velocity trended and was not stable over the cycle. Without an explanation of velocity the theory was incomplete in an important sense.

Friedman-Meiselman did not rout the Keynesians as they had hoped but their work was still an extremely telling critique. The Keynesians began to revise the monetary side of their models in ways that preserved short run fiscal effects while continuing to plan more detailed policies through the disaggregation of each sector. Friedman did not engage in extensive econometric work after this time but other monetarists attempted multi-equation extensions of the quantity theory to make it an operational short run policy tool. Hence *both* sides in the debate were compelled to specify and estimate larger and more complex *systems* of equations with all the attending problems of inference that have been discussed so far.[77]

4.4.1.4 The Exit of Frisch and Haavelmo from Econometrics

In a remarkable essay in 1961, Ragnar Frisch chose not to mention econometrics in a survey of types of economic forecasting methods and dismissed what he called the method of trend extrapolation for not analyzing the detailed mechanisms of policy.[78] He had come to believe that the models were hollow numerical exercises because they seldom represented the effective institutional and political constraints on feasible economic policies. This was a hard disappointment for the economist who had once argued the most forcefully for the value of structural estimation.

Haavelmo (1958) had also argued that weak theoretical economic foundations rendered suspect the policy value of most econometric models. He was devoting the end of his career to re-examining the neoclassical theory of investment. The easy optimism in the years immediately following the

1938 League of Nations conference was gone. When this essay appeared none of the original corps of econometricians, with the exception of Lawrence Klein, was still involved with building structural equation systems.[79]

The Oslo professors did not equate the practical failure of their econometric research with the infeasibility of designing effective government policies. Their interests turned more towards the implementation of a system of democratic central planning where key variables could be controlled directly. In the United States, on the other hand, the feeling grew among the Keynesian economists that the prospects for successful, truly "complete" macroeconomic models were about to be realized.

4.4.2 Triumph and Crisis of Large Models

It was argued in section 3.1 that the ideals of structural estimation resonated with much of the early post-War liberal economic program. As we have seen, the Cowles Commission found it nearly impossible to demonstrate a realistic capacity for their methods to guide the kinds of "social engineering" projects which Marschak had discussed in 1941. Simultaneity bias only added to the long-standing problems of weak theoretical models and poor data as obstacles to meaningful statistical inference in macroeconomics. It would have been extraordinary if the first products of Klein and others played a significant role in the actual policy process or in private business planning.

The relationship between academic work in econometrics and the outside world started to change dramatically during the 1960's. Econometrics quickly grew as a most prestigious and financially well-supported specialty. Progress in computer technology suddenly made the everyday use of econometric methods feasible and sparked a general interest among non-statistically trained economists in what had formerly been a comparatively arcane and controversial subject. Journals swelled and multiplied to keep up with the immensely varied outpouring of theoretical and applied research.[80] The huge project mounted at Brookings, published as Duesenberry, Klein, and Fromm (1965), epitomized the confidence of the Keynesian practitioners of the era: a model involving dozens of collaborators whose efforts were expected to hold the attention of the nation's highest economic policy makers. The most important monetarist model was about to be constructed by the St. Louis Federal Reserve Bank. The smooth trend of Great Society prosperity seemingly confirmed the skills of the macroeconomic forecasters and encouraged belief in the practicability of optimal control methods for guiding economic policy. Coincidentally, this last development was almost on schedule for Marschak's "theory of rational policy," mentioned above in section 2.2.1, which had been envisioned as a fifteen year research effort.[81]

Advances in econometric theory per se in these years consisted mostly of rather straightforward innovations in existing estimation procedures, e.g. random coefficients, seemingly unrelated regressions, and three-stage least squares. These could almost be considered as ingenious uses of algebra rather than statistics. Such estimators were really generalized forms of OLS, when derived for the asymptotic case. The theory of identification was carried forward by Wegge (1965) to cover arbitrary non-linear systems but work of this sort was already extremely recondite and of little interest to most investigators.[82] The critical *statistical* problems of correct finite sample hypothesis tests, surely the foundation for studying model selection, were too complicated to solve analytically and extensive Monte Carlo studies seldom produced definitive results.

A handful of theoretical econometricians kept working on what Koopmans had left as the "remaining statistical problems" but the extreme mathematical difficulty of such work virtually assured little interaction with more mainstream researchers. The first advance in a small sample theory for structural estimators was Basmann (1961), who found the exact distribution of the 2SLS estimator for particular models that he called "leading cases." His article demonstrated the special power of the new level of mathematical sophistication. The variance of the 2SLS estimator was shown not to exist for equations with a single overidentifying restriction. Earlier workers had assumed 2SLS could be meaningfully compared to OLS in this case using mean-squared error criteria. Moreover, analytical formulae could resolve many conflicting Monte Carlo simulation studies by revealing the precise implications of different assumptions about underlying parameter values.[83] Bergstrom (1962) was able to derive the exact distribution of the MPC estimated by OLS and LIML in Haavelmo's (1947) simple Keynesian model. Bergstrom's principal result was that LIML was median unbiased but had thicker tails than OLS, implying a greater probability of outlier estimates. This behavior had been noticed at an early stage, as attested by Solow's (1951) review, but workers in the late 1950's often thought it due to LIML being somehow more affected by collinearity than OLS.[84] If knowledge of the exact distribution of the available estimators is viewed as part of the fund of prior information, this kind of research is in keeping with Haavelmo's (1944) insistence on using all such knowledge in order to lessen the number of spurious inferences made by econometricians.[85] In an sustained research effort that extended into the early 1980's, the theoreticians had remarkable success in attacking further unfinished problems in identification and estimation of models formulated in continuous time.[86]

But the 1960's above all was the blossoming of the applied econometrician as an expert consultant to government on a huge variety of economic and social questions. The studies that were regularly produced recall Marschak's disclaimer, mentioned in section 2.3.1, that applied work often defied interpretation in terms of rigorous prior economic and statistical theory (and so had an inevitably ad hoc quality). To be sure, there were successes in macroforecasting and other applications. It can be argued, however, that these projects also served to retard the scientific progress of the subject. The fascination with attempts to estimate an aggregate Phillips curve, the level of many econometric policy discussions during the 1960's, was symptomatic of a major change in research emphasis compared to the early work by Tinbergen and the Cowles Commission. It marked the extreme concern with model *estimation* as distinct from model *evaluation.*[87] The Phillips curve was actually a prime example of all the conceptual difficulties encountered in estimating structural relations: autonomy, exogeneity, structural change, aggregation, and expectations. The enormous number of different curves that were estimated, as in Perry (1966), would indicate that multiple hypotheses and costs of model misspecification were still pressing problems. As a general matter, however, most studies hardly seemed to be aware of these issues and they seldom indicated the robustness of their results or the (true) levels of the reported significance tests.

The harshest professional scepticism towards the large models since Friedman-Meiselman came in a mid 1960's conference paper published as Basmann (1972). Not referring explicitly to multiple hypotheses, Basmann nonetheless accused the Brookings project leaders of practicing "number mysticism" and intimated that the science was being undermined by premature efforts to market econometric techniques to politicians. The charge was reminiscent of Keynes's description of Tinbergen as an astrologer. The prominence of these models made them natural targets for such attacks, even though they were built far more carefully than many others. In marked contrast to the humility of the early Cowles staff, the reaction of Klein and Fromm (1972) displayed a fierce defensiveness, but one which ultimately failed to silence a growing professional disquiet with their approach to modeling.

The 1970's witnessed a flood of criticism that commenced even before the OPEC crisis. The papers in Hickman (1972) were typical of a renewed interest in ex post testing in the manner of Christ (1951). A new generation of naive time series models frequently appeared to offer comparable short run forecasting ability.[88] The subsequent forecasting debacles might have been valuable as "disconfirmations" of the theories embodied in the models but there is little indication in the many published acknowledgments of "structural breaks" after 1973 as to the precise lessons that were learned.[89]

The past decade has served to bring into the open the economic and statistical deficiencies of much modern applied econometric work. Very large models now are not so much the object of reform as abandonment by many academic researchers. In part due to the Lucas (1976) critique, attention is turning to smaller systems that have more explicit and tractably rigorous microeconomic foundations. These models are at the new frontier of applied research by making use of increasingly available panel data sets. Because these efforts are so recent it is still too early to assess their potential contribution. One might expect that multiple hypotheses will still be an important issue, particularly when the sample contains individuals with heterogeneous underlying behavior patterns. Aggregation and nonlinearities will almost surely rise again as major concerns in interpretation of the results.

The smaller, more microeconomic oriented systems may be able to draw on a larger fund of prior economic theory than the large macro models to produce more satisfactory policy analyses. In addition, limiting the focus to particular markets or geographical areas may allow greater representation of institutional constraints that are crucial for designing appropriate interventions. Clarification of the links between these models and the behavior of the macroeconomic aggregates would also seem to pose challenges for the econometrician as great as the analysis of "complete" systems of linear difference equations that commenced with Mann and Wald in 1943. For these reasons, the panel models promise to offer a significant research program whose value will only become clear after comparable expenditures of intellectual energy.

The most welcome change in recent econometric practice is the new focus on within sample model evaluation. The econometric literature on non-nested hypothesis tests has sprung from the work of the statistician Cox (1961). Since only asymptotic distribution theory exists for many of these tests it is still a very open question as to their power in small samples. Competing models presumably fit well in a given sample so that choosing one on purely statistical grounds would seem to suffer from what might be termed highly collinear hypotheses.[90] It hardly seems likely that all econometric investigators will ever arrive at the same conclusions, as Klein (1947) had hoped. The emphasis on model evaluation should have scientific value, however, both for possibly reducing the number of acceptable competing models and for simply better indicating the true extent of the uncertainty about economic structure.

It is clear that the range of empirical questions economists would like to be able to answer is still far beyond the current capability of econometrics. The experiences of the last generation have shown this much. The basic task of the subject still remains as Koopmans (1949b) described: (1) to formulate all hypotheses of interest, (2) to devise appropriate estimation procedures, (3) to select all hypotheses best, or equally, supported, and (4) to establish confidence levels for the results. Recent years have witnessed a quantum advance in technique.[91] This book has tried to show the vitality of this research when the need is to evaluate substantively different theories of the economic world. One may fairly wonder whether the attempt to estimate structural equations will ever be rewarded by a solid quantitative understanding of the workings of real policies. There seems little other way to find out than to continue developing appropriate statistical methods to investigate hypotheses of interest. The key technical problems will continue to be the derivation of more finite sample distributions of estimators and test statistics in conjunction with further development of temporally finer disaggregate data bases. From this perspective, structural estimation is still in a developmental stage which may make it unrealistic to expect very compelling practical results for some time yet.

NOTES TO CHAPTER 4

[1]This comment seems to have been the germ for Koopmans and Reiersøl (1950).

[2]Frisch (1934, p. 84) had also made this point but a rigorous argument and demonstration in the econometrics literature was not advanced until James and Stein (1961). Stein also attended the 1946 conferences; Wald may have had influence on him as well.

[3]Cf. the arguments of Stone and the "English school" discussed in the next chapter.

[4]"Minutes of Discussion of Papers on Multivariate Analysis for Non-Experimental Data and Related Problems of Matrix Computation," 23 August 1946, CCA, CCDP Statistics volume I. Girschick's initial enthusiasm for structural estimation in the New York "seminar" had cooled considerably by this time.

[5]John W. Tukey, "Further Remarks on the Cowles Commission's Multivariate Problems," CC 2.8, August 1946, CCA, CCDP Statistics volume I.

[6]Minutes of Staff Meeting, 8 February 1946, CCA, CCDP Minutes 1945-46.

[7]See, e.g., Hildreth and Jarrett (1955) and Anderson et al. (1983).

[8]Bergstrom (1976) has discussed this difference in outlook in the context of continuous time econometric models.

[9]This approach was later formalized with appropriate test statistics by Wegge (1978) in an independent development.

[10]Tukey, loc. cit.

[11]Marschak, "Quantitative Studies in Economic Behavior," Memorandum to SSRC, 6 June 1946, CCA, RFN.

[12]Theodore Yntema, "The Problem of Unemployed Resources," 10 March 1941, CCA, folder: Research Plans, miscellaneous old ones.

[13]Ibid.

[14]These letters are quoted in excerpt by Marschak, Memorandum re

Schumpeter, 23 November 1946, CCA. The other main problem concerned the treatment of agents' expectations and is discussed in section 6.4.1.2.

[15]See Schumpeter (1951).

[16]Irving Fisher to Alfred Cowles, 4 April 1946, Container 24, Irving Fisher Papers, Yale University Library.

[17]Fisher to Max Sasuly, 2 April 1946, Container 24, Fisher Papers.

[18]Irving Fisher, *The Rate of Interest* (New York: MacMillan, 1931).

[19]Chester Bowles, the OPA administrator, also understood the problem in terms of a psychology of inflation expectations that did not enter econometric models for another 30 years:

> [The public has] vast buying power ... liquid assets at 300 billion. Today these dollars are held safely in savings accounts and in securities because people have confidence in the inflation control program. ... If that confidence falters, ... it will produce just the inflation that is feared. These dollars will be stampeded into a mad scramble.

From "Extension of Remarks by Alben Barkley," *Congressional Record Appendix*, 21 June 1945, p. A2964.

[20]Minutes of Staff Meeting, 11 January 1946, CCA.

[21]Minutes of Cowles Commission Conference, 19 September 1946, CCA.

[22]Minutes of Staff Meeting, 6 December 1946, CCA.

[23]Minutes of Staff Meeting, 5 March 1947, CCA.

[24]Marschak, Memorandum to SSRC, 6 February 1946, CCA, ACN.

[25]From an unsigned memorandum probably written by Marschak in 1943 titled "Outline for Theoretical and Statistical Research in the Explanation of Business Cycles and Connected Policy Problems," n.d., CCA: folder Cowles Commission Research Programs.

[26]Christ, *Economic Theory and Measurement*, p. 41.

[27]Don Patinkin, "Manufacturing 1921–1941: Preliminary Report," 27 February 1948, CCA, CCSP Econ. 218.

[28]Marschak, "Quantitative Studies in Economic Behavior."

[29]Staff Meeting on Statistics Paper 107, 12 June 1947, CCA, Minutes of Staff Meetings (hereafter cited as MSM).

[30]See "Discussion of Colin Clark's Macro Model of the U.S. 1920–1940," 8 October 1947, CCA, MSM.

[31]Minutes of Cowles Commission Conference, 20 September 1946, CCA, MSM.

[32]One solution to the problem might be to provide an economic argument to explain the generation of all the variables under examination. But as argued in chapter 6, this solution would require the exogenous variables to be modeled as well: an extreme demand that the econometricians hoped was unnecessary for estimation of "complete systems." The "encompassing principle" for model selection put forward by Hendry and Richard (1982) and Hendry (1983) appears to call for such analyses. It seems that selecting a unique model when several appear to satisfy purely statistical selection criteria (such as serially random estimated residuals) must ultimately invoke some form of prior economic theory to resolve what is at bottom a problem of collinearity.

[33]Koopmans, "Statistical Problems of Importance to the Cowles Commission Program," January 1947, CCA.

[34]The Cowles Commission *Annual Report* for 1948 states "The economist is faced with a wide variety between individuals . . . [but] he can examine his own motivation." But see the quotation from Katona on "wishful thinking," section 3.2 above.

[35]See Koopmans, "Notes of Conversation with M. A. Girschick," 5 January 1947, CCA, CCDP Minutes 1947-49.

[36]Leamer's (1982) extreme bounds analysis (EBA) has a similar basis in concern over selective reporting of results in applied work. The method computes the range over which an estimated coefficient varies after inclusion or exclusion of all combinations of the other variables in the equation. As an attempt to trace the effects of collinearity in the sample, however, it disregards the potentially different costs of specification error and attaches equal weight to all estimates. Moreover, the EBA provides a striking contrast to Koopmans's 1941 essay by making no use of prior information on expected signs or serial correlation properties of the residuals. A telling critique of the EBA when such information is available is McAleer, Pagan, and Volcker (1985).

[37]See Friedman (1953), p. 12.

[38]His study of the consumption function, Friedman (1957), was intended

to explode the theoretical basis of Klein's models.

[39]See Friedman (1951). Rutledge Vining (1949, 1956) wrote in very similar terms, condemning the idea that aggregate data revealed any unique "underlying behavior patterns."

[40]Milton Friedman, "Methods of Predicting the Onset of Inflation," in *Taxing to Prevent Inflation,* ed. Carl Shoup (New York: Columbia University Press, 1943), p. 114.

[41]From Minutes of Cowles Commission Conference, 20 September 1946, CCA, MSM.

[42]His comment was in regard to Colin Clark's macro model of the U.S. for 1920-1940. From Discussion Meeting, Minutes of 8 October 1947, CCA.

[43]Marschak to Domar, 11 April 1947, CCA.

[44]From unpublished draft of Cowles Commission annual report for 1944, 10 January 1945, CCA.

[45]Cf. Marschak's approach to policy, discussed in section 2.3.1, which consisted of manipulating indices of aggregate variables.

[46]"Discussion to Size-up Results of Business Cycle Conference," Staff Memorandum, December 1949, CCA. Leontief (1971) reiterated the point that "in no other field of empirical inquiry has so massive and sophisticated a statistical machinery been used with such indifferent results." Hatanaka (1975) showed that a priori unknown lag lengths greatly restricted the use of lagged endogenous variables for purposes of identification.

[47]A project called "Statistical Inference Regarding Stochastic Processes" was considered along with the recruitment of Ulf Grenander as a Cowles staff member. Koopmans to W. A. Wallis, 21 July 1950, CCA, folder: Cowles Commission research programs.

[48]"Comments on Macroeconomic Model Construction," [1951?], CCA, CCDP Econ. 2008.

[49]This repeated objection by Wold and his followers is discussed in the next chapter.

[50]Koopmans' exposition (1945) used *artificial* data to create an example where the OLS estimators were biased as much as 40 percent below the true parameter values. Basmann (1963a) indicated how the solution to

this puzzle depended on a quantity called the concentration parameter, which may be interpreted as the amount of information in the over-identifying restrictions. A lucid discussion of its importance in determining the characteristics of estimated parameters is Anderson et al. (1983).

[51]This review was apparently intended for publication in the journal *Skandinavisk Aktuarietijdskrift* but was not printed there. A mimeograph copy is in CCA, folder: reviews of Cowles Commission monographs.

[52]His fundamental criticism of exogeneity assumptions in structural estimation is discussed in chapter 6.

[53]See Friedman (1953), p. 12.

[54]The theory presented in *Activity Analysis of Production,* Cowles Commission Monograph 13, aimed to avoid "the specific difficulty of the diversity of individual interests." From Cowles Commission, *19th Annual Report for 1951*, p. 16, CCA.

[55]From "Statistical Methods of Measuring Economic Relationships," Lecture Notes taken by Carl Christ, Autumn 1947, CCA, CCDP Stat. 310, p. 45.

[56]This essay reads as a rejoinder to Friedman (1953). I thank David Weiman for this connection.

[57]From Cowles Foundation Discussion Paper No. 12, 10 May 1956, Cowles Foundation Library.

[58]The lecture notes of Marschak's macroeconomics course at Chicago in 1948, published as Marschak (1951), were remarkably ahead of their time for concentrating on the full aggregate demand–aggregate supply model that has overtaken IS–LM analysis in recent years.

[59]From Klein and Goldberger (1955), p. 1.

[60]The quoted phrases are from Klein and Goldberger (1955), pp. 1, 47, 72, and 68.

[61]See section 4.2.1 above.

[62]The monetary theory represented by the revised Klein-Goldberger model appended to Klein (1966) bore even less resemblance to that of Keynes or anyone else. It dispensed with the liquidity trap and appeared to be the product of many hours of fishing in a sea of data.

[63]This outcome, which is intuitively plausible, received more analytical support twenty years later in the work by Hale, Mariano, and Ramage (1980).

[64]Carl Christ, "A Revised Klein Econometric Model for the U.S.," 7 October 1949, CCA, CCDP Econ. 269. A revised version was published as Christ (1951).

[65]A virtual "lone wolf" in his emphasis on testing the restrictions rather than estimating the parameters was Basmann (1965b).

[66]The next subsection discusses how these research priorities started to be reversed in the 1970's.

[67]Only when attention was refocused on sampling theory could this view be properly qualified. See section 4.4.2 below.

[68]Marschak once rebutted this last point of Liu's by arguing:

> The structural parameters may still be necessary if there are changes in structure due to causes other than policy, e.g. if [with] a linear in parameters equation ... we have moved to a different region of the curve so that extrapolation fails.

From Minutes of Discussion 137 on Paper Econ. 259, "What kind of Econometric Research is Required for Economic Policy," 22 April 1949, CCA. Accurate estimation of such non-linearities, however, is seldom possible and Marschak did not recommend it in the surviving memoranda on Klein's empirical work.

[69]T. W. Schultz remarked concerning business cycle analysis:

> Neo-classical economics gives us a powerful concept to understand the long-run, but is not very effective for short-run quick changes. We cannot describe and identify the variables that affect the short run, they are too complex.

From Minutes of 12th Meeting of the University of Chicago Advisory Committee, 24 March 1947, CCA, ACN.

[70]It had first been developed by Friedman in the late 1930's (published as part of Friedman and Kuznets [1945]) to explain the pattern of earnings for different occupational groups.

[71]From Friedman and Becker (1957).

[72]See Kuh (1958) and Johnston (1958).

[73]The classic reference is Friedman (1956).

[74]See section 4.2.3 above.

[75]From Friedman and Meiselman (1963), p. 186 (emphasis added).

[76]By exploiting subperiods as a test for structural changes in the reduced form Friedman seemed to share Tukey's opinion, mentioned in section 4.1, that convincing interpretation of macroeconomic data would have to "detour" the details of identification.

[77]For a post-script on Friedman-Meiselman, see section 6.3.3 below on Granger causality testing and section 6.4.2.1 on rational expectations.

[78]Ragnar Frisch, "A Survey of Types of Economic Forecasting and Programming," (Oslo: University Economics Institute, 1961).

[79]T. W. Anderson, however, continued theoretical work in time-series. He and a number of his students trained as mathematical statisticians returned to fundamental study of the LIML estimator in the 1970's.

[80]It is not our purpose here to give an account of all of these developments.

[81]The specifications of these models are of some historical interest but they will not be discussed in detail. The Brookings model contained some important improvements over Klein-Goldberger, most notably Jorgenson's (1963) "cost of capital" approach that restored the interest rate as a significant determinant of investment. Klein eventually was awarded the Nobel Memorial Prize for integrating separate national models into a "world model": Project LINK.

[82]Fisher's (1966) notion of identification in a block recursive structure of course was useful in building large models. Identification problems did not again seem very urgent until the proliferation of rational expectations models in the 1970's. See section 6.4 below.

[83]For a forceful discussion of this point see Maasoumi and Phillips (1982).

[84]They were not altogether wrong in so far as high collinearity between included and excluded exogenous variables implies a lower value of the concentration parameter, hence greater dispersion of the estimators. Of course, the key role of the concentration parameter was only discovered in the course of study of the exact distributions.

[85]For example, longstanding conflicting views about the efficiency of forecasts from unrestricted OLS reduced forms and solved reduced forms began to be settled in a note by McCarthy (1972), who showed that the solved reduced form coefficients computed with 2SLS structural estimates do not possess finite variances when the structural equations are

overidentified. For an authoritative survey of the entire field of finite sample distribution theory see Phillips (1984).

[86]See, e.g., Bergstrom (1976) and Bergstrom (1983). These models are likely to find especially fruitful application in finance.

[87]Sargan (1964) was a significant exception that unfortunately was not more influential in keeping the main focus of econometrics on critical testing of hypotheses.

[88]Cf. the discussion of Orcutt (1948) and Box and Jenkins (1970) in chapter 5. Friedman's naive model in many cases only required the fitting of a second order autoregressive term to perform very well in the "horse races" reported in Nelson (1972).

[89]Cf. section 6.8 on the shortcomings of the alternative methodology of VAR models in this regard.

[90]For a current discussion and references of available techniques see Chow and Corsi (1983). A "model reduction" strategy such as Sargan's COMFAC procedure, discussed in section 5.1.4.2 below, differs in that it assumes a correct initial specification.

[91]The current state of the art is well represented by the contributions to the *Handbook of Econometrics*, Zvi Griliches and Michael Intriligator eds., 3 vols. (Amsterdam: North Holland, 1985) and the literature referenced in Judge et al. (1985).

CHAPTER 5

CONTEMPORARY ALTERNATIVES TO SIMULTANEOUS
EQUATIONS ESTIMATION

5.1 Comparative Developments in England 1939–54

5.1.1 *Introduction*

A style of econometrics began to emerge in England towards the end of the 1930's that differed substantially from earlier developments in Holland and the United States. The initial center for this work was the Department of Applied Economics founded at Cambridge University in 1939. Unlike the Cowles Commission, its efforts were not motivated by the problem of inference in simultaneous equations models. Furthermore, although Cambridge was the home of Keynes, the work there did not take the form of testing business cycle theories. The character of the English school derived from the native strength in theoretical statistics and the long standing practical impulse to quantify the tradition of economic analysis which is represented by Marshall, Pigou, and Hicks. When the Department began effective operation in April 1946, after overcoming many delays caused by the War, it concentrated its research activities in the main areas of theoretical time series analysis, improved methods of data collection, and detailed empirical investigations.[1]

The war years, however, greatly influenced its various endeavors. The study of economic time series was intensified, as in the United States, by the successful applications of prediction theory in electrical engineering and ballistics. The interest in econometric models seems initally to have taken two principal forms. The first was the compilation of a trustworthy set of national income accounts. Richard Stone, who became the first Department director in 1946, was a central figure in such work as Stone et al. (1942), which found immediate use in war finance policy. This use of the data, in conjunction with input-output analysis after the War, provided a basis for development planning models. The second was the quantification of models of consumer demand. This project was undertaken towards the end of the War and was originally intended to aid in the administration of what was expected to be a prolonged period of rationing of consumer goods. It evolved by degrees into an effort to scientifically test the validity of microeconomic demand theory as reformulated by Hicks (1939). The influence of this English work as it developed after 1946 was comparable to that of the Cowles Commission in establishing directions for econometric research.

5.1.2 *Research Orientation at Cambridge*

5.1.2.1 Keynesian Influence

There is some evidence to suggest that the Department of Applied Economics was intended at its inception to provide empirical alternatives to Tinbergen's macrodynamic models, on the one hand, and to Henry Schultz's single-market demand studies on the other. Keynes began to advocate the creation of such a department early in 1938, when these two investigators were receiving maximum attention. In a letter on business cycles to Colin Clark, objecting to the assumption of a constant MPC in empirical work, Keynes pointedly wrote:

> It is very necessary to lay the foundations for a proper department of statistical realistic economics at Cambridge.[2]

Keynes's correspondence over the next two years reveals a ferocious campaign to discredit the activities of Tinbergen and, later, Kalecki. Roy Harrod, Keynes's disciple at Cambridge, was more favorably disposed to their efforts but they apparently shared the opinion that Schultz's work was "a waste of time." Keynes may have desired the creation of an opposite pole to the Oxford Institute of Statistics where Marschak had just been appointed director. Harrod was of the opinion that Marschak was a "kind of minor Tinbergen" but this was not entirely just: Marschak worked best when developing the ideas of others and his later contributions to other parts of economic theory, especially the area of information, were deservedly influential.[3] But Keynes's influence seemed quite decisive at Cambridge: the *General Theory* was never treated there with Tinbergen's methods. The new Department came into being in 1939 with Keynes as chairman, who chose to refer to it as "Realistic Economics" instead of using the official name.[4] Until the end of the War it led a "purely formal existence" but this quickly changed in 1946 when Stone, who had worked closely with Keynes on the war budgets, became the active director of its research program.[5]

Stone often paid tribute to Keynes's devotion to empirical research but, unlike Keynes, he saw multiple correlation analysis as an essential tool for this work. Keynes's opposition to this method was extraordinarily unyielding.[6] He seemed to view quantitative policy problems as very concrete issues to be analyzed with some form of a balance sheet, as suggested in Keynes (1939b). One empirical project that received his active support was experimenting with the method of "mass observation," i.e. surveys, for discovering expenditure patterns and preferences regarding rationing, taxes, and wage deferrals in the wartime anti-inflation program. He utilized some of this work in preparing his 1941 war budget proposals. The continued tension with regression methods can be noted in Keynes's condemnation of other work on savings behavior by Mendershausen (1940), who by then was at the Cowles Commission, for using multiple correlation analysis that was "too elaborate and adds little or nothing."[7] Stone (1954a) carefully distanced his Department from this attitude. Although engaged in different pursuits from the Cowles Commission, both groups shared the new faith that econometric modeling would provide a valuable basis for post-War economic policy.

Stone and his group did not follow the precedents set by the Dutch and American work that often displayed little direct connection to the formal body of then recognized economic theory. The methodological difference arose in that much of this earlier work consisted of searching through a list of lags and other regressors until the "explained" variance of a particular variable was maximized. Tinbergen (1940), in his rejoinder to Keynes, appeared to equate this procedure with maximization of the true likelihood function for the variable in question.

The English approach instead placed greater emphasis on a rigorously formulated a priori economic model. Residual variance was not a primary criterion for model selection because non-economic forces were allowed to play a potentially major role in the actual determination of the dependent variable. The almost certain omission of such variables from the analysis was handled by first differencing the model to help reduce them to statistically random shocks rather than systematic influences. By eventually concentrating on the estimation of the models that have since been called "expenditure systems," it was also possible to lessen the acute statistical problem of multiple hypotheses that Koopmans (1949a) summarized as the proper level of confidence in a hypothesis that was both suggested and tested by the same set of data.

5.1.2.2 Statistical Traditions

The Statistics Laboratory within the Department of Applied Economics concentrated on problems of inference in single equation time series models. In large part this orientation was the legacy of Yule's (1927) research into univariate autoregressive models. His work showed them to be highly descriptive of many kinds of data but their exact statistical properties were not well understood. Kendall (1946) seems to have intended to show, among other things, that traditional methods of interpreting time series, such as correlogram and periodogram analysis, harmonic analysis, counting of peaks and troughs, and variate-differencing were likely to suggest false inferences when the underlying mechanism was of the autoregressive type. This influential work, in conjunction with the theoretical advances in Sweden represented by Wold (1938), set the stage for more mathematically sophisticated analyses of time series economic models at Cambridge and elsewhere.

The Department focused from the beginning on the problem of inference when only short time series were available. This was in keeping with an English tradition in statistics dating back to Edgeworth (1904) and was no doubt reinforced by the presence of the eminent statistician J. Wishart on the Department's advisory committee. They did not argue that structure frequently changed, as did Keynes and the early Cowles Commission, but simply that data had not been gathered over a long enough period to warrant uncritical application of asymptotic distribution theory. Their early approach was to perform Monte Carlo analyses of selected cases. They soon discovered, like the Cowles Commission, that small sample bias was not necessarily negligible when OLS was used to estimate autoregressive models. This seems to be a major reason why the work of Mann and Wald (1943) did not become the template for the structure of English models. The English applied work of this period is in fact notable for not using lagged variables, except for the first difference transformation discussed below.

The Department also devoted considerable attention to the older econometric problem of errors in variables. Geary (1949) described his research as a staff member there, which is especially notable for helping to bring the method of instrumental variables to the attention of econometricians.[8] Gerhard Tintner, who specialized in this area, was also a guest in 1947-48. Unlike the theoretical work represented by Koopmans (1937), Stone and his colleagues maintained that observation errors were likely to be serially correlated although it does not seem that either Geary or Tintner studied this case. This error structure would provide still another reason for the English school to favor using the first difference transformation. If the structural shocks were serially independent, however, it is readily seen that the transformation would introduce a moving average error component. In addition, data constructed as moving averages to reduce measurement errors would again tend to introduce a moving average error. Complications like these may help to explain the considerable interest of English econometricians in moving average models and general time series methods after the War.[9] On the other hand, if the structural shocks were also serially correlated then the transformation served a double corrective purpose. Although serially correlated observation errors could pose a complicated identification problem in structural estimation, the English school seemed unconcerned at this time with such issues. Given their focus on single equation methods, they instead argued generally that the advantages of consistent systems estimation methods were not necessarily compelling in small samples if the biases due to errors in variables are sizable.[10]

5.1.3 *Empirical Work*

The experience of compiling national income statistics played a major role in shaping the empirical work of the Department of Applied Economics. This work was continued after the War and developed into the analysis of economic growth in terms of alternative scenarios within a growth accounting framework.[11] The econometric models developed by the Department, perhaps to be expected given this background, were greatly influenced by the quality of existing economic data. Collinearity was attacked by collecting survey data directly, following the principles of experimental design, and then deriving extraneous estimates for use in time series work. This work was very much in the spirit of Marschak (1939) and a host of other studies that investigated the composition of family budgets during the Depression. Much research was directed at exploring the importance of serial correlation and observation error in models, such as the early Cowles Commission work, where these problems had been assumed absent. Part of the English work started out as an examination of the stochastic assumptions in regression analysis but it developed into a wide-ranging critique of the use of simultaneous equations methodology.

Guy Orcutt joined the Department in 1946 at first to develop novel econometric models of the consumption function. This lone piece of

Keynesian econometrics, done in collaboration with James Duesenberry, was aimed at testing the relative income hypothesis. As part of this work he was estimating equations using monthly data over the 1935-46 period.[12] His published work, however, did not report this research but instead read as a kind of statistical warning to anyone who might undertake similar macroeconomic studies. Indeed, poor data was the main reason why subsequent English work avoided macroeconomic policy models until better series became available in the late 1950's as the result of Stone's non-econometric initiatives.[13]

5.1.3.1 Distributional Assumptions — Orcutt and Cochrane

Orcutt (1948) discovered that nearly all the series used by Tinbergen satisfied the purely empirical equation

$$x_t = x_{t-1} + .3(x_{t-1} - x_{t-2}) + \epsilon_t \tag{5.1}$$

where ϵ_t appeared to be a random error. The roots of unity and 0.3 reasonably implied a damped movement around trend growth. Cochrane and Orcutt (1949a) argued from this result that regression errors should be autocorrelated since misspecification through omission of similarly autocorrelated variables was almost inevitable. They computed von Neumann ratios for the equations published by Klein, Colin Clark, and others that tended to support their conjecture. Of course, they became famous for presenting what is now called the Cochrane-Orcutt procedure. But in an apparent reference to prevalent estimation practices they admonished:

> If error terms are autocorrelated then it would frequently be a mistake to attempt to justify the statistical requirements of randomness by adding more explanatory variables or by experimenting with different combinations of the variables. . . . Owing to the shortness of economic time series high accidental correlations may be obtained. . . .

This caution should be compared to the memoranda on the specification of the Klein models, discussed above in section 4.2.1, where it appeared that serial correlation was used to rationalize the introduction of more variables into the model. The English work may be interpreted in this context as an approach to the problem of multiple hypotheses. A careful theoretical model may only relate a small number of variables (or only a few *kinds* of variables, e.g. the prices and income in Stone's work described below). The error term not only must account for all other economic forces but also the non-economic influences that might never be subject to rigorous analysis. Klein's new variables would be little more than Friedman's "tentative hypotheses" in the absence of a detailed prior theory. When the scale of an empirical study is limited either by lack of theory or by few observations it seems more prudent to allow latitude in the structure of the error term than to run the risk of specious structural coefficients.[14]

The concern with "accidental correlations" had begun in Orcutt and James (1948). The argument was that sample correlations of random series generated according to the the above scheme yielded a disproportionate number of Type I errors. Their simulations suggested that this serial correlation structure in the variables reduced the effective degrees of freedom in the data by almost 95 percent, so that even a length of 90 artificial observations was still statistically short. This result provided another justification of the English school to run all regressions as first differences.[15]

Cochrane and Orcutt (1949b) then turned directly to the Cowles Commission methods. They examined an exactly identified two equation model containing first-order autocorrelated errors with the serial correlation coefficient equal to unity. Even with the correct first difference transformation, the mean squared error of the structural estimates using indirect least squares ranged from 1.5 to 8 times those obtained through direct use of OLS. It should be observed that such studies cannot be definitive because they combined the separate effects of small sample biases, nonnormal rectangular errors, particular parameter environments, and absence of overidentification. But having generated their data to fit the Tinbergen pattern, Cochrane and Orcutt concluded pessimistically:

> Unless it is possible to specify with some degree of accuracy the intercorrelation between error terms of a set of relations and unless it is possible to choose approximately the correct autoregressive transformation . . . scepticism is justified concerning estimating structural parameters from only twenty observations. . . .

This demonstration that the biased OLS estimator could be preferable to FIML in terms of mean squared error for short series complements Wald's observation at the Ithaca conference cited in section 4.1 above. It was to remain a major justification for later work at Cambridge that relied upon single equation methods.

5.1.3.2 Econometrics of Consumer Demand

Demand studies grew out of wartime analysis of consumer budgets to plan rationing programs. As in the United States, this work started as a study of the demand for food. American workers quickly lost interest in the problem after controls ended there in 1946. It remained current in England because rationing was not fully removed until July 1954. The last major analysis of the subject was Tobin (1952), completing work that he had begun as a visitor to the Department in the late 1940's. But this avenue of inquiry soon ended with the coming of post-War prosperity.

The greatest empirical achievement of the Department of Applied Economics in this period was the work on consumer expenditure carried out under Richard Stone and published as Stone (1954a). It appears intended to replace Schultz (1938), which Stone praised for being "inspirational," as the exemplar for demand studies. As such, it offers a remarkable methodological contrast to the Cowles Commission in the emphasis it places on econometric issues apart from simultaneity bias.

Stone wrote that "although the aim of simultaneous equations methods is clear there remains some doubt as to their practical value" and decided that "there are other dangers to be guarded against [which place] a greater burden on the investigator."[16] Interdependence did enter the structure in so far as theory imposed cross equation restrictions to produce symmetry in the substitution matrix. Indeed, this was one of the most important cases of a priori cross equation restrictions in econometrics and Stone was concerned about the failure to completely implement them in the Department's early work because of the burden of computation.[17] One of the tractable problems was serial correlation and every equation was estimated in first differences. A consequence of this, in notable distinction to all the studies done by Tinbergen and Cowles, was that the equations did not use any lagged variables. Trend and cyclical behavior were presumably controlled for by the income variable and the linearization due to first differencing.

Quantities were regressed on real incomes, a trend, and real prices. It was precisely this issue, of course, that motivated Haavelmo's original article in 1943. Girschick and Haavelmo (1947) had insisted in their food demand study:

> It is impossible to derive statistically the demand function from market data without specification of the supply function.

It will be recalled from Chapter 2 that Moore and other workers in the 1920's had implicitly assumed supply functions for agricultural products that did in fact make it possible to use single equation methods to estimate demand curves. Stone analyzed such commodities but he also devoted a great deal of attention to manufactured and processed goods for which it was much more natural to assume the "market equilibrium." He did not deny the arguments for simultaneity in such cases but, as was argued in section 1.2.3 with regard to Henry Schultz, Stone believed that the lack of an adequate theory of supply behavior would likely cause problems for systems estimation due to specification errors that were no more acceptable than OLS bias. As will be seen in the next section, Tinbergen also preferred OLS in the belief that it yielded more reliable results in the presence of specification error. Stone also had the results of Tobin (1950), from which it appeared that this bias was not serious for aggregate food demand. With highly disaggregated product groupings (the study analyzed 46 of them) it was no doubt difficult to specify producer behavior given the possibilities of capital investment, joint production, and inventory accumulation. This level of commodity detail stands in notable contrast to the Cowles Commission work. Marschak had placed single market studies last on his list of research priorities probably because of the difficulty of the associated identification problems and increased data requirements.[18]

Although LIML was developed in part to avoid the need to specify equations in the system whose form was uncertain, Stone advanced four reasons why it still was not attractive for his investigation. First, he insisted that the errors in variables problem was so severe as to likely nullify the advantage of an otherwise consistent estimation method. Second, the distinction between statistically endogenous and exogenous variables was often doubtful and virtually untestable, as it required the orthogonality of their disturbances. Third, apparently referring to Cochrane and Orcutt (1949b), the consistent estimators in small samples were "demonstrably highly inefficient" while OLS was plausibly "relatively accurate."[19] His particular concern with specification error set him apart from the simultaneous equations theorists who up to that time had nearly always proceeded as though the true model were known.[20] Fourth, OLS and consistent estimators often produced about the same results in practice.

This critique is substantial and seems to have been influential among econometricians generally (cf. the comments by Clifford Hildreth in section 4.4.1 above). In later years the Department chose to focus its efforts on collecting proper national income accounts data, first in England and eventually around the world under United Nations auspices. Sophisticated econometrics was not seen as offering a great return in terms of devising development strategies and other very ambitious economic policies. The problems of statistical theory uncovered by Stone's demand work were left for others to tackle. For example, only with research in the 1970's into the finite sample behavior of alternative estimators has it been formally shown that LIML tends to be better centered but with greater dispersion than OLS.[21] The judgment that detailed commodity demands are best modeled by single equations has continued through the present day, although Deaton and Muellbauer (1980) note in their survey of the subject that even with the rigor of the neoclassical paradigm, "[economic] theory is used in a highly cavalier fashion" in many studies.[22] Moreover, they indicate that serial correlation remains a pervasive problem with many demand studies, possibly invalidating many statistical inferences, such as rejection of homogeneity and symmetry restrictions by means of F tests.

Although problems of interpretation still remain, particularly with respect to the treatment of consumer durables, the early statistical practice of using the first difference transformation appears to have found recent unexpected economic support in the consumption function of Hall (1978). Applying his rationale to the work of Stone, the transformed dependent variable would correctly incorporate the rational expectations type restriction that its one period lag enter the equation with a coefficient of unity. The other transformed variables would be correctly measured as the incremental information available to the system since period t-1. The transformation is one of the few pure time series techniques that has found continued structural economic justification.

Research on consumer demand has never been subjected to the withering attacks that have been aimed at structural estimation over the years. The wide acceptance of microeconomic theory is one part of the explanation. The belief in the symmetry of the substitution matrix was never shaken by years of estimation results that appeared to reject this hypothesis.[23] Another strength of consumer demand studies has been that they readily made the transition to cross section and panel data, unlike the large macroeconomic models. The basic specification of these models has not greatly changed since Stone except for experimentation with alternative functional forms for prices and incomes and the inclusion of demographic variables. This stability stands in marked contrast to the continual massive restructuring of the macro–models. The degree of empirical success in very different international contexts suggests a universality that has not been as well established for much other economic theory.

5.1.4 *Theoretical Statistical Work*

5.1.4.1 Distributional Assumptions — Durbin and Watson

The study of serial correlation in terms of the distribution of a test statistic was undertaken at the Department after the initial focus on errors in variables. The simulation approach of Cochrane and Orcutt was not suited for solving a problem of this kind. The distribution of an easily computable test statistic for first order serial correlation in regression residuals in finite samples was derived by Durbin and Watson (1950), who built on the results of T. W. Anderson (1948). This test was an improvement over the earlier von Neumann (1942) ratio in that it incorporated a degrees of freedom correction for the exogenous variables. In addition the statistic could be used to provide an estimate of the autoregressive parameter to transform an equation and so move away from the danger of overdifferencing with first differences.

Although the Department of Applied Economics was soon overshadowed by the emergence of other university research centers, the Durbin and Watson work revealed a closeness between English econometricians and mathematical statisticians that had no analog in the United States. This association was also particularly strong in Commonwealth countries such as Australia and New Zealand. The depth of the background in statistical theory of the Cowles Commission members was entirely atypical for the next generation of American econometricians, who were generally trained in separate economics departments. This influence resulted in particular English strengths in spectral theory and time series econometrics.[24] The sophistication of this theoretical work stands in notable contrast to applied models, especially in the U.S., that were concerned almost entirely with first-order Markov processes through the 1970's.

5.1.4.2 Spread of Time Series Methodology in English Econometrics

It is somewhat ironic that although this "English school" was not so concerned with the discovery of macroeconomic structure it had perhaps the greatest impact on modern economic policy through the "discovery" of the Phillips curve by A. W. Phillips (1958). The history of this construct actually provides a remarkable example of the problem of interpretation of a relationship not traced back to an autonomous structure. But the Phillips curve was not characteristic of the sort of work that was generally conducted. The source for the specification of many of the English models was most often the rigorous and successful development of communication and optimal control theory during the 1950's by mathematical engineers and statisticians, not economists.[25]

Kendall (1960) produced a kind of manifesto calling for the intensive study of "closed loop control systems" as the most fruitful analysis of economic policy problems. This would seem to consist of administering "shocks" to particular equations to alter their time paths while assuming the stability of the time series structures in the face of such interventions.

The justification for this approach was the analogy to a servo-mechanism with little appeal to economic theory. Box and Jenkins (1970) largely represented the culmination of this single equation time series work. Although initially resisted by most econometricians, the apparent usefulness of these methods for short term forecasting has instigated multi-equation extensions during the 1970's that have become extremely influential.

The work of Box and Jenkins (1970) and Granger and Newbold (1977) has led to the construction of elaborate models of the error term as autonomous structures within conventional structural models. Sargan's (1980) COMFAC procedure is perhaps the most interesting example where serial correlation is deliberately introduced as a "model reduction" device: the autoregressive error summarizes the common information contained in the lag structure for all the explanatory variables. In the context of Mann and Wald case (2), discussed in section 2.1.2, the lag length p is reduced to p-k while the formerly serially independent error is made autoregressive of order k. The practical effect is to reduce the number of estimated parameters in the equation by m(k-1), where m is the number of explanatory variables. The other principal economic justification for complicated models of the errors is that they constitute a sophisticated adjustment for seasonality, e.g. fourth order serial correlation. One should also consider that the error will include all non-economic influences that have not been explicitly modeled. Hendry (1983) emphasizes the disturbance as reflecting all the non-economic forces that influence the dependent variable, and so allows extremely complex specifications based on "error correction" dynamics. These treatments of the correlation structure of the error term are important extensions of structural modeling that also seem free from the conventional reproach that pure time series methods are too divorced from economic considerations.

5.2 Tinbergen and the Netherlands Central Planning Bureau

An employment act was passed in the Netherlands after World War II which created a *Centraal Planbureau* with duties similar to the American Council of Economic Advisors. Like its American counterpart, the Dutch body was authorized to carry out statistical investigations and to draw up a coordinated "national budget" but had no direct role in the making of actual economic policy. Jan Tinbergen was director of the research activities of the Bureau through the mid 1950's. The work performed there provides another instance of applied econometrics outside of the Cowles

Commission methodology. The basis for the following discussion is the system of equations used for the Central Economic Plan for 1955 as published in 1956.[26]

This macroeconomic model was constructed as a "complete" system of 27 equations in 27 endogenous variables plus numerous exogenous variables. The similarity to the Cowles work and to Tinbergen's own studies from the 1930's largely stops here, however. Like the work of Richard Stone, all variables were taken as first differences to approximately linearize the system.[27] Otherwise the system did not employ any lagged variables. Regressions of this form are analogous to Orcutt's in that they imply a unit root, hence non-stationarity, in the levels of the variables. This difficulty apparently is handled by treating the model as applicable only in the short run. This interpretation is supported by the fact that the 1956 report also includes a "Macro Model 1970" that appears to satisfy stability conditions. The short run model stands in remarkable contrast to Tinbergen's earlier work using linear difference equations which was preoccupied with the discovery of endogenous cyclical movements. And while the *Planbureau* sponsored research into simultaneous equations estimation, most notably with Henri Theil (1953) and the development of two-stage least squares, even the Bureau's 1955 model was estimated by OLS.[28]

Tinbergen adopted a very different position in this period towards the nature of economic policy. The regression coefficients in his League of Nations work represented for him the economic structure of society. Policy was theoretically intended to change these coefficients so as to damp down the oscillations generated by the model. The Cowles method was intended to yield correct, i.e. consistent, estimates of these coefficients both for proper estimation of the autoregressive representation of the reduced form and for even bolder interventions that would eliminate some of the structural equations entirely. As we have seen, the Cowles group kept yielding ground on this point and eventually allowed that policy measures, such as tax rates, were best introduced as separate exogenous variables and not as structural behavioral parameters. Tinbergen himself seems independently to have come to this view as well.

Tinbergen (1952b) outlined his new theory of policy based on what he described as the interactions between "instruments," or exogenous variables, and "targets," or endogenous variables. This again was nothing more than the the algebra of n equations in n unknowns, where the unknowns were the values of the instruments. The approach passed over questions about the dynamic behavior of the system by assuming the exogenous variables would be effective in determining the values of the targets in every period. By merely requiring algebraic completeness of the system, in principle any combination of targets was attainable in the short run. Policy seen in this way seems very clearly akin to standard set-ups in control theory but Tinbergen seems to have believed it was possible to finesse the natural questions of stability and the role of expectations in determining the period by period outcomes.

For long run policy analysis Tinbergen did not employ these ideas but instead used the concept of "system invariances." These seem to correspond more to the Cowles interpretation of a structural parameter. They included such quantities as price elasticities of exports, the rate of population growth, and the capital-output ratio. These elements formed the basis of a growth model to forecast the effects of the long-standing national interest in encouraging emigration.

The statistical simplification of Tinbergen's post-War models, indeed his emphasis on such simplicity, is one of the main messages of Tinbergen (1951), the first textbook on econometrics. To the limited extent this book describes simultaneous equations methodology, it devotes equal space to the special cases where it yields the same results as OLS. He specifically doubted the importance of "very elaborate statistical methods" when the models themselves were so tentative and in any case only approximately true. Focusing as did Stone on the likelihood of misspecification he emphasized:

> The first thing to be done in any particular application is to give a correct economic analysis of the relation to be investigated ... Many young investigators seem to overlook this.

The text also argued that OLS was more resistant to specification error than other estimation methods.

We have already seen how Koopmans thought the "multi-model" hybrid estimate was a possible scientific resolution of the problem of model selection. Tinbergen instead formally introduced the idea of a scenario. His textbook example of policy through instruments and targets treated six different cases of the values of four key coefficients because of "the uncertainty margin."[29] This approach accords well with the *Planbureau's* role as advisor to policy makers rather than being itself a policy making body. The political leadership, perhaps with its own data resources, then assumes the risk and responsibility for model selection. Tinbergen's views here possibly influenced Marschak (1953), who no longer spoke of directing "social engineering" but rather the more modest goal of letting "alternative decisions be ranked [econometrically] according to their desirability by the policy maker." By the time of his Nobel prize acceptance speech, Tinbergen (1969) placed considerable distance between his early econometric studies and his later preoccupation with direct central planning and government involvement in economic development. This later experience convinced him that the critical policy problem was to devise appropriate institutional arrangements for an economy, for which econometric studies did not often seem directly useful.[30]

5.3 The Swedish School: Recursive Models and OLS

5.3.1 Introduction

Herman Wold of Uppsala University in Sweden was for many years the leader of a crusade against the structural estimation methodology. After completing an influential dissertation on theoretical time series analysis in 1938 he directed his attention to the study of consumer demand in Wold (1943). His first published comments on the work of Haavelmo and the Cowles Commission appeared as a defense of the single equation methods he had used in these inquiries. Wold and Bentzel (1946) is in several respects the most interesting statement of a critique that was repeated with little variation for over twenty years.[31]

This article presented what is now familiar as the recursive system of simultaneous equations. It is a special case of Mann and Wald (1943) in which the $A^{(0)}$ matrix of current endogenous coefficients is lower triangular and the covariance matrix of the errors is diagonal. The proof that OLS on a single equation of this system is equivalent to MLE under normality of the errors was trivial.

Wold felt that his special case was actually the most general model that was economically or statistically justifiable. His critique has always been highly idiosyncratic. The 1946 article made the point, later elaborated by Bentzel and Hansen (1954), that the "Haavelmo bias" could affect the estimates of the recursive system in the guise of a specification error if the available observations were computed over a longer interval than a hypothetical market period. The Swedish school tended to study empirically only consumer demand, where the recursive model often appeared well confirmed, and shunned other areas, particularly macroeconomics, where theory and data argued for the use of different methods.

Wold parted company with the Cowles Commission and, indeed, with the English school on account of a fundamental difference over a basic point of economic theory. This difference explains much in his approach but it was never brought out in years of otherwise telling attacks by his chief methodological enemy Basmann (1963b, 1965a). Wold specifically rejected the Marshallian and Walrasian view that the economy is essentially always in a state of competitive equilibrium. He was very much a product of the Swedish school of economic theory that flowered after Wicksell.[32] Instead of equilibrium concepts, the Swedish school worked in terms of "cumulative causation" and, most importantly for Wold's work, "sequence analysis." It considered equilibrium to be a transient or nonexistent state, so that it was permissible to model the dynamics that moved the system without the powerful restrictions implied by neo-classical equilibrium conditions. Wold also suggested that the economy was dominated by monopolistic sellers who only imperfectly maintained a profit maximizing position. These ideas are evident in Wold and Bentzel (1946) but are not clearly repeated in Wold's later writing.

5.3.2 *The Recursive Model*

The disequilibrium aspect of Swedish econometrics contrasts very strongly with the Cowles Commission work which was often expounded as the statistical embodiment of the Walrasian general equilibrium system.[33] Wold and Bentzel (1946) wrote:

> There is in general a marked difference between quantities supplied and quantities demanded. The chief cause of this discrepancy is that the production process requires time. . . . The unrealistic implication of [Haavelmo and Koopmans] is a consequence of using the same variable for demand and supply.

They presented the following model as the basis for their understanding of market behavior (variables are logs and deviations from mean):

$$s = b_1 P_{t-1} + b_2 l_{t-1} + e_1$$

$$P = g_1 P_{t-1} + g_2 s_t + g_3 l_{t-1} + e_2$$

$$d = a P_t + e_3$$

$$l = d l_{t-1} + s_t - d_t + e_4 \qquad\qquad (5.2)$$

with equations for production, price, demand, and inventory accumulation, respectively. With a storable good there is no condition that production equal demand. Comparing the price equation above to the one implied by market clearing:

$$model: \quad P = (g_1 + g_2 b_1)P_{t-1} + (g_3 + g_2 b_2)l_{t-1} + e_2 + g_2 e_1$$

$$market\ clearing: \quad P = b_1/aP_{t-1} + b_2/al_t\ -1. + (e_1 - e_3)/a \qquad (5.3)$$

there is no reason for these two expressions to be equal or even to have the same signs for the lagged variables. Disequilibrium may be rationalized for a single market in this way although it does not necessarily follow that data for spatially and temporally aggregated markets would display the same properties. The Swedish school did not consider arguments of this kind that would rehabilitate more classical analysis.

Allocating production between market sale and inventory investment inescapably leads to the question of the price expected to prevail in future periods compared to the current price. Wold and Bentzel (1946) believed that a suitable expectations mechanism would pose no problem for the recursive model because it would only concern additional lagged, not contemporaneous, variables. They simply assumed that the price equation was a useful approximation of supplier behavior when modeling the process of *tatonnement* in the typical retail market: "Under ordinary market condtions the prices are determined first and the consumers react afterwards." Wold's earlier demand work attempted to measure the own–price and income elasticities of various consumer commodities. These articles always stressed the need for demand to be "free," i.e. unrationed, for the analysis to yield accurate results. This condition seems to have been carried over as an assumption imposed on the recursive model. For all observed points to lie on the demand curve it would be necessary for suppliers to meet excess demand out of an inexhaustible inventory when market price was below equilibrium.[34]

This basis for the recursive system was repeated in Wold and Jureen (1953), where it was stated that the analysis was meant to apply to retail markets. This book again considers only problems of microeconomic consumer demand. It offers Wold's only published qualification of the claimed universal applicability of the recursive model. On the question of whether an observed scatter of price against quantity could represent a hybrid of supply and demand curves he wrote:

> [This is] a question in demand analysis that cannot be dealt with on a purely statistical basis but calls for subject matter consideration.[35]

In particular he allowed that wholesale, or more generally auction, markets might in principle be more accurately described by a non-recursive simultaneous system. The importance of this distinction for guiding applied work was completely lost in the decade of methodological polemics that followed.

The recursive system seems to have a priori plausibility on institutional grounds in certain contexts. As discussed previously in section 5.1.3.2, a number of the English demand studies provided some empirical evidence that current price was not very important in the supply function for food products. On the other hand, one might expect that macroeconomic variables such as money and interest rates or income and consumption are essentially simultaneous. An ideal procedure would be to endogenize a recursive relationship and test for significant simultaneity. Haavelmo (1944) had already discussed this in regard to his provisional assumption of exogenous investment. Wold, however, never viewed the recursive system as something to be tested. Rather than treating alternative specifications as hypotheses to be tested by the data, Wold and Jureen (1953) began a peculiar debate over the non-empirical philosophical superiority of recursive modeling.

5.3.3 *Critique of Interdependent Systems*

The appearance of Cowles Monograph 10 prompted many discussions in the early 1950's on the interpretation of cause and effect within a multi-equation econometric model. Nearly all of this work attempted to find a parallel to the stimulus–response structure of a conventional laboratory experiment. Chapter 6 analyzes the role of exogeneity in this context. Wold put out a veritable flood of articles that argued the logical superiority of the "causal chain" nature of the recursive model over jointly determined relationships.

This claim bears some additional commentary beyond the sober analyses by Basmann cited above. Basmann (1963b) patiently presented the case for simultaneity but in a market ruled by equilibrium relations. Except for the one instance in 1953 this case simply failed to impress Wold as economically meaningful. Wold ultimately seemed to advocate the recursive system because it conceded a certain degree of simultaneity without losing the property that it could be consistently estimated by OLS. He insisted somewhat oddly that the supreme advantage of the system was that its equations had a "more direct" interpretation than other simultaneous structures. The idea of testing proposed structures, central to the Cowles Commission approach, is absent from Wold's work. Indeed, the recursive school put forward very few empirical models to substantiate their theoretical positions.[36]

The denial of structural estimation was combined with apparent failure to appreciate a basic issue in the related statistical theory. In the only mention of the identification problem in Wold and Jureen (1953), Wold claimed that recursive systems avoided the problems of identification. This is only true, however, if the coefficient matrix for the endogenous variables is triangular and the covariance matrix for the error terms is diagonal. It would be more accurate to say that recursive systems must contain n(n-1) zero restrictions to achieve exact global identification.[37] Since exact identification cannot be tested, it should be recognized that an alternative exactly identified structural system can be formulated to receive the identical degree of confirmation from the data.[38] Moreover, the recursive system still leaves open the problem of incorporating overidentifying restrictions into the model.

The explanation for Wold's intransigence seems to be that single equations, stacked to form a causal chain, meet an a priori standard for simplicity in scientific explanation. How else can one interpret Wold's statements that the recursive demand function is "more direct" than any other? The passage to the reduced form is a necessary operation to determine the equilibrium values of, for example, supply and demand. The estimation of a recursive system may be mathematically simpler compared to a structural system but the question is whether a particular model is able to represent a phenomenon of interest. If it cannot then its relative simplicity merely becomes an absolute inadequacy. Wold, however, excludes phenomena from consideration for which his model is not suited.[39]

A key point of contention with structural estimation is revealed in the following passage from Wold and Jureen (1953):

> Can a relation in the [interdependent] system be used for estimating one variable in terms of the other ones? . . . If it cannot, for what purpose can the structural system then be used? . . . The passage from a structural system to its reduced form is a purely formal operation, the economic significance of which is not immediately obvious.

This failure to comprehend one of the basic premises of structural estimation was repeated in numerous later articles. The obvious answer is that the structure is used to deduce the values of parameters of interest, e.g. elasticities, while the reduced form predicts the values of the endogenous variables. By automatically equating the structural system with the reduced form Wold left no place for the concept of the relative autonomy of the two sets of equations. Only by assuming no structural change will one set be redundant for forecasting purposes.

Structural change has subtle implications for simultaneous systems because a change in one parameter can affect every coefficient in the reduced form. A recursive system has the special property that all the information contained in a structural change is incorporated into the altered value of one dependent variable which is then used further down the causal chain. The remaining coefficients are unaffected. This restriction of the possible scope of structural change was simply not contemplated in the initial work of the Cowles Commission.

5.3.3.1 Rejection of Maximum Likelihood Estimation

A striking number of the econometricians who have had wide experience in the collection of actual economic data have not been attracted to systems estimations methods. Wold, Stone, and even Klein, to name the most prominent examples, were among those for whom this observation seems justified. The problem of errors in variables was but one aspect of their reluctance to abandon traditional regression methods. Wold, and the early Klein, rejected Haavelmo's "probability approach" in so far as the investigator was called upon to specify a particular distribution for the disturbance term in the model.[40] This specification does not necessarily vitiate an asymptotic estimation theory. Mann and Wald (1943) had shown that serially independent errors that possessed sufficient moments were the key requirements for obtaining asymptotically valid test procedures. Haavelmo used the probability distribution to derive the maximum likelihood solution but this part of his work seems less important than the demonstration of inconsistent OLS parameter estimates. There can be little doubt, however, that part of the resistance to maximum likelihood stemmed from the difficulty of computing the estimates even under the assumption of normal errors.

Wold was particularly critical of small sample hypothesis tests that were based on assumed normal errors and this point does have some force:

> For small sample tests, in particular, the accuracy attained will as a rule be illusory since such tests require a full specification of the regression residuals. . . .[41]

As a time series specialist he was also well aware of the unknown small sample behavior of OLS estimators in autoregressive models. He did not advance similar objections to hypothesis testing in time series analysis of other phenomena, e.g. tides or rainfall, when long observation series were available. Wold thought that confidence in an econometric model came from using it in a variety of situations and checking for similarity in the results. This approach was exploited in his earlier budget survey work. As a general philosophy of economic modeling it is notable because it does not automatically concede that experimentation is impossible in economic research.

It is not clear, however, how the understandable objection to spurious precision implies a rejection of systems modeling. The Cowles Commission theorists themselves always viewed their asymptotic distribution theory as a prologue to the development of exact finite sample test procedures. Wold seemed to think that assuming normality for the use of FIML was unsupportably arbitrary, although the practical effect was only to apply the least squares principle in minimizing the generalized variance of the reduced form. In other contexts, e.g. Wold (1945), he was satisfied with the use of an estimation procedure whose sampling properties were only known for the asymptotic case. Consequently, he was not averse to estimation in the absence of proper tests for significance.

Another factor is suggested by the procedure Wold chose to test the symmetry of the Slutsky substitution matrix. A system of demand equations seems to constitute one of the most intuitively reasonable examples of a multivariate regression problem with cross equation constraints. Wold, however, tested the hypothesis by constructing the substitution terms from unconstrained single equation estimates and "eyeballing" whether their ratio in a two-good case was near unity. He accepted the null hypothesis after liberal adjustments of the estimates.[42] Provided OLS was consistent, Wold saw no need to employ more sophisticated procedures whose efficiency depended on the unknown error distributions. Thus the Swedish school in the 1950's grew away from maximum likelihood methods in econometrics. The emphasis on more simple, but not necessarily more efficient, estimation techniques based on OLS was a major characteristic of that era.[43]

5.3.4 *Soft Modeling and Partial Least Squares*

5.3.4.1 Background

In a surprising change of pace in the mid 1960's, Wold proposed a new method that he called the "fix point" for estimating an entire system of structural equations. It was based on two-stage least squares and provided a computationally simple approximation to FIML.[44] Remarkably, Wold still saw no merit to the structural system per se but interpreted an included endogenous variable as causal if it took on the value that would be implied by the reduced form. This view perpetuates a confusion about the meaning of autonomy and behavioral equations and need not be discussed any further here.

The import of this new method lies elsewhere. It is connected with the theme of Wold (1945), namely, the problem of the selection of regressors when the available data will not permit the use of all of them. This issue resurfaced in the 1960's for large conventional models like the Brookings project, where the number of variables in the reduced form would frequently approach or exceed the number of observations.[45] The same problem seemingly would afflict the recursive system as well, because it was obvious that the number of variables in each equation increased as one moved down the causal chain, although Wold did not mention it explicitly. The "fix point" constituted a new solution to the problem of undersized samples.[46]

Wold's approach anticipated his most recent views on economic modeling. It was based on the construction of instruments that are akin to the latent variables of factor analysis. They are defined in terms of orthogonality conditions with respect to the structural errors.[47] Estimation of the reduced form was unnecessary except perhaps to provide initial estimates of the IV's for the iterative solution. This aspect of the "fix point" method pointed the way to a new model reduction strategy that Wold has developed under the banner of "soft modeling."

5.3.4.2 Soft Modeling

"Soft modeling" emerged as a method to preserve the causal chain structure in models with a large number of variables but little information concerning the place of each variable in the chain. It seems particulary intended for the socioeconomic models that started to appear with the development of very large computerized data bases in the 1960's. Interest in these models, coinciding with a growing concern in government and academic circles over increasing social unrest around the world, often lacked extensive theoretical foundations. By the late 1960's Wold had abandoned the kind of empirical work, such as demand analysis, for which economic theory might provide very specific prior restrictions. The social and political phenomena under investigation required a way to interpret great masses of data that had not previously been the subject of theoretical analysis or detailed field investigations.

Wold (1982) explained that "parsimony in the use of parameters is a key feature of soft modeling." It is achieved by building causal chains of a particularly simple form. The procedure divides all the observed variables of interest, the "indicators," into groups with hypothetical interpretations as functional "blocks." For example, household characteristics (such as income, education of parents, and number of children) might be considered part of the group for "family background." A child's performance on a number of tests could part of the group for school ability. The causal chain would regress school ability on family background with no other included exogenous variables: a single estimated coefficient for a model with potentially dozens of variables. In essence the method is an extension of classical factor analysis where the latent variables form the chain. The estimation procedure is a clever use of a sequence of iterated OLS regressions that avoids the complications of MLE. Rather than maximize a likelihood function, with the attendant identification problems and nonlinear computations, soft modeling only constructs latent variables that obey the orthogonality requirements of a causal chain structure. The parsimony is due to the fundamental assumption that the causal chain connects only latent variables which, as common factors, are expected to subsume large numbers of the "indicator" variables that are the real focus of the investigation.

It is still premature to assess the value of the soft model for economics. The factors may in some cases have interesting causal interpretations as indices, similar to the index of consumer sentiment.[48] But the method departs considerably from the earlier causal chain systems that treated the indicators as autonomous explanatory variables. For example, Wold (1982) used the first principle component of a set of indicators as the common factor, although the coefficients on the indicators are not consistent estimators of their effects taken separately. It is not clear how to guide policy intervention in this framework, in so far as policy consists of altering the values of particular indicator variables. The problem of interpretation for policy is made more confusing by the possibility that a set of indicators can require more than a single common factor to summarize the useful information contained in it. Moreover, a key assumption of the method is that a given indicator variable may appear in only one group so as to preserve orthogonality of the block structure. This is a very stringent requirement which is exactly the reverse of the condition for the causal chain when Wold advocated it as the appropriate model for applied economic work. A "true" model would surely display a pattern of exclusion restrictions between these two extremes, but Wold's methods allow no middle ground on what seems to be a key issue of specification.

Most importantly, "soft" investigations do not stress the critical testing of hypotheses. Wold (1982) describes the practical working of the method as a constant "give and take" in a "dialogue with the computer." Presumably many tentative models are tried before one is selected. Indeed, the process of selection from a multitude of results seems to be the softest part of the methodology. The published examples of soft models that seem most convincing have dealt with problems in chemistry and pollution engineering where in actuality considerable prior information was available to provide restrictions on the structure.[49] For economic applications the method seems open to the same critique of traditional econometric models that emphasize coefficient estimation over hypothesis testing and model evaluation.

NOTES TO CHAPTER 5

[1]University of Cambridge, Department of Applied Economics, *First Report 1946-48* (November 1948), p. 6.

[2]Keynes to Colin Clark, *Collected Works,* 12:801.

[3]See Keynes, *Collected Works,* 12:829-41, 14:285-305. It will be recalled that Koopmans was to take up residence at Oxford to carry on Tinbergen's work for the British case. This investigation was eventually undertaken by Klein at Oxford while in refuge during the McCarthyist persecutions in the United States and was published as Klein, Ball, et al. (1961).

[4]Keynes to Geoffrey Crowther, *Collected Works,* 12:813.

[5]The Rockefeller Foundation played a key role by providing an initial grant of £23,500. From *First Report,* p. 9.

[6]Lawson and Pesaran (1985) contains a number of informative essays on different dimensions of Keynes's own methodological thinking.

[7]See Keynes, *Collected Works,* 12:821. Mendershausen used cross section data from the 1937 U. S. census to discover apparent differences in regional savings patterns. After acknowledging severe shortcomings of the data for this purpose, he was left with the unambiguous conclusion that the black population had a lower average standard of living than the white.

[8]See also section 6.3.1.

[9]English attention was refocused on autoregressive errors through work by Sargan (1959).

[10]Stone (1954a), p. 298 reports that the Department experimented with Geary's instrumental variable procedures to correct for errors in variables bias but found the resulting estimates with annual data had excessive variance.

[11]Stone has discussed well the origin of this activity with benefit of his personal experience. See his essay "The Use and Development of National Income and Expenditure Statistics," in *Lessons of the British War Economy,* ed. D. N. Chester (Cambridge: Cambridge U. Press, 1951),

pp. 83-101.

[12]*First Report*, p. 19.

[13]See the interview with Sargan in Phillips (1985).

[14]Cf. the remarks on "multi-model" estimates in section 4.2.2.1 above.

[15]This article bears uncanny similarity to the later critique of Granger and Newbold (1974), which also recommended differencing to avoid "spurious regressions." Orcutt and his associates seemed to favor first differences, despite their development of the autoregressive procedure, because of computational simplicity and the belief that such an approximate correction was adequate for the models they were examining. Viewed as an approximation, the first difference may of course overcorrect and introduce an error of its own in hypothesis testing. This danger seems more likely for models that use quarterly or finer data, where the equation disturbances may be more complicated than a simple Markov or random walk process. Sargan and Bhargava (1983) have recently shown that such overdifferencing may be difficult to detect because standard test statistics can have low power to reject the null hypothesis of a random walk when the true serial correlation coefficient is even as low as 0.4.

[16]From Stone (1954a), p. 249.

[17]*First Report*, p. 20. The nonlinear constraints were successfully handled by a simple iterative procedure in the linear expenditure system presented in Stone (1954b). Later specifications grew more flexible as a result of increasing computational capacity.

[18]See Minutes of Staff Meeting, 22 March 1946, CCA, MSM.

[19]From Stone (1954a), p. 286.

[20]This issue has been illuminated in detail recently and it appears that in models with false exclusion restrictions OLS can be a superior estimator to TSLS and FIML. See Hale, Mariano, and Ramage (1980).

[21]See Phillips (1984) for a survey of recent achievements in this area.

[22]See Deaton and Muellbauer (1980), pp. 77–80.

[23]Recent research on the small sample behavior of the asymptotic Wald, likelihood ratio, and Lagrange multiplier test statistics has indicated that the null hypothesis of symmetry was incorrectly rejected far too often in

past work.

[24]See especially the work of the Australian Hannan (1970) and the New Zealander Whittle (1963).

[25]The vector ARMA model of A. W. Phillips (1966) is the obvious generalization of Mann and Wald (1943) but, like Orcutt (1948), the parameters did not always have a ready economic interpretation.

[26]Netherlands Central Planning Bureau, *Scope and Methods of the Central Planning Bureau* (The Hague, 1956), pp. 70-82.

[27]See section 2.1 above for an argument that this procedure may have been inferior to his earlier use of deviations from nine year moving averages.

[28]Theil (1966) was not optimistic that TSLS would provide much better estimates of structural coefficients, given available sample sizes, but recommended the method as a relatively simple way to impose prior restrictions on the reduced form. He seemed to advocate the pragmatic course of estimating structural equations by OLS but inflating the estimated standard errors by a subjective factor to broaden confidence intervals.

[29]See Tinbergen (1951), pp. 168-207. Research described in section 5.1.3.2 also argues in favor of OLS for this reason.

[30]Cf. his reply (1940) to Keynes, advanced during the most optimistic period in econometrics. The argument of chapter 3 also stresses a role for institutional studies.

[31]Cf. the similar arguments in Strotz and Wold (1960).

[32]See Knut Wicksell, *Geldzins und Güterpreise* [Interest and Prices] (Jena: G. Fischer, 1898); Erik Lindahl, *Studies in the Theory of Money and Capital* (London: Allen and Unwin, 1939); Gunnar Myrdal, *Monetary Equilibrium* (London: W. Hodge, 1939); Erik Lundberg, *Studies in the Theory of Economic Expansion* (London: P. King, 1937).

[33]Swedish econometricians have tended to be very sophisticated in the use of pure time series analysis without similar regard for a priori economic theories.

[34]More general models of market disequilibrium have now become major items on the econometric research agenda. By allowing observed points to lie either on a demand or a supply curve they are inherent multi-

equation estimation problems. See, e.g., Eaton and Quandt (1983).

[35]From Wold and Jureen (1950), p. 11.

[36]In one of the few published critical studies, L'Esperance (1964) compared OLS, LIML, and recursive models of the watermelon market and found LIML to predict best.

[37]The question of the structural interpretation of coefficients in a Wold ordering recurs in the discussion of VAR's in section 6.7 below.

[38]Cf. Basmann (1965a). The econometric models formulated in continuous time of the type advocated by A. W. Phillips (1959) were assumed recursive in part to avoid the identification problem. P. C. B. Phillips (1973) began the rigorous extension of the theory of identification to continuous time models.

[39]Fisher (1965) adapted the principle of a causal ordering in proposing "block recursiveness" of instrumental variables to facilitate estimation of large conventional macro models. Unlike Wold, Fisher was very cautious about the plausibility of assuming a diagonal error covariance matrix across different blocks.

[40]Cf. Klein (1960), discussed in the previous chapter, to Klein (1943), written before he joined the Cowles Commission:

> [The] assumptions needed to apply his [Haavelmo's] method may be quite arbitrary. . . . [One] must also assume the probability distribution of the random elements . . . [an assumption] not needed for regression.

[41]See Wold and Jureen (1950), p. 23.

[42]See Wold and Jureen (1950), p. 301. His intuition accords with recent research into the true size of more formal tests that would now reject symmetry far less frequently in small samples.

[43]Cf. the parallel development of TSLS, discussed in section 4.4, and instrumental variables, discussed in section 6.3.1.

[44]See the discussion and references in Wold (1980). Dhrymes (1974) has analysed this method as "iterated instrumental variables."

[45]The previous chapter discussed how conventional econometricians like Klein saw the resulting near equivalence of OLS and TSLS as a reason to abandon systems methods. See above, section 4.4.1.

[46]Cf. the use of principal components in TSLS by Kloek and Mannes (1960).

[47]See Wold (1980) for a detailed description of the estimation procedure.

[48]Sargent and Sims (1977) also proposed models based on factors extracted from macroeconomic data as an alternative to conventional structural estimation. Factor methods in macroeconomics seem most easily rationalized in Stone (1947) who searched for agglomerations of variables to represent the 3 traditional notions of underlying trend, cyclical, and seasonal movements.

[49]See Wold (1982) for examples and an extensive list of references.

CHAPTER 6

EXOGENEITY

6.1 Introduction

Tinbergen originally introduced the concept of exogenous variables in econometric models. Their major function was to increase the descriptive power of a complete system without adding to the number of equations to be estimated. Tinbergen was primarily interested in estimating the coefficients of the lagged endogenous variables that determined the oscillatory behavior of the system. The exogenous variables represented specific outside economic shocks that excited the equations. At that time estimation of their coefficients was not understood to involve any further statistical assumptions about the model.

As discussed in chapter 2, Koopmans (1950) extended the model of Mann and Wald to include exogenous variables also. This development played two vital roles in the emerging methodology of structural estimation. First, it offered a solution to the identification problem that seemed not to depend on the often quite uncertain a priori restrictions on the lags of the endogenous variables. Second, it provided the means to represent the direct instruments of economic policy. For these purposes exogenous variables were not viewed as shocks so much as the independent variables in a classical scientific experiment.[1]

Exogenous variables became the foundation stones for the Cowles Commission method. Koopmans derived the statistical requirements for exogeneity but was not optimistic that they would be fulfilled in many applications with available data. The problematic nature of the concept has aroused three major critical reactions in later practice. Orcutt (1952b, c) called for the use of panel data to replace a priori categorizations of exogeneity. Granger (1969) in effect suggested a return to the basic Mann and Wald model stripped of Koopmans's extensions. The rational expectations literature of the 1970's offered theoretical grounds for questioning the autonomy of structural equations when a model contained exogenous variables as Koopmans defined them. The force of these criticisms has recently grown in parallel with the empirical problems of structural estimation discussed in chapters 4 and 7.

6.2 A Priori Exogeneity

Koopmans (1950) analyzed exogeneity in terms of its statistical implications within the simultaneous equations framework. His approach centered on the statistical requirements for consistent maximum likelihood estimation of the structural coefficients associated with a contemporaneous variable in the system. He identified two possible cases.

The first dealt with "variables which influence the remaining (endogenous) variables but are not influenced thereby." Koopmans specifically named this the "causal principle" in keeping with the image of an experimental set-up. Such variables posed no special problems for inference in simultaneous equations. If the causal variable was an "uncontrolled" random process, its stochastic element was assumed to be uncorrelated with the endogenous disturbances. This eliminated biased inferences due to unspecified third causes. Exogeneity in these terms ruled out "feedforwards" of any kind between current endogenous and future exogenous variables. Equivalently, a current exogenous variable was not supposed to be determined by any present or past values of the endogenous variables. This condition may be termed "strict" exogeneity.

While this definition corresponded to an experimental stimulus, it drastically limited the number of economic factors that could be considered exogenous in a macroeconomic model. Koopmans gave examples of exogeneity in this sense that included only natural phenomena such as temperature, rainfall, and earthquake intensities. However, climate and geology were not adequate to accomplish the main goal of identification of structure. Adherence to the traditional concept of a cause in a laboratory experiment would make inference impossible in the simultaneous equations framework. Koopmans instead considered how the effect of an given variable, that did not fulfill the above requirements for exogeneity, could be statistically equivalent to the same series generated by a truly exogenous process. The approach complemented his other work on identification problems.

The second case generalized what Koopmans called predetermined variables. Let the model contain G current variables, none of which is known to be "strictly" exogenous. The system must then contain G equations to be complete. The estimation problem can be simplified if g variables appear only with a lag (if at all) in G-g equations. The remaining g equations may contain all G variables in both current and lagged form. In this case the current values of G-g variables in the g equations are statistically indistinguishable from exogenous variables as initially defined, provided the two sets of errors for the two blocks are again uncorrelated. The effect is to reduce the necessary number of equations to be estimated by G-g and to provide as many variables to aid in identification.

Let the complete, unrestricted structural system for G variables be:

$$A^{(0)}x_t = A^{(1)}x_{t-1} + \ldots + A^{(P)}x_{t-p} + \epsilon_t \tag{6.1}$$

where $A^{(i)}$ are $G \times G$ coefficient matrices, ϵ is Gaussian i.i.d. with mean zero and positive definite covariance matrix Σ, the lag order p is known, and the autoregressive process is stationary and invertible (assumptions identical to the Mann and Wald model discussed in section 2.1.2). The reduced form as defined by Mann and Wald is:

$$x_t = A^{(0)-1}A^{(1)}x_{t-1} + \ldots + A^{(0)-1}A^{(P)}x_{t-p} + A^{(0)-1}\epsilon_t \tag{6.2}$$

assuming $A^{(0)-1}$ exists. Consider a partition of x_t into two subvectors $x_{1,t}$ and $x_{2,t}$ with lengths G-g and g, respectively. For convenience, let (6.2) be rewritten as:

$$(x'_{1,t}, x'_{2,t})' = G^{(1)}x_{t-1} + \ldots + G^{(P)}x_{t-p} + u \tag{6.2b}$$

where $E(uu') = \Omega = A^{(0)-1}\Sigma A^{(0)-1'}$ and all matrices are conformably partitioned with x_1 and x_2. Let $G^{(j)}_{i\cdot} = (G^{(j)}_{i1}, G^{(j)}_{i2})$. Mann and Wald showed that the best linear predictor of the vector $x_{2,t}$ when the vector $x_{1,t}$ was already observed was:

$$x_{2,t} = \Omega_{21}\Omega_{11}^{-1}x_{1,t} + \Sigma_{j=1}^p(G^{(j)}_{2\cdot} - \Omega_{21}\Omega_{11}^{-1}G^{(j)}_{1\cdot})x_{t-j} \tag{6.3}$$

which follows by conditional expectations of jointly normal variables. Since the parameters of (6.2) are always identified, they can be estimated consistently and transformed to yield the predictors (6.3). Equations (6.3) could also be consistently estimated directly by OLS because the residual in the regression would be orthogonal to $x_{1,t}$ by construction.

The parameters of (6.3) evidently are functions of all the original parameters of the structural system (6.1).[2] Koopmans's approach may be understood as finding a set of a priori restrictions on (6.1) that would imply a parameterization of (6.3) solely in terms of the parameters of the g equations that define the endogenous block. The restrictions serve to map the relation (6.3) into:

$$x_{2,t} = A_{22}^{(0)-1}[A_{22}^{(1)}x_{2,t-1} + \ldots + A_{22}^{(p)}x_{2,t-p}] + A_{22}^{(0)-1}[-A_{21}^{(0)}x_{1,t} +$$
$$\ldots + A_{21}^{(p)}x_{1,t-p}] + A_{22}^{(0)-1}\epsilon_{2,t} \qquad (6.4)$$

which is the structure more commonly called the reduced form although it is actually a special case of (6.3). Alternatively, as proved by Hatanaka and Odaki (1983), the restrictions may be thought of as sufficient conditions to equate the parameters of the special structure (6.4) to those of (6.3), which is the correct conditional predictor with the the given assumptions for the model (6.1).[3] Only the values of $x_{1,t}$ are needed in (6.4). This is the important case where the parameters of the process which determine $x_{1,t}$ do not play a role, which clarifies when an exogenous variable does not have to be modeled for the system to be complete.

The particular restrictions used by Koopmans to identify (6.4) with (6.3) were that $A_{12}^{(0)}$ and Σ_{12} contained all zeros, which implied that the likelihood function for the complete system admitted the factorization:

$$f(x_2, x_1|X_{t-1}, \delta_1, \delta_2) = f_1(x_2|x_1, X_{t-1}, \delta_2) \, f_2(x_1|X_{t-1}, \delta_1) \qquad (6.5)$$

where X_{t-1} represents all lagged values of x, and δ_1 and δ_2 are the parameters from the exogenous and endogenous blocks, respectively. Since Koopmans (1950) assumed that f_1 and f_2 "depend on entirely different sets of parameters," i.e. that δ_1 and δ_2 were not linked by any constraints, efficient maximum likelihood estimation of (6.4) could "disregard entirely" the estimation of the processes for the exogenous variables. In Koopmans's phrase, when such restrictions were available to make the smaller system (6.4) "complete for statistical purposes," the variables in x_1 could be termed exogenous with respect to it. With additional identifying restrictions, the parameters of the endogenous block could be estimated from the reduced form (6.4).

More recent analysis of exogeneity has made it clear that Koopmans's conditions are sufficient but not necessary for consistent or efficient estimation of the g equations for the endogenous variables on the basis of the system (6.4). The sufficient condition for consistent estimation of the coefficients of $x_{1,t}$ in (6.4) is only that $x_{1,t}$ and $\epsilon_{2,t}$ be uncorrelated. Hatanaka and Odaki (1983) showed that predeterminedness defined this way depended only on the condition:

$$\Sigma_{12} = A_{12}^{(0)}A_{22}^{(0)-1}\Sigma_{22} \qquad (6.6)$$

for which Koopmans's restrictions were a special case. Hatanaka and Odaki pointed out that this minimal relation implied consistent, but not necessarily efficient, estimation. Engle, Hendry, and Richard (1983) called a current period variable "weakly" exogenous if it appeared in f_2, and found two other sets of special restrictions on the system contemporaneous covariance matrix that implied Koopmans's factorization without using his assumptions on structure. They extended the definition of "strict" exogeneity similarly to cover "weakly" exogenous variables that were not determined by past values of the endogenous variables. This last case they termed "strong" exogeneity.[4]

By viewing exogeneity as a statistical property it is possible to introduce many economic factors into a model that have the same interpretation as laboratory stimuli.[5] This extension can only be achieved by making prior assumptions about economic structure similar to the exclusion restrictions used to solve identification problems. These exogeneity assumptions are often tenuous, however, in so far as they concern lag lengths and cross equation error covariances. The zero covariance assumption seems particularly liable to invalidate exogeneity through omitted variables, which seems a likely possibility when a model is deliberately kept small because of limited amounts of data. For example, let the true complete system consist of three variables with $A^{(0)}$ equal to:

$$
\begin{matrix}
1 & 0 & a_{13} \\
a_{21} & 1 & 0 \\
0 & a_{32} & 1
\end{matrix}
\tag{6.7}
$$

and a diagonal Σ so that no variable is exogenous. Misspecification of only a two variable model with $A^{(0)}$ equal to:

$$
\begin{matrix}
1 & 0 \\
a_{21} & 1
\end{matrix}
\tag{6.8}
$$

will not identify (6.4) because exogeneity of the first variable in (6.8) is spurious.

Exogeneity as a model reduction device is clearly very problematical. Considering the complete system (6.1), the assumption $A_{12}^{(0)}$ equals zero entails $(G-g)g$ restrictions that may not be very strongly motivated by economic theory, particularly if $A_{12}^{(1)} \ldots A_{12}^{(p)}$ are plausibly not zero a priori. The best candidate exogenous variables in this connection might be the active instruments of government policy such as taxes, public expenditure, and immigration quotas that do not react instantaneously to other economic factors. In principle they could even be subjected to experimental controls. The presumed exogeneity of these instruments was the entire basis for Tinbergen's "instruments and targets" approach to policy that was discussed in section 5.2.

It is unclear how useful the other weak exogeneity conditions studied by Engle, Hendry, and Richard will prove in specifying actual models. Their examples, which often do not clearly distinguish the structure from the reduced form, seem most striking for confirming Tukey's opinion that structural estimation was pointless if no trustworthy prior identifying restrictions were available.[6] The "parameters of interest" they discuss ultimately seem meaningful only as the hypothetical constructs that are *defined* in the context of a particular model. One may surmise that their results were not unknown to Koopmans but that he felt it most worthwhile to formulate conditions that emphasized concrete economic, as distinct from statistical, interpretation. Rather than extend his study of exogeneity in the difference equation framework, however, Koopmans believed the associated conceptual problems made it more important to develop an estimation theory for models such as the "complete" reduced form (6.2) but formulated in continuous time.

6.3 Testing Exogeneity

6.3.1 *Direct Tests of Structural Models*

Statistical exogeneity assumptions are part of the body of maintained hypotheses that underlie any econometric investigation. A natural question, in keeping with the the central focus of the Cowles Commission philosophy of econometric research, would be the extent to which they are subject to test. Koopmans, however, never expressed optimism regarding the feasibility of testing exogeneity assumptions. In Koopmans, Rubin, and Leipnik (1950) he described them as "theoretical, a priori . . . [for] which statistical evidence may or may not be obtained at a later date." In his comments (1952) on a paper by Orcutt (1952b) Koopmans doubted that a suitable test could be formulated because the available estimation procedures, FIML and LIML, yielded inconsistent estimates when the null hypothesis of exogeneity for a particular variable was false. Consequently with these methods it did not seem possible to construct power functions to make a test informative. The lags in the system (6.2) could be estimated as a partial test of "strict" but this information was of little value in itself. "Strict" exogeneity was not necessary for consistent estimation and without prior information (6.2) could not identify the crucial parameters of the simultaneous relations. It is a real advance that later researchers succeeded in finding several avenues of solution for the technical problem of testing for exogeneity.

The central problem, as Koopmans recognized, was to obtain consistent estimates of a structural equation when the null hypothesis was false. The theoretical key to the breakthrough was provided by Sargan (1958), who introduced econometricians to instrumental variables (IV) estimation. The method had first been proposed in its modern form by the statistician Reiersøl (1945) to deal with the errors in variables problem. It is perhaps another sign of the exhaustion at the Cowles Commission by the early 1950's that IV estimation was not discovered there, particularly in view of the collaboration between Koopmans and Reiersøl (1950).[7] No doubt the exclusive attention at Cowles to maximum likelihood and the associated computation problems also had become a kind of methodological trap which was not sprung until Theil's (1954) 2SLS. Sargan's article presented the general asymptotic distribution theory for IV estimators. Sargan (1964) derived an asymptotic chi-square test to test the predeterminedness of instruments but, as section 4.4.2 discussed, the mainstream of econometrics at that time did not share this concern for hypothesis testing.

Although an IV test for independence between regressors and disturbances was suggested by Durbin (1954), such procedures did not receive much attention in econometrics until the article by Wu (1973).[8] Wu's procedures estimate an equation by OLS and IV and derive asymptotic chi-square tests of the hypothesis that there is no significant difference between the two estimates. This idea also became the basis for the more general approach to specification testing developed by Hausman (1978). Engle, Hendry, and Richard (1983) point out that the Wu-Hausman procedures are tests for predeterminedness, i.e. the Hatanaka and Odaki condition, rather than "weak" or "strong" exogeneity, but they surely can be very informative since rejection is sufficient to reject either premise of exogeneity. The validity of these tests is of course contingent upon the availability of suitable instruments but viewed as potential empirical tools they comprise one of the significant additions to econometrics since the Cowles Commission work.

6.3.2 Panel Data and Interviews

Exogeneity was essential in the simultaneous equations methodology because it provided the conceptual basis for understanding economic data as the results of experiments. Koopmans's analysis made it appear unlikely that very many uncontrolled economic quantities could plausibly serve as independent variables in this context. The situation is reminiscent of Schumpeter's criticism that aggregates seldom act directly on each other. Causal mechanisms would have to be specified more finely in order to elucidate satisfactory explanantions of economic phenomena.

Guy Orcutt made the problem of exogeneity his second major reason for rejecting the Cowles method after his earlier investigations (1948, 1949a, b) into the poor statistical quality of most aggregate economic data. Orcutt accepted the formulation of simultaneous equations models, unlike other methodological opponents, e.g. Wold and Bentzel (1946) and Stone (1954a). He focused instead on the need for imposing a detailed probability structure on the model. His critique stands in an interesting relation to Marschak's assertion that the Cowles method constituted the only rational approach to empirical research.

In his review (1952a) of Cowles Monograph 10 Orcutt listed four problematic assumptions about the nature of the stochastic terms in the structural equations. These were that (1) they did not contain errors of observation, (2) they were uncorrelated with each other at all lags, (3) they were jointly normally distributed, and (4) they were distributed independently of the disturbances in whatever system determined the exogenous variables.

As evidence that the first two assumptions were often not valid Orcutt was able to cite Morgenstern (1950) and his own earlier studies, respectively. It is fair to note that some theoretical work had already commenced at that time to discover ways to lessen the need for them.[9] Normality is bound up with the question of the interpretation of outliers. Markedly non-normal errors in macroeconomic models seem better resolved economically by modifying the behavioral relations, especially their linearity, rather than by assuming extremely asymmetric or thick-tailed distributions.[10] The key point is that empirical evidence can be marshalled to examine these problems. By contrast, Orcutt doubted that the fourth assumption "has or can readily be given an operational meaning."

He modified this last view slightly in (1952b). His argument was that in regard to macroeconomic variables not directly controllable by some agent there was little reason to believe that any of them satisfied the requirements for statistical exogeneity. In other words, an entire prior stage of inference was needed before Marschak's "rational inductive" claim becomes justifiable. Orcutt wrote:

To label some piece of knowledge as being given a priori can hardly add any support to its validity over and above the evidence which has been used to establish it. We still somehow must learn from experience.

The question became the source of this knowledge, since Koopmans had denied that it could be gleaned from the data used to construct the typical model.

In this sense exogeneity is part of the general problem of choosing a model specification. Earlier chapters have described the problems of the Cowles Commission in formulating rigorous models containing many restrictions. It will be recalled from section 4.2.2.1 that by 1948 Koopmans was defending the personal experiences of the econometrician as a source for these hypotheses. Orcutt (1952c) came around to this view as well:

> This source of experience may be and has been useful in constructing causal relations in precisely the same way as experimental evidence is useful. In fact it would be reasonable to classify it under experimental data.

Orcutt's proposed solution to the exogeneity problem that emerged from these ideas was to turn to the development of panel data for making studies of this kind. No doubt he was influenced by the economic survey work that was being conducted in England at the time.[11] The large number of observations in a panel might provide a surer basis for a priori assumptions because the subjective notions of the investigator could be tested against data at the individual level where competitive markets assured that key data, such as wages, prices, and interest rates, would in fact be (weakly) exogenous.

This approach is a striking parallel to Marschak's call for interviews with businessmen in order to clarify specification of the investment function. The difficulty in each case was that satisfactory a priori knowledge was seldom available to make compelling identification of behavioral explanations linking economic aggregates. The early econometricians were agreed that such knowledge was a prerequisite for rational policy formation. In its absence the Cowles Commission turned to research in pure economic theory, where no data were needed, and activity analysis, where all data were available. The twin problems of exogeneity and behavior specification had to be solved before efficient estimation could become of primary importance for policy analysis. The attempt to solve them through intensive data collection is a possible explanation for why pure statistical theory was not a major research interest for most econometricians in the decade after the publication of Monograph 10.

6.3.3 *Granger Causality and Exogeneity*

Granger's (1969) test for causality in an econometric model is an important break with the concept of exogeneity as propounded by the Cowles Commission. He rejected the analogy of an experimental setup and wrote that his theory was "not relevant for non-stochastic variables." Moreover, like Herman Wold he believed that most economic systems were not simultaneously determined so the considerations associated with the need for identification do not enter. Granger plausibly argues that "there appears to be little common ground" between his approach and the previous econometric literature.[12]

The essence of Granger's idea is illustrated by a simple model. He considered two stationary time-series each with mean zero generated as follows:

$$x_{1,t} = \Sigma a_i x_{1,t-i} + \Sigma b_i x_{2,t-i} + e_t$$

$$x_{2,t} = \Sigma c_i x_{1,t-i} + \Sigma d_i x_{2,t-i} + u_t \qquad (6.9)$$

There are two crucial assumptions. The first is that e and u are orthogonal white noise series. Second is that the model uses the correct lag length although in practice it is set at a largely arbitrary value that depends on the available degrees of freedom. All that is needed for x_2 to cause x_1 in Granger's terms is that at least one b_i in (6.9) not equal zero.

The model is seen to be identical to case (1) of Mann and Wald from section 2.1.2. Far from lacking common ground with the Cowles Commission work, Granger's model is rooted in the same soil. However, Granger appears to reject the use of prior restrictions to extend the Mann and Wald results along the lines laid out by the Cowles Commission. Since his approach does not emphasize the role of economic structure, it is not clear whether it remains within the framework of testing specific theories of behavior. For example, if Granger's model is given a structural interpretation then it corresponds to the "complete" system (6.1) above with diagonal $A^{(0)}$ and diagonal Σ. In this case the structural equations could be estimated consistently by OLS and the finding that x_2 does not "Granger cause" x_1 would accord with Koopmans's definition of x_1 as a strictly exogenous variable. There is an identification problem, however, if simultaneous relations are admitted so that Granger's model must be interpreted as a reduced form like (6.2). A diagonal covariance matrix in (6.2) could result either from diagonal $A^{(0)}$ and diagonal Σ or arbitrary positive definite Σ and columns of $A^{(0)}$ equal to eigenvectors of Σ. Moreover, $G_{12}^{(i)} = 0$, $i = 1, \ldots p$, the condition for Granger non-causality in this context, need not imply $A_{12}^{(i)} = 0$ in the structural equation for x_1. Consider a two variable complete model where the lag length p is unity. In the previous notation, $G^{(1)} = A^{(0)-1}A^{(1)}$. Assume that $A^{(0)-1}$ exists and that no structural coefficient equals zero. The necessary and sufficient condition for $g_{121} = 0$ is only that $a_{121} = a_{120}a_{221} / a_{220}$ (where the third subscript indexes the relevant matrix). It is certainly conceivable that an agent constrained to have a non-zero a_{120} may choose a non-zero a_{121} so as to neutralize the effects of lagged x_2. Here is a nice instance of the importance of autonomy: x_2 Granger causes x_1 in the structure but not in the reduced form.

The foregoing again highlights the importance of structural assumptions when interpreting economic data. The non-diagonal covariance matrix that is typically observed in applications of Granger causality tests could imply that a reduced form was being observed, or common variables were omitted from a non-simultaneous system, or both. Granger (1969) acknowledged that it was more relevant in many applications to assume that one would be dealing with a reduced form but he did not emphasize the behavioral and statistical implications of this case.[13] In particular, section 6.2 above discussed that, when simultaneous relations are considered, Granger non-causality is neither necessary nor sufficient for weak exogeneity and consistent estimation of structure. Limitations to the usefulness of "Granger causality" as a causal rather than predictive concept emerge when policy may consist precisely of introducing or eliminating feedbacks, e.g. links between the money supply and interest rates. Furthermore, if no a priori restrictions are used the size of the reduced form (6.2) for a plausible complete system quickly makes estimation infeasible with the usual amounts of time series data. The value of the weak exogeneity assumption in part is that it can exclude variables from the system (6.4) that affect x_2 only through x_1. The small "unrestricted" reduced forms that are typically used for tests of Granger causality really invoke many restrictions in the form of exclusions. The consequences of these exclusions when they are false are unpredictable, especially in finite samples. Granger's (1969) discussion of specification is confined to the crucial observation that "if relevant data has not been included in this set [of lagged explanatory variables] then spurious causality could arise . . . similar to spurious correlation."

The Granger approach is conceptually appealing in certain economic contexts. The goal is to discover feedbacks among variables in the manner of a control engineer. If x_1 Granger causes x_2 while x_2 does not Granger cause x_1, then, provided the orthogonality conditions hold for e and u, x_1 can be used as a control variable for x_2. Economic policy would consist of inducing deviations in the evolution of the "causal" process through additive shocks to its disturbance term. Since the parameters of Granger's model are identified, in principle they can be estimated to test for absence of feedbacks between variables although the available procedures are open to serious statistical objections.

First, even if the models were correctly specified the small sample distributions of the estimators are not known exactly. Making inferences of Granger causality with F statistics, when the model contains lagged endogenous variables, may be very inappropriate. In particular, these asymptotic chi-square tests become progressively less accurate as a root of the system approaches unity.

Second, since the true lag length for the lagged dependent variable is seldom known a priori, the usual procedure is to increase it until the estimated residuals appear serially random. This outcome is certain in a finite sample but is hazardous without an underlying economic theory.[14] For example, Sims (1972) used 8 quarterly lags on nominal money and real GNP with no other economic variables to claim causal priority of money stock over income. This was an important application of Granger's approach as a further attempt to resolve the Friedman-Meiselman debates discussed in section 4.4.1.3 above. Sims defended the F tests used to make the inference in part because the estimated errors appeared to be white noise. This priority disappeared in Sims (1980b), however, when several lagged nominal interest rates were added to the equation. The later model used fewer lags but also appeared to have independent residuals. If it is correct to include interest rates then the 1972 work demonstrates the fact that serial correlation due to omitted variables can always be masked by using enough lagged dependent variables. The key point is that F tests would not appear to be very powerful tests of specification in this context.

Third, economic theory seldom would predict the complete absence of feedbacks among the major macro aggregates. Lagged variables are frequently significant until the inclusion of lagged endogenous, indicating possible identification problems. For example, income in period t-1 will Granger cause money in a simple bivariate regression. In addition, the method is data intensive and must omit some variables altogether to allow long lags on others.

We have seen how the modeling strategy of the Cowles Commission was fundamentally determined by the the presumed availability of identifying restrictions, and hence a rather detailed economic theory, in advance of estimation. One might interpret the Granger causality test as a conservative, alternative strategy that places less faith in the prior restrictions.

Regressions in this set-up would be more in the nature of exploratory data analysis, but guided, of course, by economic considerations. In this context, a "reasonable" lag length for the dependent variable could serve as a pragmatic screen against acceptance of the "spurious regressions" discussed by Granger and Newbold (1974).[15] But as this section has tried to argue, the difficulties raised by multiple hypotheses are no less acute here than elsewhere in econometrics.[16]

6.3.3.1 Granger Causality, Reduced Forms, and Forecasting

For Koopmans, an exogenous variable x_1 could in principle be set at will in each future period regardless of the stochastic process that generated it historically. The coefficients in the endogenous block were presumed to remain unaffected by even complete randomization of x_1, as would be done in a classical experimental design. Indeed, the writings of many econometricians, e.g. Orcutt (1952b), suggest that this would be the ideal solution to the problem of multicollinearity in time series. For these reasons Koopmans thought that the past behavior of explanatory variables was immaterial and focused on consistent estimation of their structural coefficients. Forecasts of endogenous variables would then be based on the reduced form (4). This reasoning is most compelling for the policy variables entirely under the control of a policy maker that were discussed as "instrumental" exogenous variables in section 6.2.

By contrast, Granger views all variables as inherently stochastic processes.[17] He specifically does not consider the exogenous variables that can be fixed as in a laboratory experiment. Moreover, he seems to suggest that all the historical stochastic structure is a fixed state of nature. Policy in the Granger setup is most naturally understood as a shock to an otherwise autonomous process that ideally might serve as a control variable. For example, the stock price index in Tinbergen's model is an exogenous variable that can be influenced but not determined by a policy maker. Forecasts in this case would have to be generated by a simulation of the complete reduced form (6.2) for all variables in the system. Indeed, there seems little alternative interpretation within the limits of the Mann and Wald model.

Hatanaka and Odaki (1983) combined these two viewpoints in an important analysis of prediction of future endogenous variables with reduced forms. As discussed in section 2.1.1, Koopmans stressed the estimation of structural parameters but was not very hopeful for accurate long range ex ante forecasts on account of the accumulation of future disturbances in autoregressive models. Hatanaka and Odaki demonstrated a more fundamental problem in this context.

Let x_1 be weakly exogenous so that the reduced form (6.4) is identified. It is clear that as an autoregressive model (6.4) can be rewritten to express $x_{2,t}$ in terms of lags of x_1, ϵ_2, and higher order lags of itself. Consider the most simple example to eliminate $x_{2,t-1}$:

$$x_{2,t} = x_{1,t} + \epsilon_{2,t} + \epsilon_{2,t-1} \qquad (6.10)$$

where $x_{1,t-1}$ and the higher order lags in all variables are suppressed. The usual forecasting procedure supplies values for future x_1 and assumes that in period $t+\tau$ ($\tau > 1$):

$$E(x_{2,t+\tau}/x_{1,t+\tau}) = x_{1,t+\tau} \qquad (6.11)$$

so that the conditional forecasts are unbiased. The critical issue is whether:

$$E(\epsilon_{2,t+\tau}/x_{1,t+\tau}) = 0 \qquad (6.12)$$

$$E(\epsilon_{2,t+\tau-1}/x_{1,t+\tau}) = 0 \qquad (6.13)$$

or whether $x_{1,t+\tau}$ is uncorrelated with the future structural disturbances for x_2.

Hatanaka and Odaki proved that (6.12) holds in the forecast horizon provided x_1 is predetermined, as indeed it must be for (6.4) to be identified. The condition (6.13) is only valid in general, however, if x_2 does not Granger cause x_1 in the forecast period. Intuitively, when x_2 Granger causes x_1, the path of x_1 must be correlated with past shocks to x_2, namely ϵ_2. The only path for x_1 consistent with unbiased forecasts in (6.10) is the one implied by the simulation of the complete system in (6.2), which presumably would not be available. Assuming an arbitrary path for x_1 in policy simulations, when it actually will be Granger–caused by x_2 in an autonomous stochastic process, will not produce valid forecasts in (6.11). This dilemma brings out how solving the *estimation* problem for only part of the structure of the complete system may not suffice for attacking the *prediction* problem in the subsystem (6.4).

Hatanaka and Odaki suggested that if the exogenous variables were in fact controllable through policy rules, i.e. were "instrumental" in Tinbergen's sense, then in principle one could specify the parameters of structural equations for x_1 directly, combine them with the estimated A_2, and use system (6.2) to generate unbiased conditional forecasts. This solution seems to require that the remaining "non-instrumental" exogenous variables not be Granger caused by the endogenous variables, i.e. that they be strictly exogenous. Hence the proposed solution may not often have very convincing application.

A purely formal solution exists to this forecasting problem that was also discussed by Hatanaka and Odaki. The idea is a generalization of the conditional predictor equations (6.3). They extended the Mann and Wald results to generate predictor equations when future x_1 was known for s periods in advance. The coefficients for the expression $E(x_{2,t}|X_{t-1},x_{1,t},...,x_{1,t+s})$ can be derived from the identified structure (6.2). This procedure may be viewed as a more sophisticated analysis of Tinbergen's "scenarios" that were discussed in section 5.2. In effect it adds correction terms to (6.4) by predicting the unobserved future ϵ_2 using the information that x_1 will actually follow the assumed path. A crucial point is that knowledge of only the reduced form (6.4) is insufficient to derive these forecast equations. Forecasting can require a structure that was irrelevant for estimation. Moreover, in so far as the future ϵ_2 generate the future x_1, the correct predictions are conditional on a pattern of x_1 that there is no a priori guarantee of observing.

6.4 Rational Expectations

Since the rational expectations revolution is still in progress, a historical analysis of it can only be highly tentative. This book will not attempt a full treatment of the subject. A number of important background essays and critical interpretations already exist, for example the introduction by Lucas and Sargent (1981) to their essential collection of readings and the article by Sims (1982). This literature has grown enormously and now covers an exceedingly wide range of issues in pure economic theory, econometrics, and policy.[18] The following discussion focuses on the historical relationship of rational expectations to structural estimation and earlier work on errors in variables models. This is one area that has not been explored in as much detail in the work of others.

6.4.1 *Structural Autonomy and Exogeneity*

The Cowles Commission did not undertake to explain the particular values of structural parameters aside from locating their ultimate basis in the technical, institutional, and behavioral relations of society. Their methodology concerned identification and estimation of a given structure which otherwise remained largely a phenomenon. In this respect their approach was in the spirit of the scientific experiments that measured such intangibles as the gravitational constant and the energy in a photon. But the view of a model as a representation of optimizing behavior naturally raises the possibility that the parameters of the structural equations might not be independent of the processes generating the exogenous variables, even if the conditions for consistent estimation were satisfied. It is worth trying to infer the attitude of the Cowles Commission on the question, especially as it pertains to their stated concerns with the analysis of structural change.

Marschak (1950) supplied the basic discussion of the relationships between exogenous variables and structure in the Cowles methodology. He wrote (using an obvious notation):

> The observable vector [Y] can always be represented as a product of a conditional and a marginal distribution . . . [e.g.] $f(Y,Z) = g(Y|Z;\delta)h(Z)$.

> The parameters of the ("subsidiary") marginal distribution $h(Z)$ are not related to the parameters δ of . . . the conditional distribution of the endogenous variables.

> For the purpose of estimating [the endogenous structure] we have to consider not the joint distribution $f(Y,Z)$ but merely the conditional distribution . . . we can *disregard* the possibly random character of Z and treat Z as if it were fixed in repeated samples of Y.[19]

Marschak was restating Koopmans's result that efficient estimation of the structure did not require information about $h(Z)$, given their statistical definition of exogeneity. As they were well aware, for the model to display this property it is essential to rule out cross equation restrictions connecting the parameters of the endogenous and exogenous blocks. Failure to model structural non-linearities was regarded as the main source of apparent dependencies of this kind.[20] The time varying parameter models explored by the Commission were of the form:

$$Y = (b_1 + b_2t + b_3X_1)X_2 \qquad (6.14)$$

which was used really to justify nonlinear interaction terms. In correctly specified structural equations, the coefficients were still assumed to be "autonomous" in Frisch's sense and accordingly were not restricted by the distribution of the exogenous variables.

The Cowles Commission did not employ cross equation restrictions even within the endogenous block partly because Koopmans had not developed the theory of identification for this problem in detail but also because they doubted that such structural restrictions were well motivated by economic theory.[21] The reduced form, of course, was their example of a less autonomous equation system that was subject to cross equation restrictions that could be imposed using FIML for efficient estimation. Marschak clearly implied, however, that the exogenous variables were to be viewed as experimental stimuli whose distributions implied nothing about the structural parameters.

The question becomes more complicated when policies of explicit structural change are considered. The original discussions of economic policy in econometrics put primary emphasis on this goal. It was seldom specified, however, how it could be achieved. Action to accomplish it would seem to involve manipulation of some instrument under the control of a policy maker. Accordingly, there appears to be an inherent possibility that an exogenous variable can affect structural parameters. The Cowles memoranda cited above in section 4.2.2 and Marschak (1953) in fact allow the same quantity, frequently a tax rate in their expositions, to represent both a structural parameter and an exogenous variable. Koopmans seemed to allude to this kind of ambiguity in other comments on Klein's early models:

> An empirical relationship between personal and business cash balances is quoted to justify the use of their sum as a variable in the consumption function. What is the "theory" of this relationship? Can it be relied upon to persist under the policies discussed, e.g. deficit spending and easy money?[22]

Haavelmo was also conscious of this difficulty in establishing a basis of neoclassical utility maximization for aggregate policy analysis:

> Before using "old" structural equations under a new policy it is therefore important to specify exactly the *conditions of free choice* (the maximizing conditions) of the N groups under the new policy and to compare these conditions with the conditions of choice that prevailed before the policy change was made.[23]

It will be recalled from section 2.1 that Tinbergen had also left it an open question whether policy could change a single structural parameter without affecting other parts of the system.

These statements provide no assurance that structural parameters will not respond to changes in the distribution of the exogenous variables. It seems that all of these researchers considered the invariance of the structure to such changes to be part of the prior information that defined the model in the first place. In this formulation it would be a problem for economic theorists to ascertain whether invariance had a sound basis in advance of statistical estimation.[24] As such it was not further investigated by the Cowles Commission.

There are two immediate areas of uncertainty regarding the interpretation of the conditional distribution even when it is estimated with infinitely many samples of Y with a fixed regressor set Z. First is the effect of a controllable variable Z_1 when set to occur with an unprecedented combination of values of the other exogenous variables. Second is the effect of Z_1 when made to follow an unprecedented time sequence of values. These questions are related to the problem of out of sample extrapolation. The difference is that the extrapolation can be along dimensions for which Z_1 remains within the range of observed values. Given that structural equations describe optimizing behavior, it is not obvious that the coefficients that determine optimal responses in these cases are the same as those implied by infinite repetitions of the fixed regressor set.[25] Moreover, orthogonalization of the regressors as a cure for multicollinearity is not certain a priori to leave unaffected the structural parameters under investigation. The historical covariation of the exogenous variables may itself be an important characteristic of the structure.

These questions about structural invariance were never deeply discussed in the writings of the Cowles Commission, although in recent years they have loomed large in the rational expectations literature. The original equations of "macrodynamics" were patterned after the analysis of driven harmonic oscillators in physics. Exogenous variables corresponded to external driving forces which did not themselves require explanation for a study of their effects. In particular, the oscillator in physics is not conditioned by an anticipation of future driving forces. This view of behavior may not be appropriate when studying adaptation to altered environments in social or biological science, which might be thought a natural complement to the study of dynamic economics. The theory of rational expectations places central importance on these adjustment processes. By strictly adhering to principles of rational behavior at the individual's level it has revealed important conceptual limitations of the analogy to experiments in physical science for economics.

6.4.2 *Analysis of Structure Under Rational Expectations*

This book has discussed two instances in which expectations (i.e. forecasts) have seemed to play an overriding role in a particular economic problem. The first, mentioned in section 1.2.2, was Holbrook Working's concern that the standard "market equilibrium" story did not satisfactorily explain the level of demand for purposes of inventory speculation. Implicitly, this was also a critique of Moore's supply function which made the expected future price equal simply to the current market price. The other case was Friedman's consumption function, in which the household (and the econometrician) had to predict permanent income on the basis of past values of actual income.[26]

By the late 1950's a variety of "expectations hypotheses" had come into use that were much more sophisticated than Moore's. Friedman and many others adopted a distributed lag with exponential weights:

$$x_t^e = \beta \Sigma_{i=1}^{\infty} (1-\beta)^{i-1} x_{t-i} \tag{6.15}$$

where x_t^e denoted the expected future value of x as of the preceding period. This could be obtained from different forms of the adaptive expectations hypothesis.[27] Two main considerations argued in its favor. First, it plausibly modeled expectations as averages of past experience with less weight given to more remote history. More specifically, since the weights summed to unity it seemed that (6.15) had to be "unbiased" in that x^e *exactly* equalled x_t in the hypothetical steady-state (where x_t equalled x_{t-1}). Second, (6.15) had the property that persistent forecast errors eventually would be corrected. The "speed of adjustment" of expectations obviously depended on the parameter β. For example, in a jump from one steady-state up to another, a small value of β implied many periods of underestimation while convergence was approached from below. This was not an attractive feature from a decision-theoretic point of view but perhaps it could be dismissed if such jumps were not very probable. As a structural parameter, β was assumed to depend mainly on unspecified adjustment or learning costs stemming from institutional factors or "noise" in the data. Some processes, e.g. hyperinflation, would have a β close to unity. Others, such as Friedman's permanent income expectation, were reasonably believed to be more damped. The precise value of β was not otherwise explained.

This particular formulation often received good empirical support, so it was assumed to be an adequate approximation to whatever process generated expectations in reality. John Muth (1960a) was the first researcher to ask for which specific stochastic processes the exponential forecast was in fact the *optimal* prediction (in a minimum mean square error sense). The answer he found was that the prediction was optimal for infinite moving averages of i.i.d. shocks of the form:

$$x_t = \epsilon_t + \beta \Sigma \epsilon_{t-i} \tag{6.16}$$

which was perhaps a surprisingly restrictive condition. Muth pointed out, however, that as a mixture of transitory shocks (ϵ_i) and permanent effects ($\beta \epsilon_i$) the process (6.16) could have an economic application, for example in

Friedman's consumption function. He respecified the process slightly more generally as

$$x_t = \eta_t + \epsilon_t + \sum_{i=1}^{\infty} \epsilon_{t-i} \qquad (6.17)$$

with η_t and ϵ_t statistically independent, corresponding to Friedman's assumption that shocks to permanent and transitory income were uncorrelated. The exponential forecast again was optimal but the lag weights became a function of the ratio of the variances of the two contemporaneous shocks. This "signal to noise" interpretation was reasonable but it had a more important implication in that the coefficient β explicitly became a function of other parameters of the system. Muth's analysis implied that structural models of expectations were not likely to display as high a degree of autonomy as other parts of a complete model, with potentially serious problems for statistical inference.

Muth was not wedded to a particular empirical model of expectations. He emphatically rejected the appeal to institutional factors or other unmodeled phenomena as an economic basis for mechanisms such as the exponential forecast. Instead, he viewed expectations as an economic good, the quality of which could be judged by definite statistical criteria. His argument at bottom was a striking new use of the old errors in variables approach in econometrics. The core proposition was that an optimal (mean squared error) forecast should display the property:

$$x_t = x_t^e + u_t \qquad (6.18)$$

where the forecast error u_t had zero mean, was serially uncorrelated, and had zero correlation with the forecast itself. The first condition implied unbiased forecasts, the second implied that systematic overprediction or underprediction should not exist, and the third meant that all information through period t-1 useful in forecasting x_t would be utilized. Hence u_t would comprise only the component of x_t that could not possibly have been (linearly) predicted in advance. Nothing in (6.18) implied a specific expression for x^e. In fact, the analogy to errors in variables suggested that "optimal" expectations in general were *unobservable* data that at best could be measured with error by using the actual realizations. Presumably, estimation procedures for models with expectations terms could be revised to handle this setup correctly.

In this context, however, direct use of the standard errors in variable specification would encounter major problems. Most importantly, using x_t as an instrument for x^e when x_t itself was the dependent variable almost surely would destroy the identifiability of the model, e.g.:

$$x_t = \alpha x^e + \beta z_t + u_t \tag{6.19}$$

would reduce to

$$x_t = \beta/(1-\alpha)z_t + 1/(1-\alpha)u_t \tag{6.19b}$$

In models where x_t was not the dependent variable, using it instead of x^e of course simply led to an inconsistent estimator of α. Identifiability would still be a problem, however, if expected and actual values entered separately in the equation:

$$y_t = \alpha_1 x_t + \alpha_2 x^e + u_t \tag{6.20}$$

Muth indicated that such would be the case for a wide variety of models intended for optimal control purposes, where in particular $\alpha_1 + \alpha_2$ might equal zero. It was clear that a different approach was needed to solve this version of the errors in variables problem. But it was not clear at this stage how important this line of research would prove to be. The role of expectations variables was not emphasized in most existing economic theories and errors in variables up to that time had appeared to be a relatively minor nuisance. The full consequences of the "optimal" forecasting assumption remained to be explored.

Like Koopmans, Haavelmo, and Wright, Muth was defining and classifying variables on the basis of their stochastic properties. In the case of Friedman's consumption function, Muth showed that the expectations mechanism happened to coincide with the "optimal" forecast under the assumed covariance structure of permanent and transitory income. For the bulk of other applied models, however, there seemed little reason to believe a priori that the expectations variables at all satisfied the conditions in (6.18). Hence there was likely to be extreme uncertainty in these cases regarding estimated parameters of expectations mechanisms, their potential inconsistency, their structural autonomy, and the extent to which the forecasts actually described the beliefs of economic agents.[28]

The open question was how to derive optimal forecasts in general if the exponential lag and other devices were valid only for special cases. Of course, Muth (1961) has become famous for arguing that in a model designed to predict a variable x, the "rational" forecast must coincide with the prediction of the model itself. This reasoning can again be related to the logic of (6.18). Let a complete structural model be denoted by:

$$BY + \Gamma Z = u \tag{6.21}$$

with the usual assumptions of nonsingular B, i.i.d. u with mean zero and

covariance matrix Σ of full rank, and Z a matrix of exogenous and predetermined variables. To simplify matters, assume that expectations variables
do not enter the specification (this does not preclude the existence of a
rational expectation). Compare the reduced form to (6.18):

$$(i) \quad Y = \Pi Z + v$$

$$(ii) \quad Y = Y^e + u \qquad\qquad (6.22)$$

The connection between these two expressions becomes apparent when
the reduced form is written as:

$$Y = [\pi_1 Z_{t-1} + \pi_2 E(Z_t|Z_{t-1})] + [\pi_2(Z_t - E(Z_t|Z_{t-1}) + v_t] \qquad (6.23)$$

The first bracketed expression is the reduced form prediction of Y based on
all information available prior to the current period. The notation
$E(Z_t|Z_{t-1})$ is the expected value of the current exogenous variables conditional upon all past Z. The second set of brackets is the ex post forecast
error.[29] It follows immediately that the optimal forecast, or the ex ante
"rational" expectation of Y, is simply the first expression in brackets.[30]
This analysis indicates that the rational expectation is a reduced form prediction augmented by forecasts of the future values of the exogenous variables. The key result is that the expectation becomes a function of the
parameters of the process for Z.

It is clear that the "rational expectations" hypothesis in these terms does
not necessarily invalidate the ad hoc mechanisms utilized in, for example,
the Klein-Goldberger or the Brookings work. As approximations they may
have been quite close to the rational result. In fact, in Muth's (1961) analysis
of the speculative inventory problem, a one period lag to model expected
price turned out to be optimal for an interesting case. The important differences concerned deeper issues of interpretation of structure and structural
change.

Earlier econometric practice had considered the structural parameters to
have the highest level of autonomy in a model. The dependency of expectations on the parameters of the Z process, i.e. cross equation restrictions
spanning the endogenous and exogenous blocks, changed this notion
substantially. Structural parameters could no longer be assumed to be
given in the absolute by technology and human nature. The cross equation
restrictions amounted to a (not necessarily complete) model for them. The
most autonomous relations in effect become the strongly exogenous variables.

Rational expectations models considerably lessen the power of Koopmans's analysis of exogeneity. He attempted to find a way to reduce the necessary size of a complete system for statistically consistent and efficient estimation procedures. Under rational expectations it would no longer be possible to follow him and Marschak in disregarding the stochastic nature of Z. At best, his methods would provide consistent but inefficient estimates of structural parameters. This followed only if the Z process remained unchanged over the sample period. Efficient estimation would require correct specification of all variables in the system, the difficulty of which for empirical work was precisely the problem that Koopmans sought to avoid.

In addition, the Cowles focus on structural change suggests a further conceptual role for Koopmans's approach that is undermined by rational expectations. His theory allowed the investigator to ignore all structural changes in the exogenous block with no statistical penalty. Isolating relevant structural change to the endogenous relations is an important analytical simplification. In a large macroeconomic model, for example, the exogenous variables typically vastly outnumber the endogenous ones. If structural changes in their processes also had to be considered, the complexity of the analysis would be unmanageable.[31]

The hypothesis of rational expectations can explain the seeming paradox of structural change that was discussed in the preceding section. It compels a revision of the analogy between exogenous variables and experimental stimuli. The earlier view of the autonomy of structural relations in part was derived from the wish to preserve the separation of the observer from the object. Rational expectations critiques the behavioristic psychology that seems to underlie this separation. Structural relations from the rational expectations perspective are ultimately the rules for rational behavior in the environment defined by the exogenous variables and the stochastic disturbances. It has aroused much controversy largely because of its strong result in some policy models that predictable movements in "instrumental" exogenous variables can have no real effects. Frequent changes of policy in effect can lead agents to develop strategies to neutralize their exposure to such variations. It recalls another property of the harmonic oscillator where the amplitude of the effect of the driving force approaches zero as its frequency approaches infinity. The paradox of structural change takes on a new form: too much becomes indistinguishable from none at all.

6.4.2.1 Rational Expectations and Early Structural Estimation

Viewed in this light, the rational expectations school provides a basis for structural equations in a framework of optimizing behavior by individuals. It is surprisingly similar to the general program that the Cowles researchers initially contemplated. Marschak plainly anticipated the point of departure for Muth (1961) in a letter to Schumpeter in 1946:

> The great difficulty in deriving a macro-dynamic system from the postulate of individual rational behavior consists (apart from the aggregation question) in the fact that the equations of rational behavior relate optimal (i.e. profit maximizing) values of certain measurable variables to certain variables that are mere expectations of individuals.
>
> One might look for help from the principle of rational behavior in the following way: one assumes the individuals to handle their past experience in the way a rational inductive investigator, i.e. a statistician, would do it. But this complete substitution of rational for traditional behavior . . . goes probably too far. Give it up and you are faced with an enormous variety of equally eligible "psychological" expectation equations.[32]

This statement comes remarkably close to expressing the rational expectations hypothesis but it does not seem that Marschak recognized the scope of its importance. Samuelson (1983) has suggested that Marschak recruited Klein to build models that would support Keynesian ideas empirically on a more microeconomic level. Hurwicz (1946) was also asked to try this. Such models had to devise expectations variables for the theories of investment and liquidity preference. They may have preserved Marschak's distinction between rational and traditional behavior because of the acceptance of money illusion in the consumption and labor supply functions. Marschak's later work in economic theory emphasized the role of information and uncertainty in investment and organization behavior but the problem of expectations in econometrics ironically was not subjected to comparable analysis for another generation.

There is some evidence for believing that the Cowles researchers and the other early Keynesians would not necessarily have rejected Lucas's (1976) characterization of effective policy as a "surprise" or unexpected shock to the system. Consider this correspondence between Alvin Hansen and Lawrence Klein after the apparent disconfirmation of many forecasts of an immediate post-War depression. Hansen wrote:

> Could it not be argued that the pessimistic forecast . . . was basically correct and the policies [concerning taxes and price and wage controls] introduced were also correct, leading to a condition of full employment. . . .
>
> One of the functions of forecasting [is] to insure that (by introducing appropriate policy) the forecast shall not turn out as anticipated.

Klein's answer was quite direct:

I agree that correct policy on the basis of a forecast changes the behavior of the
system so that the forecast is wrong.[33]

Both writers seem close to suggesting that effective policy in part depended
on its "unpredictable" component. They did not proceed to the full
"rational expectations" notion, however, that strictly systematic policies
may be neutralized by private agents' own forecasts of the behavior of the
policymaker.

This lack of concern with private forecasts was typical for the the
Keynesians of the time, who viewed macroeconomics as the special
domain of the policy maker that was largely independent of the volition of
individual agents. The systems of difference equations displayed cyclical
patterns that had no clear rationale in terms of the maximization of individual utilities, as Schumpeter had observed in 1937. They appeared quite
similar in nature to the contemporary Swedish concept of "cumulative
causation," which brought out the unintentional and irrational element in
macroeconomic phenomena.[34] This idea suggests that individual agents
may be unable to prevent an event such as a general downturn in spite of
accurate perceptions of its imminence, thereby justifying a role for policy as
a necessary countermeasure to an inherent potential for instability in the
growth of a competitive economy.

In this connection it is interesting to note that Klein's analysis of liquidity preference was initially cast in terms of the maximization of a utility
function for goods, bonds, and money over a T period horizon using what
he termed anticipations variables for prices, income, and interest rates.[35]
He included an unconstrained one period lag for each variable to model the
anticipated value for it. Statistically significant lags would be retained as
predictors. However, this formulation was not retained in the final work
reported in Klein (1950), presumably because too few degrees of freedom
made it impossible to estimate a detailed lag structure. There was little
concern at the time over this point because the chosen money demand
function happened to fit well over the sample period. To the extent that
later applied studies did utilize the mechanical extrapolative expectations
mechanism, they did not appear to imply the individual inductive rational-
ity that is indispensable in microeconomic analysis.[36]

Econometrics may be understood, as Marschak implied, as the study of
the most efficient utilization of the information available to an economic
agent. In this sense rational expectations commands attention as part of
the theory of maximizing behavior. One purely technical reason may be
offered for why it did not sweep econometrics for over a decade after
Muth's insight. The theory of identification in the presence of cross equa-

tion restrictions only started to develop beyond Koopmans's notes in Monograph 10 with the contributions by Wegge (1965). This was extended and made more accessible by Rothenberg (1973). Application to larger models followed with the work of Sargent (1976) and Hansen and Sargent (1980) and others. Since then it has become a familiar item in the tool kit. It was a notable advance for a problem of pure econometric theory that Koopmans had set aside as "pretty hopeless."[37]

6.4.2.2 Rational Expectations and a Return to Structure

Structural estimation began as the analysis of policies for introducing structural changes into an economic system, particularly through changing coefficients of the endogenous variables. The coefficients of the exogenous variables were important in so far as they determined the parameters of the reduced form for prediction and control purposes. As section 4.2.2 suggested, policy soon came to be conceived in terms of Lerner's (1941) "economic steering wheel," as in Marschak's (1953) paraphrase:

> The motorist, ignorant of the car mechanism, steers his wheel quite successfully, responding instantaneously to changes in the surface and the direction of the road.

Here the car mechanism stood for economic structure and the steering wheel represented all the "instrumental" exogenous variables. Estimation of the reduced form was believed sufficient to learn how to "drive" the economy.[38] A crucial assumption in this approach was Marschak's (1953) assertion that "there is a difference between changing the exogenous variables and changing the structure."

Hatanaka and Odaki (1983) and Engle, Hendry, and Richard (1983) in effect returned to study Marschak's claim that the distribution of the exogenous variables was irrelevant for the estimation of the reduced form or for the inference of structural parameters. They established that the necessary and sufficient condition was weak exogeneity, essentially what Koopmans had already discovered. The two articles reminded econometricians that ignoring valid cross equation restrictions between the endogenous and exogenous blocks would yield consistent but inefficient estimates, much like any other restrictions when the structural parameters were otherwise identified. Muth (1960b) made this point as well in early work that has been published only recently. Rational expectations has provided powerful economic arguments that such restrictions should be present in many complete equation systems. The hypothesis is noteworthy for introducing a new form of interdependence in econometric models through the parameters, in addition to simultaneity in the variables. Such linkages suggest that in many contexts the notion would be limited merely to predetermined (lagged) variables.

The most drastic consequence of valid rational expectations type restrictions is that the analysis of structural change can no longer be confined to the equations of the endogenous block. Changes in the distribution of the exogenous variables would force changes in the parameters of the structural equations and, accordingly, the parameters of a reduced form such as (6.4). The experimental analogy breaks down for the case it was thought most suitable, namely the orthogonalization of the "instrumental" exogenous variables. Ironically, such manipulation virtually defines a category of structural change in rational expectations models.

Hatanaka and Odaki (1983) completed their analysis of forecasting with reduced forms by noting that rational expectations introduces another level of complication. As with the case of changed policy rules, knowledge of the entire complete structural system (6.1) would be necessary. With rational expectations, however, substituting the new parameters for the exogenous processes must be followed by adjusting all the structural coefficients in accordance with the cross equation restrictions. Then the complete reduced form (6.2) would again be solved to generate predictions. These restrictions conceivably could imply large changes in structural coefficients under a new exogenous regime but the difficulty of incorporating them in current large macro models is a formidable obstacle to application.[39]

In this one is also reminded of Tukey's question, discussed in section 4.1, whether a large change in a structural parameter necessarily leads to a significantly different reduced form. The small rational expectations models of Sargent and Wallace (1975), for example, with radical implications of "policy ineffectiveness" are reminiscent of Koopmans's first efforts to prove the importance of simultaneity bias. In both cases, startling formal statistical results can be produced from models whose economic foundations are perhaps open to question.

Rational expectations is most powerful as a sort of comparative statics of dynamic equilibria. The theory does not determine a priori the speeds of adjustment to changes in the exogenous regimes. Since agents must now also make inferences about behavioral parameters of exogenous processes, full adjustment to a change in regimes need not be instantaneous. Many examples in the literature of the effects of a credible announced change in an established government policy "rule," e.g. money supply growth targets, have been constructed to make such a learning process unnecessary.

Announcements of this sort could lead to immediate revisions in the structure along the lines indicated by Hatanaka and Odaki (1983). The key issue in these examples is the information content of such announcements. There is little evidence that such rules have ever existed in the macroeconomic context. If adjustment costs are high or the information in the process is low, the original estimated structural equations may still provide a useful approximation to optimal behavior over a horizon of interest for policy.[40] Indeed, if exogenous regimes change frequently and costs of adjustment slow the approach to the full rational expectations equilibrium, Tinbergen's original use of data as deviations from long moving averages might allow an unrestricted model to perform tolerably well. Not surprisingly, financial markets have best exhibited the efficient reactions idealized in rational expectations theory. The force of the rational expectations critique remains, however, that in the absence of a model of the "learning" process, confidence intervals for forecasts from the original reduced forms are subject to an additional but unmeasured source of uncertainty.[41]

As a general proposition, however, rational expectations in the form given in (6.21) does not seem especially controversial if one is otherwise prepared to accept the idea of structural estimation. The question of greater interest is the particular economic hypothesis embodied in the use of expectations variables. In the Keynesian models of the 1950's and 1960's the role of expectations was so circumscribed as to make little difference in any simulation exercises. The main consequence of rational expectations seemed to be only a minor reparameterization of the identifiable structure (as in Muth[1960b]). That situation could radically change, of course, as demonstrated by Sargent and Wallace (1975) and others. In such a context the problem of hypothesis testing again comes to the fore. If the rational expectations restrictions are overidentifying they can serve as maintained hypotheses to test the validity of the rest of the model. The view taken here is that such a procedure would test the least certain parts of the specification.

It should be noted that rational expectations can be tested as a behavioral hypothesis if appropriate survey data are available. Muth himself once tested the orthogonality of survey forecast errors to the forecasts and found, contrary to rational expectations, that his sample did not possess this property.[42] Of the three conditions in (6.18), this one was the most restrictive and could be termed the "strong form" of rational expectations. Muth concluded that actual expectations should be interpreted as the rational expectation plus a disturbance, so that x^e in (6.18) generally is not available to agents. In other words, the agent himself (as well as the econometrician) might be understood as observing the rational expectation with error. This result suggests that agents in fact typically do not make use of all relevant information to form predictions, due presumably to costs of observing or processing a vast data set.

It is not clear, however, what the alternative hypothesis should be in such a case. The forecast error is still likely to be serially uncorrelated so that recourse to a simple distributed lag scheme would not be justified. This problem recalls the arguments by Keynes in section 5.1 against structural modeling where the number of *important* explanatory variables was very large. But even if the strong form of rational expectations is not a realistic assumption, so that actual models are chronically misspecified with too few variables, the forecast obtained with a given information set, along the lines of (6.21), may be the best one possible. But the effects of this sort of specification error are not at all clear.

The rational expectations hypothesis has suggested telling criticisms of the Keynesian models that have been associated with the origins of structural estimation. But it is striking how the hypothesis actually refocuses attention on the analysis of underlying structural parameters to evaluate the real and lasting effects of any type of economic policy. One recalls the original Cowles research agenda: the distribution of income, monopoly and industrial structure, wage and price rigidities, the burden of taxation. Such problems are still treated very schematically in the large macroeconomic models.[43] One might expect that the reinterpretation of the Phillips curve by the rational expectations movement will only be the beginning of a new study of policy based on more detailed knowledge of economic behavior under institutional constraints.[44]

This renewed attention on structure would possibly return applied econometrics to the kind of policy discussions that were more usual in the 1940's and 1950's, as outlined in chapter 3. Indeed, Sargent and Wallace (1975) can be read as a further development of the monetary arguments of Friedman and Meiselman (1963) discussed in section 4.4.1.3. The partisans of rational expectations are often hostile to much of the economic structure that is the legacy of the New Deal, the Full Employment Act, and other reforms. Their program has come as a shock to liberal macroeconomists for whom policy was primarily a question of appropriate Keynesian deficits and monetary policy, within a basically unquestioned post-New Deal institutional framework. The liberal response has usually invoked notions of imperfect or missing markets, non-optimizing behavior, and social welfare to prove that, in Marschak's phrase, rational expectations "goes probably too far."[45] It is a worthy challenge for econometrics to evaluate empirical arguments on these issues. The aggregate linear difference equation model of Mann and Wald may not prove to be a completely satisfactory tool for this purpose, but the clear understanding of exogeneity assumptions should help in deciding when and how it is appropriate.

NOTES TO CHAPTER 6

[1]The asymptotic estimation theory for the Mann and Wald model with exogenous variables was the main contribution of the thesis by Herman Rubin (1948).

[2]This paragraph draws on the exposition in Hatanaka and Odaki (1983).

[3]Important considerations in the multi-period prediction problem are discussed in section 6.3.3.1 below.

[4]What they call "superexogeneity" will be discussed in subsection 6.4.4.1 below.

[5]Simon (1953) seemed to have this idea in mind when interpreting simultaneous equations as a kind of "causal chain." He was defending the Cowles Commission approach against the critique made by Herman Wold that was discussed in the preceding chapter.

[6]Tukey, "Further Remarks on the Cowles Commission's Multivariate Problems," CC 2.8, August 1946, CCA, CCDP Stats. volume I.

[7]In an interview with the author, Sewall Wright reported that he once gave a seminar on path coefficients to the Cowles Commission but could not remember the year. One may hazard it was in 1943 or 1944. Evidently neither side saw particular merit in the other's methods. See section 1.2.4 above.

[8]Nakamura and Nakamura (1981) show the equivalence of Durbin, Wu, and Hausman tests in certain contexts. See section 5.1.2.2 for mention of use of Durbin's work by Stone in England.

[9]An unpublished paper by Anderson and Hurwicz titled "Statistical Models with Disturbances in Equations and/or Disturbances in Variables" dated Spring 1946 is in CCA, folder: Statistics, papers. See also Herman Rubin, "Identification Problems with Serially Correlated Disturbances," 18 November 1948, CCA, CCDP Stat. 319. Chernoff and Rubin (1953) also dealt with some of these issues.

[10]For example, Tobin (1958) initiated the study of panel models using the truncated normal distribution for the errors. Bassett and Koenker (1978)

have made fundamental contributions to the theory of robust regression which are of value when the errors are obviously non-normal and no prior economic theory can be utilized to otherwise refine the model.

[11]See section 5.1.3.

[12]For frequency domain extensions of Granger's work see Geweke (1982) and the references cited there.

[13]Zellner (1979b) interpreted Granger non-causality as a property of the reduced form. Engle, Hendry, and Richard (1983) seem to view it as pertaining to a structural equation. Many discussions in the literature are confusing for not making a clear distinction between the two possibilities.

[14]Cf. the work of Cochrane and Orcutt (1949a) discussed in section 5.1.3.1 above.

[15]For an important new analysis of the "spurious regression" problem see Phillips (1986).

[16]Much of the discussion of vector autoregressions in section 6.5 below is also pertinent for Granger causality.

[17]Cf. Friedman's emphasis on "transmission mechanisms" in section 4.2.3 above.

[18]Among the more interesting recent contributions are Lucas (1987) and Pesaran (1987). Many surveys of the literature now exist; a good starting place is Shiller (1978).

[19]From Marschak (1950), p. 24 (emphasis added).

[20]While commenting on one of Klein's early models Koopmans wondered "what happens if the value of N [a labor supply function] exceeds the existing labor force?" In "Comments on 'The Use of Econometric Models,'" January 1947, CCA, CCSP Economics 1946–1947. Koopmans (1957) was still repeating his concern, first expressed in his *Tanker Freight Rates*, over this deficiency in business cycle models and emphasized the econometric implications of sectoral capacity constraints.

[21]Cf. the English consumer demand work discussed in section 5.1.3.2 that made use of cross equation restrictions in the context of *non-simultaneous* models.

[22]Koopmans, "Comments on 'The Use of Econometric Models.'"

[23]Haavelmo, "Note on Structural Equations and Economic Policies," 2 December 1946, CCA, CCSP Economics 1946-47, (emphasis in original).

[24]Cf. section 6.4.1.2 below.

[25]Lipsey (1960) shrewdly observed that the Phillips (1958) curve provided no information on the rate of inflation implied by holding unemployment at the same level for many periods. Unfortunately this insight was forgotten for a generation.

[26]Note also the discussion in section 4.2.1 on Irving Fisher.

[27]Koyck (1954) and Nerlove (1956) are standard references. This formulation was also widely used for "production smoothing" in the operations research literature.

[28]An especially clear example of this problem is offered in Sargent (1971).

[29]If Z_t is observed prior to y_t then the rational expectation is just the reduced form prediction in period t.

[30]If the structural error was serially correlated then x^e would be modified to contain lagged values of v as additional predictors of the reduced form disturbances.

[31]Engle, Hendry, and Richard (1983) define a "superexogenous" variable as one that is weakly exogenous and has the additional property that changes in its distribution do not imply changes in the structural parameters. It is a testable hypothesis if the model can be estimated over subperiods between which the equation for the exogenous variable is known to have changed. The power of such tests in practice is likely to be rather low, as acknowledged by Hendry (1983).

[32]Jacob Marschak, Memorandum re Joseph Schumpeter, 23 November 1946, CCA.

[33]Hansen to Klein, 7 October 1946; Klein to Hansen, 10 October 1946, CCA, CCSP Economics 1946-47.

[34]See Gunnar Myrdal, *Monetary Equilibrium* (London: W. Hodge, 1939).

[35]Klein, "Memorandum on the Money Market for a Cowles Commission Staff Meeting," October 1946, CCA, CCSP Economics 1946-47.

[36]For thoughtful, indeed chastened, view of these mechanisms in econometrics see Nerlove (1979).

[37]Koopmans, "Statistical Problems."

[38]The difference between valid estimation and valid forecasting was not sufficiently appreciated until the analysis by Hatanaka and Odaki (1983) discussed in section 6.3.3.1.

[39]See Eckstein (1984) for an example of a smaller, more micro oriented system that makes effective use of rational expectations restrictions and Granger non-causality to model agricultural production.

[40]Sims (1982) has made this argument at some length.

[41]Keynes himself perhaps would have found the rational expectations critique compatible with his own theories concerning expectations and the business cycle. The following note written in 1938 is typical of his explications of the *General Theory:*

> In short, an unforeseen change in the situation leads to temporary anomalous values of propensity to consume, rate of investment and liquidity preference and there is a time lag before these anomalies cure themselves.
> How long these anomalous values persist . . . is a matter of practical importance for forecasting but it does not really affect the central theory. When there is an unforeseen change of conditions the propensity to consume departs from its normal value and there is a time lag before it resumes it.

From Keynes, "Comments on [Colin] Clark," *Collected Works*, 12:804. In 1941-42 he briefly supported the idea of his disciple James Mead to vary the MPC as a countercyclical tool through changes in the social security tax rate but, as discussed above in section 4.1, he eventually preferred a high and *steady* rate of public investment instead.

[42]See Muth (n.d.).

[43]Cf. Malinvaud (1981) who pointed out, however, that present rational expectations models are too crude to settle many relevant policy problems.

[44]The reliance on money illusion as a basis for employment policies in many Keynesian models has always contrasted rather strongly with the clear awareness of real wages on the part of both organized and unorganized labor. The full employment proposals of the CIO during its more aggressive period stressed maintenance of real wages *and* structural reforms such as a national jobs registry, etc. See Congress of Industrial Organizations, *The People's Program for 1946*, Pamphlet No. 11 (Washington D.C.: CIO Political Action Committee, 1946).

[45]See, e.g., Tobin (1980).

CHAPTER 7

VECTOR AUTOREGRESSIONS

7.1 Background

The confidence of the applied econometricians did not last long into the 1970's. The economic shocks of the decade began to invalidate the forecasts from the large structural macro models and drove researchers to constant respecification and re-estimation of their systems. This work was accompanied by a growing number of studies that compared the forecasting quality of the large models to a new generation of univariate time series "naive" models. These comparisons still often showed that the structural models predicted no better than the naive models, in apparent confirmation of Friedman's predictions made in 1949. As the inadequate modeling particularly of price relations and financial sector behavior became apparent, the model builders continually announced that "the" key variable which would set matters right had finally been located.[1]

Sims (1980a) challenged this whole line of activity. He wrote in recognition of a "deep vein of scepticism" about the large models that he felt had surfaced within the academic economic community.[2] He asserted that as representations of economic behavior their "claims for identification cannot be taken seriously." He denied that their identifying restrictions were derived "by invoking economic theory." These objections seemed equally intended for the ostensibly Keynesian and the strictly monetarist econometricians. The implication for econometric modeling in his view was simple. By rejecting all identifying restrictions as "incredible," all variables should then appear without lags in all equations. The category of exogenous variables does not exist for models constructed on this basis. With no prior information as to lag lengths, only a set of reduced form equations with identical lags for all variables could be estimated. He called this "alternative style" of econometrics a "vector autoregression" or VAR.

The Sims critique is the most recent, and in many respects the most influential, of all the objections to structural estimation that we have traced.

It is a much more radical break than the *Econometrica* symposium papers. It takes a position of directly making "everything a function of everything else," and in so doing goes beyond what even T. C. Liu thought was advisable.[3] We see in effect that after 40 years of development, econometrics was relegated back to case 2 of Mann and Wald (1943), a very provisional framework for representing economic hypotheses. The Cowles Commission extension of using economic theory to suggest exogenous variables to determine structure is essentially dismissed. From this perspective, even though Sims remarkably does not refer to Mann and Wald, the adoption of VAR methodology in place of structural estimation amounts to one of the clearest instances of abandoning a longstanding research program in the history of modern science. A detailed discussion of the critique is therefore justified.

7.2 Critique of Identification

Sims does not give statistical evidence to support his statement that many identifying restrictions in macroeconomic models are invalid. However, he does give a theoretical example of a particular continuous time model that is formally unidentified if estimated with discrete data, a demonstration not greatly different from the cases of underidentification discussed by the Cowles Commission. But in the absence of such rigorous economic theory to establish the unidentifiability of parameters, the identifying restrictions might better be viewed as the *definition* of the economic theory embodied in the model. As such, the econometrician should view them as hypotheses to be tested as critically as available data and statistical techniques will allow.[4] At the same time it does not follow that putting every variable in a structural equation, as in a VAR, is more acceptable theoretically than leaving a given one out. The criterion in each case is whether a *reason* can be supplied for the particular decision. The examination of the early work by Klein and Patinkin in section 4.2.2 above has shown the characteristic uncertainties that confront macroeconomic modelers in this regard.

Sims could charge with some justification that the chosen specifications are often held with little confidence even by their originators. But more importantly, it has been statistically verified that the economic theories represented by overidentifying restrictions are rejected in the vast majority of published tests. As was argued earlier in section 4.1, this outcome must also cast serious doubt on the untestable exactly identifying restrictions.

Sims does not evaluate this evidence but Koopmans and Hood (1953) had already called it "natural" to abandon restrictions that were "strongly rejected by the data." One of the major scientific uses of structural estimation is to falsify proffered economic theories on sound statistical grounds. It is therefore important to have learned in this way that many macroeconomic models are in fact poorly identified.

The Sims critique has real force in light of the empirical work of two generations which attempted to overcome similar objections to the earliest Cowles Commission studies. The original goal of structural estimation of identifying the separate behavior of different classes of economic actors has hardly been achieved. Sims correctly denies that reliable macroeconomic information has been found to justify unique transformation of reduced forms into structural equations. In this respect, the state of economic knowledge has not greatly improved since 1943, when Marschak admitted that no single theory deserved special credence.[5]

We have seen that the Cowles Commission method was based on a belief that the critical testing of hypotheses was the foundation on which economic science would be built. Sims does not appear to reject this orientation but he definitely abandons the hope of eventually discovering meaningful structural equations that possess Frisch's "autonomy." As a matter of research strategy, he chooses not to conceptualize macroeconomics as the resolvable interaction of individual tastes, institutions, and technologies.

7.3 An Alternative Time-Series Methodology

The essence of Sims's approach is to forecast the joint movements of selected macroeconomic variables without tracing the causes back to microeconomic factors. The model is driven by stochastic shocks, as were the original macrodynamic systems, but it is not intended to analyze even a component of these shocks in terms of the effects of policy or structural changes. The purpose is instead to trace out the reaction of a vector stochastic process to a random impulse, under the unstated assumption that the behavior of the system is not sensitive to the underlying economic origin or nature of the shock. For example, Sims does not make any distinction between a shock of the classical statistical type, composed of innumerable small perturbing effects, and one that is a large change in a single variable that is not otherwise modeled. The consequences of the specification error when a VAR may not plausibly be regarded as a "complete" system are explored below.

For forecasting on this basis Sims ideally would utilize frequency domain time series methods to derive the transfer function of the vector process. The obstacle, apart from enormously difficult computation, is that spectral estimation is non-parametric and accordingly requires a very large number of observations before it can produce very definite results. In practice, Sims stays with the use of unconstrained linear difference equations in the time domain. They have lag lengths that reduce the degrees of freedom in the system to near zero, apparently drawing on the ideal result that infinitely long lags would provide the same information as knowledge of the cross-spectral densities. While deep problems with structural estimation have become apparent, it is by no means obvious that this alternative methodology offers a real advantage.

It will be recalled from section 4.3 that Ulf Grenander declined a Cowles offer to study pure time series processes. Not long afterward he completed a treatise on the subject where he pointedly noted:

> Concerning econometrics . . . the stationarity assumption will often be valid only for short time intervals [for which] we would hesitate to apply any of the statistical techniques of this book.[6]

In this connection it is worth recording that Norbert Wiener, the mathematician who in many respects was the father of modern time series prediction theory, opposed this use of the theory just as forcefully. He doubted the existence of "long runs of economic data [where] the whole of the run shall have uniform significance." It seemed obvious to him that the proper interpretation of the data was subject to "important revision, say, every ten years."[7] Furthermore, a principle result of Kendall (1946) was that hundreds of degrees of freedom were probably needed for reliable estimation of the period of even a second order difference equation.

The use of time series methods in econometrics entails assumptions as crucial as any hypothesis employed in structural estimation. For example, to obtain accurate results with them it is necessary to use far more observations compared to a parameterized structural model. But non-stationarity in this context is the counterpart to structural change. The premise of the Cowles Commission and the other time series theorists cited above was that long runs of structurally homogeneous data were not available in economics. The advantage of structural estimation was that smaller samples could be used, with a higher probability that structure was unchanged over the interval.

7.4 Contrast to Structural Methods

Sims is trying to do econometrics with a minimum of untestable a priori assumptions. One might expect that the quality of economic data and the absence of informative prior restrictions would limit the power of the inferences to be drawn from the VAR model. In particular, the available number of observations severely constrains the number of variables that can appear in the system. Sims cites the FRB-MIT model as having over 90 exogenous variables, without giving a count of the endogenous ones. Even with a two period maximum lag, it would not be possible to estimate it within the VAR framework. By eschewing admittedly uncertain assumptions about lag lengths and exogeneity, Sims appears to guarantee the omission of relevant variables for the explanation of the phenomena under consideration.

It was precisely this trade-off that motivated the Cowles Commission to analyze the implication of introducing exogenous variables into the Mann and Wald setup, with the consequent study of identification problems. We have seen that disaggregation was quickly recognized as necessary to represent the diverse patterns of behavior in a complex economy. Bergstrom (1955) indicated the potential gains from attention to this sort of detail. The large size of the models of the 1960's was in part also due to the need for many exogenous variables to legitimize the required ceteris paribus clauses of their theoretical foundations. And in a pragmatic vein, Hildreth (1960) properly observed that avoiding simultaneity bias was only one of several competing goals in any empirical investigation. The VAR therefore seems almost anachronistic when Sims uses it to estimate a six equation system of real GNP, money supply, unemployment, wage rates, general price level, and import price level. While the lagged variables are likely to be predetermined, the system is otherwise unacceptable on both Keynesian and classical grounds for not including an interest rate variable. But Sims has already declared his independence from such theoretical economic problems. His discussion in 1980 of VAR specification goes no further than the state of the art in 1943:

> In larger systems . . . some additional form of constraint will be necessary. Finding the best way to do this is very much an open problem.[8]

7.5 Estimation and Inference with a VAR

Sims initially used a lag length of 8 quarters to estimate the system for U.S. data over the period 1949:1 to 1975:4. Counting two extra terms for constant and trend, there is a total of 50 parameters to estimate with 108 observations. It does not seem surprising that he found a "relatively stringent" lag of 4 quarters did not materially affect his results. The rest of his analysis used the shorter lag. Since each variable was seasonally adjusted, it seems conservative to impute another 18 estimated parameters, again yielding a ratio of degrees of freedom to parameters of under 1.5 to 1. Sims openly makes the number of observations "explicitly a function of sample size" but even this simple application seems to have resulted statistically in a kind of nonsense regression, irrespective of its economic basis.

It is not possible to evaluate the plausibility of Sims's estimated equations because they were not printed in the article. Given that the model was not expected to conform to any a priori structure, it would also be important to know if any regressions were run other than the ones he discusses.[9] The VAR method is not immune to the problem of multiple hypotheses and, as Friedman and Koopmans insisted, a proper scientific report in econometrics must carefully document the procedures that were used to select a particular set of results.

This information would likely influence the interpretation of the VAR. Sims mentions in a footnote that it would have been better to include the behavior of the likelihood function around its computed maximum. It is almost certain to be quite flat in several directions, since he refers to a high degree of correlation among the predetermined variables. He chose not to report the estimated coefficients because they are "difficult to interpret." His meaning is not clear but a possible clue is his statement that the "implied long run behavior [is] misleading," which might imply that the sum of the lags on certain variables had the wrong sign.

Sims makes several inferences about the period of oscillation of the system. These are just point estimates but Kendall's work suggests that the confidence intervals, could they be computed, would be quite wide. There are two reasons for believing this. The first is the size of the standard errors and finite sample biases of the OLS estimators. The second is the frequency domain analog of extrapolation beyond the sample period. Sims detects a "long oscillation" of 80 quarters, or 20 years, when he had only 27 years of data to work with, although Kendall (1946) had stressed that reliable estimation of a period requires enough observations for several complete cycles to be included in the sample.[10] Sims believes that the "long run behavior of the system is nonsensical" but that it was "well behaved over a short horizon." This finding parallels Stone's work with non-stationary short-run models. Indeed, the fact that Sims characterizes the basic movement of the system as a "very slowly damped oscillation" suggests that it contains a root of near unity, although he does not make this argument. If so, it would be a striking re-confirmation of Orcutt's analysis of Tinbergen's inter-War data.

7.6 Hypothesis Testing

The major economically important hypothesis that can be tested with the VAR typically relates to whether all lags on a given variable in a particular equation are equal to zero. Sims (1980a) and later investigators have indicated how a VAR might be used to test for the independence of real macroeconomic variables such as the interest rate from their nominal counterparts. This is a very important application when one considers that Granger's (1969) proposed test for causality is actually a two variable VAR. Sims equates "exogeneity" with "Granger causal priority," which was discussed in section 6.3.3. A test for exogeneity in this sense is particularly relevant to determine the possible existence of feedbacks in policy control problems. Sims quickly points out, however, that a high order autoregressive system with few degrees of freedom "makes interpretation of the tests difficult." He cites sensitivity of the F tests to non-normality. This issue is of great importance since the system likely contains a root of modulus near unity. In this case the true finite sample distribution of the estimators is unknown but recent work, e.g. Evans and Savin (1984), makes it clear that they can be far from normal.

Bearing this in mind, it is worth examining the "two main conclusions" of Sims's hypothesis testing. The first one deals with a test of exogeneity for variables in a Phillips curve system. There are several findings here. The system "decisively rejected" the hypothesis that wages and prices have no feedbacks on unemployment, real output, and the money supply. In addition, the money supply (lagged) has a direct effect on wages, not prices. Most remarkably in this context, "unemployment is not important in the estimated wage equation, while it is of some importance in explaining prices." His last conclusion is that the money supply affects real output (in the short run).

These are not small questions. Sims appears to have intended this particular model as a separate contribution to settling the Friedman-Meiselman debate introduced in section 4.4.1.3. But the results do not provide very powerful arguments (except perhaps to invalidate the extreme rational expectations position on policy ineffectiveness). It surely is no surprise to find a link between such variables as wages and unemployment. On the other hand, to claim that the money supply has no direct effect on prices is to contradict the views of nearly every major economist since David Hume. Indeed, this claim reinforces the thoughtful paper by Basmann (1970), who argued for more scrutiny of econometric results against the background of broader historical knowledge. On the statistical plane, it is reasonable at least to ask how knowledge of the true distributions of the test statistics would qualify these results. In addition, Sims's critique of identification cites Hatanaka (1975) on the importance of knowing the "exact lag lengths and order of serial correlation." The VAR does not seem entirely free of this requirement either. Since no economic hypotheses are advanced to guide inference in the model, it becomes extremely important to explore the sensitivity of the results to changes in assumed lag lengths, pre-filtering of the data, and inclusion of additional variables. These sensitivities can be quite extreme with the usual macroeconomic data but Sims offers no information on the variations he found, assuming that more than one model was estimated.[11]

At this point the VAR method itself begins to arouse scepticism. By bringing so little information to bear on the phenomena under study it yields in effect economic "over-generalizations." Granger and Elliot (1967) did not fare much differently than Sims in their spectral analysis of the English wheat market in the eighteenth century. They concluded merely that wheat prices throughout the country tended to move together. Although they offered the reader the idea that "[merchants] made money . . . by operating the market," this inference concerning actual behavior apparently came not from their data but from a standard historical work on the period.[12] This apparently typical use of time-series and spectral methods in economics ironically confirms Wiener's belief that:

> In the social sciences we have to deal with short statistical runs. . . . We cannot afford to neglect them, neither should we build exaggerated expectations of their possibilities. There is much we must leave, whether we like it or not, to the "unscientific" narrative method of the professional historian.[13]

Conversely, to see whether the historian's conclusions warrant generalization, it would seem necessary again to return to some kind of structurally based econometrics that is able to test them critically as hypotheses.

7.7 Policy Analysis

Sims accepted that reduced forms from conventional models are useful tools in forecasting and policy analysis. His position is basically the one enunciated by Klein and Haavelmo in 1946, cited in section 4.2.2. Structure is considered to be "something which remains fixed" so that "analysis is more often . . . projecting the effect of a change in a policy variable than changing the parameters of a model equation." He wrote that "policy choice is then most easily and reliably carried out by comparing . . . conditional projections from the best existing reduced form model." It should be clear, after the discussion of the work by Hatanaka and Odaki (1983) in sections 6.2 and 6.3.3, that these practices are liable to produce misleading forecasts when the structure of the complete system is not taken into consideration.

The VAR is intended to facilitate policy analysis by estimating reduced forms that do not embody any "incredible" overidentifying restrictions. Although Sims does not use the language of complete systems, he describes his models as "unrestricted reduced forms [that] treat all variables as endogenous." It appears that since the VAR contains as many equations as it has variables, it should be interpreted as the reduced form of a hypothetically complete system.

One might immediately note how limited the direct representation of policy must be in a system that contains only six variables. For example, the system cannot explicitly treat the effects of tight money, a personal tax cut, accelerated depreciation allowances, or a large public sector deficit. These instruments would seem to be the kind that require explicit study in many policy problems. For Sims, however, policy is understood to mean only the addition of a known "innovation shock" to the reduced form disturbance for a particular variable in the current period. Policy variables in effect are merged into the reduced form errors. The response of the whole system is then traced out by experimenting with different combinations of shocks.

Sims isolates the effects of different policies by rearranging the system as a lower triangular Wold form, transforming from an autoregressive to a moving average representation, and sequentially "shocking" the variables down the causal chain. He explains this procedure as follows:

> The residuals [in the original system] are correlated across equations. In order to be able to see distinct patterns of movement the system may display [in response to an "innovation"] it is therefore useful to transform them to orthogonal form. There is no unique best way to do this. What I have done is to triangularize the system with variables ordered as M, Y, U, W, P, PM. . . . [In effect] the M innovation is assumed to disturb all other variables of the system instantly . . . while the

PM residual is only allowed to affect the PM variable in the initial period.

The 6 variables can be ordered 720 different ways in constructing a Wold form. It is clear that coefficients can be derived to reformulate the system as one of these combinations arbitrarily[14] The economic significance, if any, of choosing just one of these orderings for policy analysis requires some clarification.

The procedure to predict k current reduced form errors in a G equation system, when j of them ($j{<}G$) are already known, was given by Mann and Wald (1943). As presented in section 6.2, it is just the regression that is determined by the appropriate partitioning of the covariance matrix Ω of the reduced form errors. If the reduced form errors were orthogonal (the most simple case) then the known shocks would only affect the remaining variables beginning in the next period. This would seem to be the only procedure that is consistent with the assumed stochastic mechanism underlying the data, if no other information is available.

Sims's procedure is identical for the first variable in his ordering, i.e. in this case, the money stock. The equation for M is neither a money demand nor a money supply relation but an approximately correct reduced form that summarizes its predictable evolution. Knowledge of the current value of M yields an estimate for its disturbance that can be used to predict the current values of the other endogenous variables before they are available. Basmann (1965a) discussed this possibility, which clearly is the idea behind the procedure given by Mann and Wald. It seems most directly applicable when there is a "reporting lag" for some of the data. However, this straightforward forecasting problem is not all that Sims means by policy simulation. The question remains whether using the procedure is economically appropriate when the value of the disturbance is assumed, rather than observed.

It does not seem possible to discuss the issue without imposing more structure on the problem. Consider again the complete reduced form from section 6.2:

$$x_t = G^{(1)}x_{t-1} + \ldots + u \qquad (7.1)$$

and denote the elements of $A^{(0)-1}$ as a^{ij}. The complication in the analysis stems from the assumption that the covariance matrix Ω of the reduced form errors is not diagonal.[15] Presumably, if the shock is under the control of an economic agent, it must be a component of the error for a behavioral equation. For simplicity, denote the structural shock to the money equation as ϵ_1 and assume that it is *entirely* under the control of the monetary authority. Also, let the structural covariance matrix Σ be diagonal. It would be reasonable to assume that all other structural disturbances are equal to their expected value of zero.

The coefficient of the direct regression of u_i on u_1 in the reduced form, as would be calculated by the Mann and Wald procedure, is a ratio of weighted sums of the variances and covariances of the structural errors. There is no a priori reason to equate this coefficient to the ratio a^{i1}/a^{11}, which would seem to be the correct predictor. In fact, for general policy analysis through the "innovations" one would like all the elements of $A^{(0)-1}$ but they are of course unavailable without imposition of identifying restrictions. The computed values of u_2 through u_6 will not stand in proper proportion when generating conditional forecasts. The situation would be remedied by assuming that $a^{1j} = 0$, $j \rangle 1$, which of course would imply that money is an exogenous variable. Without this information it does not appear that the money innovations viewed as policy generate system wide shocks that are consistent with the structure of the reduced form. The analysis suggests that the economic validity of the forecast depends on this point.

A related problem concerns the ordering of the remaining non-controlled variables. While mathematically correct, the elements of the orthogonalized residuals in the Wold form have no economic interpretation. They are analogous to variables in an ordinary regression constructed as principal components. The usefulness of assuming a particular sum of fractions of behavioral shocks as a *policy* innovation seems quite limited, even non-operational. Furthermore, without additional economic theory it is entirely arbitrary to assert that one variable causally precedes another.

This issue is crucial for the intended use of the model. The innovations in the Wold ordering in effect comprise a set of initial conditions for simulating the reduced form. The pattern of initial conditions clearly determines the resulting forecast path. The sensitivity of the forecasts in part depends on the frequency response characteristics of the VAR. Even if money is granted causal autonomy, the five remaining variables can still generate 120 different forecasting models. It is not clear that any one of them really sheds light on macropolicy when the structure of the errors in terms of the policy instruments remains unspecified.

These problems do not arise if the underlying structural coefficient matrix is in fact lower triangular when the variables are ordered as Sims describes. The triangular solution is unsatisfactory, however, in so far as the VAR was intended to avoid the need for such assumptions about structure. In fact, once the system is assumed to be of this form the entire rationalization for the VAR becomes superfluous if the structural covariance is in fact diagonal. Each structural equation would be identified. Moreover, there would be no need to include all variables in all lags. Equations could be specified without concern about the symmetry of a reduced form.

The VAR considered as a reduced form system derived from structural equations leads to severe problems of interpretation when the objective is policy analysis. It may be useful to treat it without reference to structural equations at all. This approach actually seems implicit in Sims's work in that his model does not contain the standard endogenous variables of the Cowles Commission Keynesian models. For example, there are no separate behavioral equations for consumption and investment. Aggregation, the great conceptual problem with models of behavior, is not recognized in this framework.[16] But if macroeconomic structure really is not identifiable then it ceases to be an operational concept. The VAR itself becomes the structure.

Under this interpretation, it would no longer treat data as generated by an underlying behavioral process. The VAR would be an approximation to an unknown stochastic process, in effect a very elaborate trend and cyclical movement. Economic policy would then consist of attempts to deflect its course for short periods. But when policy consists of "exogenous" shocks to autonomous equations, it is not at all clear how the effects of instruments available to the policy maker could be quantified without imposing meaningful economic assumptions to identify relevant parameters.[17]

It is worth emphasizing what was first mentioned in section 6.3.3 regarding tests of Granger causality. The VAR in economic applications is very likely to be a "spuriously" complete reduced form. The symptoms of omitted variables are disguised by the long lags on the included variables that nearly exhaust the degrees of freedom and make the estimated residuals appear serially random. It was already known in the 1940's that a high order univariate estimated AR process could yield a close sample fit that nonetheless often displayed very erratic forecast behavior.[18] To the extent that policy shocks also ramify through omitted variables that "Granger cause" the system, one must be sceptical that response dynamics will be adequately modeled. The inclusion of an interest rate, for example, may be expected to change the behavior of the system substantially. "Innovations" then will confound policy effects and errors of specification. It is well to recall Koopmans's insistence that the researcher specify as carefully as possible "in what manner randomness enters into the formation of economic variables." The VAR as a policy tool does not seem able to escape this need. Without such a basis its forecasts seem little different scientifically from the "eruptions of a mysterious volcano" that Koopmans sought to plug in 1947.

7.8 Conclusions about VAR Methodology

The VAR arose as an alternative to a style of macroeconometric modeling that seemed not to produce useful forecasts in a period of rapid economic change. The major fault of these models was alleged to be the "incredible" nature of the economic theories that they represented. The response was to use no theory in a search for stable patterns in data. The system of linear difference equations used for this purpose was the one analyzed by Mann and Wald in 1943.

Many of these models were already believed to be implausible on the basis of tests of their overidentifying restrictions. It is worth exploring what alternative hypothesis might then be chosen. The logical converse of H_0: k coefficients equal to zero is simply that at least one coefficient is not equal to zero. Sims implicitly concludes that all would be different from zero. It is equally possible to proceed with additional tests of the structural hypotheses.

Since all of H_0 was not necessarily held with a great deal of confidence in the first place, one could try to discover which of the excluded variables were least compatible with the structural constraint. Koopmans, for example, very early suggested the use of a sequence of likelihood ratio tests for this case:

> The test of the [overidentifying] hypotheses, while permitting to test the a priori restrictions as a set, does not indicate which particular restriction should be dropped. Specific tests can be based on the likelihood ratio procedure.[19]

Initially doubtful restrictions could be relaxed to allow these variables into the equation. Indeed, Tukey claimed that the automatic sequential checking of restrictions was the central advantage of his alternative to the direct use of MLE.[20] It may be found that all of the "offending" variables were highly correlated so that only one of them need be included for an acceptable specification. This case is particularly important as it reveals specific regions of uncertainty in the parameter space. The investigator may accept H_0 and attribute the outcome to sampling fluctuation but specific weaknesses of the economic theory would now be more clearly understood. Structural estimation for a given model may still be abandoned after such an analysis. It must be considered an advantage, however, to base this action on tested economic criteria rather than a prioristic negative assumptions.

The VAR shuns many developments in econometrics that are not directly tied to the identification problem. For example, the earliest records of the Cowles Commission indicate the restrictive nature of linear equations. It is fair to point out that the approach described by Sims does not clarify how one might build the endemic identities and nonlinearities of conventional macroeconomics into VAR models. The reality of adding-up constraints and nonlinear relations between nominal and real quantities is surely less open to question than the validity of a particular set of over-identifying hypotheses. The most immediate consequence for Sims's policy exercises is that the shocks are assumed to have constant effects regardless of the state of the system. As a matter of economics, one might expect that a money innovation would influence real output and inflation depending on the position of the system relative to a cyclical peak or trough. The covariance matrix used to apportion the shock is an average of these responses whose applicability is uncertain for very short run forecasts.[21]

The VAR as described by Sims makes no reference to the recent literature on continuous time models, which seem directly relevant to the emulation of frequency domain procedures. One result of this work is the discovery that continuous time models estimated with discrete data in general have a moving average error component. This is important because Sims appears to select the lag length for the system on empirical grounds. If the moving average is slowly damped then a four period autoregressive lag may be a serious distortion of the implied infinite process. In view of the serious collinearity of the data, explicit specification of this error structure may be necessary to obtain proper estimates of equation dynamics. In the realm of pure forecasting, Akaike (1974) has shown that very low order ARMA schemes, typically (2,1) and (2,2), in the univariate case often approximate unknown processes better than high order strictly AR schemes. An important extension of this work would be to derive the discrete time implications of economic hypotheses formulated as tractable nonlinear differential equations.

The Cowles Commission continually emphasized that economic theory was necessary to provide explicit mechanisms for understanding the phenomena under study, particularly problems of structural change. Testing the performance of such mechanisms was one means by which economic knowledge itself would be developed. In this connection, Sims (1982) introduces an important change in the VAR approach. He abandons the premise of structural stability. Instead the coefficients of the model are assumed to follow independent random walks. This has received a more detailed defense and rationale in Doan, Litterman, and Sims (1984). Such a model can fit historical data quite well but as an explanation of economic forces it recalls Koopmans's original critique that "an observed regularity not traced to underlying behavior . . . is an instrument of unknown reliability." It should be observed that Sims (1980a) reported that the VAR appeared to suffer a structural break after 1973. His 1982 article seems to have been motivated by the further breakdown in its ability to predict well, given the subsequent economic history of the decade. The random walk structures of the coefficients at best have obscure implications for the forecast behavior of the system. Although it would be crucial to explore the effects of the policies pursued after the OPEC "shock" in as much detail as possible to improve models and plan responses for future crises, Sims's time-varying parameter scheme forsakes economic analysis altogether. It is a remarkable substitution of statistics for economic theory as an explanation of economic change.

The VAR critique arose from the slack scientific procedure of much empirical work. There can be no doubt that economic models now embody false and "incredible" premises. The key methodological point, however, is that they have been discovered through the use of appropriate statistical tests. Indeed, it is not clear how else one might acquire such information. Moreover, on this basis it has not been proven that all of the premises in the various models are false. As this book has argued throughout, an outstanding problem in the history of applied econometrics has been precisely that *not enough* differing hypotheses can be rejected by economic data. Econometrics in this respect must realistically be viewed like any other statistical tool which aims to expose error while only suggesting possible truth.

The great difficulty with the VAR is that it does not appear to provide an effective means for reducing the level of economic ignorance. Rather than resolving different theories of macroeconomic structure, it essentially ignores them and retreats to economic hypotheses that are so broad and known to be incomplete that they virtually defy critical test. The original structural models of the Cowles Commission were designed to study the partial influence of specific policy actions. Forecasting actual levels of endogenous variables was not accorded highest priority, particularly given the property that dynamic models accumulate future values of the error that tend to swamp other components of a forecast. The VAR focusses on forecasting per se but, as the above discussion has emphasized, the procedure likely suffers from grave problems of bias and economic interpretation. These considerations alone, apart from the structural changes issue, create a legitimate suspicion that VAR models may represent a new form of "number mysticism" that was justifiably censured in the work they are intended to supplant.[22]

One of the lessons of macroeconomic research is arguably that many different theories are simultaneously supported for highly aggregated data. Economists have never lacked alternative visions of reality. It now seems likely that scientific study of these differences will require a level of institutional and period detail that the econometricians of the 1940's hoped could be avoided. The challenge for econometrics will continue to be to devise accurate and powerful statistical tests to test the hypotheses that will be suggested in this research. As a return to the special case which minimizes the extent to which the more general structural system is able to model such detail, the VAR is a research strategy that is particularly ill-suited for this task of macroeconomics.

NOTES TO CHAPTER 7

[1]See, for example, *Parameters and Policies in the U.S. Economy*, ed. Otto Eckstein (Amsterdam: North Holland, 1976).

[2]Cf. the discussion in section 4.4.2 above.

[3]See section 4.4.1.1.

[4]Cf. the split that grew in the 1960's between estimation and testing of models that is discussed in section 4.4.2 above.

[5]Cf. section 2.3.1 above.

[6]Ulf Grenander and Murray Rosenblatt, *Statistical Analysis of Stationary Time Series* (New York: Wiley, 1957), p. 178.

[7]Norbert Wiener, *God and Golem, Inc.* (Cambridge: MIT Press, 1964), p. 91.

[8]Unless otherwise indicated, all references to Sims concern his essay (1980a).

[9]Sargan's (1980) COMFAC procedure, discussed above in section 5.1.4.2, would seem to provide a powerful alternative approach to model reduction. It also postulates long and identical lags for a set of variables but produces a reparameterization that perhaps more readily suggests insignificant variables and/or lags that may be dropped from the model.

[10]Pure frequency domain methods are less subject to this risk since poor estimates of autocorrelation can often yield good estimates of a properly smoothed spectrum. See R. B. Blackman and John Tukey, *The Measurement of Power Spectra* (New York: Dover, 1959), p. 12.

[11]Unrelated work by Courakis (1978) showed that the interest elasticity of demand for money could vary from 0.5 to 3.5 *depending* on the number of lagged endogenous variables. Hatanaka and Odaki (1983) proved that tests of Granger causality could depend on the nature of the filter used to transform data to stationarity series.

[12]They referred to R. B. Westerfield, *Middlemen in English Business* (New Haven: Yale U. Press, 1915).

[13]Norbert Wiener, *Cybernetics* (Cambridge: MIT Press, 1948), p. 164.

[14]See Basmann (1965a) for the algebra.

[15]Cf. the discussion in section 6.3.3 regarding this issue and Granger causality.

[16]Koopmans (1949a) cites Ezekiel's work of the 1930's as already establishing the importance of separating investment into "autonomous" and "induced" components for analysis.

[17]Akaike (1978) also derived a Wold form on account of a non-diagonal covariance matrix while using the VAR to study a problem in control engineering. He wrote that "design of a proper test input signal [i.e. policy innovation] is an important practical problem" but one that could be approached using considerable prior knowledge of the steam boiler system being analyzed.

[18]Sims does not address the important econometric question of the statistical reliability of the moving average coefficients but their asymptotic distribution was derived by Baillie (1983).

[19]Minutes of Staff Meeting, 8 February 1946, CCA, MSM.

[20]His procedure was discussed above in section 4.1.

[21]Neftci (1984) has given an example of a business cycle model driven by non-linear moving average shocks.

[22]See section 4.4.2.

CHAPTER 8

CONCLUSION

8.1 Review of the Argument

Structural estimation was founded on the belief that Tinbergen's approach to empirical economics could be adapted to yield decisive tests of different economic theories and to design effective policies for changing an economic system. It was an ingenious extension of standard statistical methods for the analysis of laboratory experiments. The "endogenous" variables under study were assumed to be generated by an equal number of co-acting "laws" that operated in the aggregate. The problem was first to determine whether these separate underlying laws were unambiguously recoverable from the observed data. If so, then their parameters could be consistently estimated by a variety of methods.

The body of statistical theory that has been developed for this purpose is a major intellectual achievement. The initial results on identification due to the Cowles Commission covered linear restrictions on the parameters of individual linear structural equations. Their estimation procedures included what are now called FIML and LIML. The crucial question of the proper inferences that could be drawn from use of these procedures was given provisional solution through the derivation of test statistics that had known asymptotic properties.

These three areas have not received equal attention in subsequent research but each one has been fundamentally advanced in the last twenty years. Identification now can be ascertained for arbitrary nonlinear restrictions on a nonlinear equation system. Estimation by instrumental variables methods, notably 3SLS and 2SLS, avoids the difficult computations of maximum likelihood techniques. Finite sample theory has established important differences between asymptotic distributions of econometric estimators and test statistics and their behavior in samples with realistically limited degrees of freedom. Not only has this work found analytic biases for the moments, it has also shown parameter dependent asymmetries in the true distributions which can be critical for actual inferences although of no importance asymptotically. The growing number of researchers with primary training in mathematical statistics and even pure mathematics may be expected to continue this progress in the tradition of the Cowles Commission and especially Abraham Wald.

Empirical experience with structural estimation has been less satisfactory. There is little evidence that the large macroeconomic models estimated to date are consistently able to forecast out of sample better than very naive alternative methods. Furthermore, contending schools of macroeconomic theory have not yet been resolved by econometric studies. A serious deficiency in much empirical work from the theory standpoint is the common emphasis on estimation of models without making use of the range of currently existing diagnostic tests to evaluate chosen specifications. A major problem at present is that adequate training in these important advances in technique have not been incorporated into the typical university courses for non-specialist econometricians. The current situation with more microeconomically oriented research is likely to be substantially similar but has received less attention in critical reviews of econometric models.

The historical analysis suggests, however, that the success in discovering the statistical properties of simultaneous equations systems has not settled many other serious methodological problems of econometric modeling. It was argued in chapter 4 and section 5.2 that the early researchers at the Cowles Commission, as well as Tinbergen and Frisch, by the early 1950's came to view these other issues as posing fundamental obstacles to the realization of their original goals. Exogeneity was one of these problems and was the subject of chapter 6. The book also stressed in chapters 2 and 4 the long-standing and still relevant debates over the use of aggregate linear difference equations as appropriate models for data generating processes in econometrics. In addition, the argument throughout the study has been that the problem of "multiple hypotheses" has proven essentially intractable in this framework and was primarily responsible for the first econometric theorists to abandon further work in the field. This problem tended to be neglected by the next generation of practitioners but urgently needs more careful attention for future modeling efforts.

8.2 Divergent Trends in Modern Econometrics

Unquestionably, it has been the empirical results that have aggravated a methodological split in the ranks of econometricians. One tendency is basically atheoretical and makes little use of economics or statistics to interpret the output of estimation procedures. Christopher Sims, with the VAR, and Herman Wold, with "soft modeling," are two principal figures in a movement away from discovering underlying economic structure. They have nearly abandoned the ideals that motivated both structural estimation and the original British work in quantification of microeconomic theory. By posing few hypotheses they have correspondingly less need for sophisti- cated statistical theory. The advantages of these methods would seem to lie in their simplicity, particularly for forecasting, but few successful and compelling economic applications have been presented so far.

It would be a remarkable reversal of the experience of applied workers since Tinbergen and Henry Schultz if econometrics could serve as a reliable forecasting and policy tool on these terms. The second major trend in econometrics is to enlarge the number of theoretically interesting models with known statistical properties to broaden the possibilities for scientific inference. In this connection, it is arguable that the aggregate linear differ- ence equation with constant coefficients has proven to be too crude a model for many important economic phenomena. There is a real scientific need for new models that clearly embody a maximum of economic and institu- tional detail and for appropriate statistical theory to test hypothesized implications. The continuing challenge for econometric theorists will remain to enable critical testing of new kinds of models, e.g. formulated with panel data and in continuous time, with the same thoroughness as is now possible for the Mann and Wald framework.

8.3 A Role for Methodological Studies

The problem of multiple hypotheses was a primary objection by mathe- matical statisticians in the 1940's to the Cowles Commission methodology. Marschak, as cited in section 4.2.2.1, interpreted this problem very nar- rowly as the proper adjustment to the size of significance tests when the same data are used repeatedly for discriminating among hypotheses. He seemed to maintain an underlying belief, however, that of the hypotheses being tested only one, or perhaps none, was actually true. This approach also seems evident in much of the current research into model selection, e.g. Pesaran (1982).

Early in this book, in section 2.1.1, it was discussed how econometrics largely adopted the Popperian viewpoint that objective scientific research in the natural sciences consists of attempts to falsify theories. Proposed economic "laws" that passed critical statistical tests would form the class of potentially "true" theories while the failures could be discarded. In general, the econometricians hoped that this process of falsification would operate as effectively for them as it had for the experimental scientists. Subsequent experience has given much reason to believe, however, that a large number of plausible competing theories cannot be rejected in econometrics.

The book has suggested at various points, viz. sections 2.1.1, 3.2, 4.2.2.1, and 4.3, that the multiple hypotheses problem might indicate precisely the conclusion that all models are true. It is submitted that economics is different from many problems in natural science because many different behavioral laws for the same phenomenon can be in force at the same time. This idea seems to have several consequences both for the interpretation of multiple hypotheses and the Popperian view of empirical economic economic research.

At one level it may be dismissed as a problem of aggregation, as seemed implicit in the letter from Marschak to Schumpeter that was discussed in section 4.2.2. Koopmans, in section 5.4, was less sure but deferred the issue as more properly economic than econometric. No doubt some quantities can be satisfactorily aggregated for certain purposes, yielding e.g. total production or per capita income. It is much less clear what is meant by aggregating different behavior patterns, as is presumably the case with structural estimation. A coefficient, such as the MPC, may represent an average propensity for the population and, given information on the income distribution, may have an acceptable economic interpretation. Aggregation procedures with such plausible properties would be important to the policymaker the Cowles Commission had in mind, i.e. one interested in forecasting the effects of various policy instruments that apply to all agents, e.g. tax and interest rates.

Aggregation procedures with comparable economic foundations have not been found for most models. If one is unwilling to accept estimation results for such models given the existence of different underlying behavior patterns then a different type of research seems necessary. Econometrics has stressed multiple hypotheses as a purely statistical problem that would be solved by accumulation of more data. The argument here is that it is as likely to represent a genuine, though perhaps unexpectedly complex, economic reality. Accordingly, a host of competing hypotheses need not be rejected asymptotically but, on the contrary, may all gain even stronger confirmation. Statistical tests on aggregate economic data may intrinsically fail to reject a large number of seemingly incompatible theories.

To analyze the real range of economic behavior it seems essential to develop models that contain far more historical and institutional structure than has so far been possible in the traditional equation systems, simultaneous or otherwise, of econometrics. The recent view of macroeconometrics as models of disequilibrium, e.g. Hendry (1980), seems to highlight a current lack of knowledge about the constraints that play fundamental roles in the economy. On a more micro level, panel data often indicate significant individual differences that are hardly explained by use of a dummy variable for each subject.

This history of structural estimation takes no issue with the highest original goals of econometrics: discovery of structure and analysis of policies. Indeed, a major problem with certain modern schools of research is their decision largely to cease these pursuits. The argument throughout, however, has been that econometric models have been extremely misleading when, as is unfortunately too common, they are not subjected to the most exhaustive statistical tests to reject as many proposed structures as possible. Furthermore, multiple hypotheses will likely remain an endemic problem with aggregate models whose solution will require new modeling strategies in addition to mere accumulation of more data.

This book cannot venture what form such new strategies may take. At this time it can only offer an inference that was suggested by this initial research into the history of econometrics and of economic thought.

Econometrics is possibly unique among the sciences for aspiring to great quantitative precision without benefit of controlled experiments or large samples from uniform, stable populations. Experience to date suggests that even the largest models have precise but simplistic structures which represent actual phenomena to a very low number of significant digits. The research program of the American Institutionalists, the comparative theme of chapter 3, by contrast was quantitatively imprecise but stressed a a complex, disaggregated, historical approach to economic structure. Their policies were most successful when the problems under attack were rather specific and allowed experimentation in the form of "learning by doing," e.g. design of an unemployment insurance program, implementation of a labor mediation board, or administration of a ration program. A further key factor was a detailed understanding of the diverse circumstances and motives of the different economic groups affected by these measures. By contrast, there is some justice to Vining's (1949) observation that the econometricians seemed to be concerned with nothing less than the "pathology of entire civilizations." This study would suggest that the imprecision of many econometric models is an inevitable result of greatly simplified explanations of economic phenomena. It may be most fruitful for econometric analyses to be conducted on a new level where institutional constraints and individual behavior are more clearly discernible.

BIBLIOGRAPHY

Akaike, Hirotugu. (1974) "A New Look at Statistical Model Identification." *IEEE Transactions on Automatic Control AC-19*. 716-723.

————. (1978) "On the Identification of State Space Models and their Use in Control." In *Directions in Time Series*. Proceedings of the IMS Special Topics Meeting on Time Series Analysis. Edited by D. R. Brillinger and G. C. Tiao. Ames, Iowa: Iowa State University.

Ames, Edward. (1948) "A Theoretical and Statistical Dilemma — The Contributions of Burns, Mitchell, and Frickey to Business Cycle Theory." *Econometrica* 16, 347-369.

Anderson, T. W. (1948) "On the Theory of Testing Serial Correlation." *Skandinavisk Aktuarietidskrift* 31, 88-116.

Anderson, T. W., K. Morimune, and T. Sawa. (1983) "The Numerical Values of Some Key Parameters in Econometric Models." *Journal of Econometrics* 21, 229-243.

Anderson, T. W. and Herman Rubin. (1949) "Estimation of the Parameters of a Single Equation in a Complete System of Stochastic Equations." *Annals of Mathematical Statistics* 20, 46-63.

Ando, Albert and Franco Modigliani. (1965) "The Relative Stability of Monetary Velocity and the Investment Multiplier." *American Economic Review* 55, 693-728.

Baillie, Richard. (1983) "Asymptotic Tests on Moving Average Representation Coefficients with an Application to Innovations on Spot and Forward Exchange Rates." *Economics Letters* 13, 201-206.

Basmann, R. L. (1957) "A Generalized Classical Method of Linear Estimation of Coefficients in a Structural Equation." *Econometrica* 25, 77-83.

————. (1961) "A Note on the Exact Finite Sample Frequency Functions of Generalized Classical Linear Estimators in Two Leading Over-Identified Cases." *JASA* 56, 619-636.

————. (1963a) "Remarks Concerning the Application of Exact Finite Sample Distribution Functions of GCL Estimators in Econometric Statistical Inference." *JASA* 58, 943-976.

————. (1963b) "The Causal Interpretation of Non-Triangular Systems of Economic Relations." *Econometrica* 31, 439-448.

————. (1965a) "A Note on the Statistical Testability of 'Explicit Causal Chains' against the Class of 'Interdependent' Models." *JASA* 60, 1080-1093.

————. (1965b) "On the Application of the Identifiability Test Statistic in Predictive Testing of Explanatory Economic Models." *Indian Economic Journal* 13, 387-423.

————. (1965c) "The Role of the Economic Historian in Predictive Testing of Proffered Economic Laws." *Explorations in Entrepreneurial History* (Second Series) 2, 159-186.

————. (1972) "The Brookings Quarterly Econometric Model: Science or Number Mysticism." In *Problems and Issues in Current Econometric Practice*. Edited by Karl Brunner. Columbus: Ohio State University, 3-51.

Bassett, Gilbert Jr. and Roger Koenker. (1978) "Asymptotic Theory of Least Absolute Error Regression." *JASA* 73, 618-622.

Bentzel, R. and B. Hansen. (1954) "On Recursiveness and Interdependency in Economic Models." *Review of Economic Studies* 22, 153-168.

Bergstrom, A. R. (1955) "An Econometric Study of Supply and Demand for New Zealand's Exports." *Econometrica* 23, 258-276.

————. (1962) "The Exact Sampling Distributions of Least Squares and Maximum Likelihood Estimators of the Marginal Propensity to Consume." *Econometrica* 30, 480-489.

———— editor. (1976) *Statistical Inference in Continuous Time Econometric Models*. Amsterdam: North Holland.

————. (1983) "Gaussian Estimation of Structural Parameters in Higher Order Continuous Time Dynamic Models." *Econometrica* 51, 117-152.

Box, G. E. P. and G. M. Jenkins. (1970) *Time Series Analysis: Forecasting and Control*. San Francisco: Holden Day.

Chernoff, Herman and Herman Rubin. (1953) "Asymptotic Properties of Limited Information Estimates under Generalized Conditions." Chapter 7 in *Studies in Econometric Method*. Cowles Commission Monograph 14. Edited by T. Koopmans and W. Hood. New Haven: Yale University Press, 200-212.

Chow, Gregory. (1981) *Econometric Analysis by Control Methods*. New York: Wiley.

Chow, Gregory and Paolo Corsi. (1982) *Evaluating the Reliability of Macroeconomic Models*. New York: Wiley.

Christ, Carl. (1951) "A Test of an Econometric Model for the United States 1921-1947." in *NBER Conference on Business Cycles*. New York: National Bureau of Economic Research, 35-106.

——. (1956) "Aggregate Econometric Models." *American Economic Review* 46, 385-408.

——. (1960) "Simultaneous Equations Estimation: Any Verdict Yet?" *Econometrica* 28, 835-845.

Cochrane, W. and Guy Orcutt. (1949a) "Application of Least Squares Regression to Relationships Containing Autocorrelated Error Terms." *JASA* 44, 32-61.

——. (1949b) "A Sampling Study of the Merits of Autoregressive and Reduced Form Transformations in Regression Analysis." *JASA* 44, 356-372.

Courakis, A. S. (1978) "Serial Correlation and a Bank of England Study of the Demand for Money: An Exercise in Measurement without Theory." *Economic Journal* 88, 537-548.

Cox, D. (1961) "Tests of Separate Families of Hypotheses." In *Proceedings of the Fourth Berkeley Symposium on Mathematical Statistics and Probability I*. Berkeley: University of California Press.

Cramer, Harald. (1946) *Mathematical Methods of Statistics*. Princeton: Princeton University Press.

Davidson, James, David Hendry, et. al. (1978) "Econometric Modeling of the Aggregate Time Series Relationship between Consumers' Expenditure and Income in the United Kingdom." *Economic Journal* 88, 661-692.

Deaton, Angus and John Muellbauer. (1980) *Economics and Consumer Behavior*. Cambridge: Cambridge University Press.

DePrano, Michael and Thomas Mayer. (1965) "Tests of the Relative Importance of Autonomous Expenditures and Money." *American Economic Review* 55, 729-752.

Dhrymes, Phoebus. (1978) *Introductory Econometrics*. New York: Springer.

Doan, Thomas, Robert Litterman, and Christopher Sims. (1984) "Forecasting and Conditional Projection using Realistic Prior Distributions." *Econometric Reviews* 3, 1-100.

Duesenberry, James, Lawrence Klein, Gary Fromm, and Edwin Kuh editors. (1965) *The Brookings Quarterly Econometric Model of the United States*. Chicago: Rand McNally.

Durbin, J. (1954) "Errors in Variables." *Review of the International Statistical Institute* 22, 23-32.

Durbin, J. and G. S. Watson. (1950) "Testing for Serial Correlation in Least Squares Regression I." *Biometrika* 37, 409-428.

Eaton, Jonathan and Richard Quandt. (1983) "A Model of Rationing and Labor Supply—Theory and Estimation." *Economica* 50, 221-233.

Eckstein, Zvi. (1984) "A Rational Expectations Model of Agricultural Supply." *Journal of Political Economy* 92, 1-19.

Edgeworth, Francis Y. (1904) "The Law of Error." *Transactions of the Cambridge Philosophical Society* 20, 36-66.

Engle, Robert, David Hendry, and Jean-Francois Richard. (1983) "Exogeneity." *Econometrica* 51, 277-304.

Evans, G. and N. E. Savin. (1984) "Testing for Unit Roots: 2." *Econometrica* 52, 1241-1270.

Ezekiel, Mordecai. (1942) "Statistical Investigations of Saving, Consumption, and Investment." *American Economic Review* 32, 272-307.

Fisher, Franklin. (1965) "Dynamic Structure and Estimation in Economy-Wide Econometric Models." Chapter 15 in *The Brookings Quarterly Econometric Model of the United States*. Edited by James Duesenberry, Lawrence Klein, and Gary Fromm. Chicago: Rand McNally, 589-636.

————. (1966a) *The Identification Problem in Econometrics*. New York: McGraw-Hill.

————. (1966b) *A Priori Information and Time-Series Analysis*. Amsterdam: North Holland.

Fisher, R. A. (1925) *Statistical Methods for Research Workers*. Edinburgh: Oliver and Boyd.

Friedman, Milton. (1940) "Review of *Business Cycles in the United States*." *American Economic Review* 30, 657-660.

————. (1948) "A Monetary and Fiscal Framework for Economic Stability." *American Economic Review* 38, 245-264.

————. (1953) "The Methodology of Positive Economics." In his *Essays in Positive Economics*. Chicago: University of Chicago Press, 3-46.

————, editor. (1956) *Studies in the Quantity Theory of Money*. Chicago: University of Chicago Press.

————. (1957) *A Theory of the Consumption Function*. Princeton: Princeton University Press.

Friedman, Milton and Gary Becker. (1957) "A Statistical Illusion in Judging Keynesian Models." *Journal of Political Economy* 65, 64-75.

Friedman, Milton and Simon Kuznets. (1945) *Income from Independent Professional Practice.* New York: National Bureau of Economic Research.

Friedman, Milton and David Meiselman. (1963) "The Relative Stability of Monetary Velocity and the Investment Multiplier in the United States, 1897–1958." Research Study Two in *Stabilization Policies.* Prepared for the Commission on Money and Credit. Englewood Cliffs, NJ: Prentice-Hall, 165-268.

————. (1965) "Reply to Ando and Modigliani and to DePrano and Mayer." *American Economic Review* 55, 753-785.

Frisch, Ragnar. (1933a) *Pitfalls in the Statistical Construction of Demand and Supply Curves.* Leipzig: Hans Buske.

————. (1933b) "Propagation Problems and Impulse Problems in Dynamic Economics." In *Economic Essays in Honor of Gustav Cassel.* London: Allen and Unwin, 171-205.

————. (1934) *Statistical Regression Analysis by Means of Complete Regression Systems.* Oslo: University Economics Institute.

————. (1938) "Statistical versus Theoretical Relations in Economic Macrodynamics." Mimeograph dated 17 July 1938. Contained in memorandum "Autonomy of Economic Relations" dated 6 November 1948. Oslo: University Institute of Economics.

Frisch, Ragnar and Frederick Waugh. (1933) "Partial Time Regressions as Compared with Individual Trends." *Econometrica* 1, 387-401.

Geary, R. C. (1948) "Studies in Relations between Economic Time Series." *Journal of the Royal Statistical Society* (series B) 10, 140-158.

Geweke, John. (1982) "Measurement of Linear Dependence and Feedback between Multiple Time Series." *JASA* 77, 304-313.

Gilbert, Christopher. (1986) "Professor Hendry's Econometric Methodology." *Oxford Bulletin of Economics and Statistics* 48, 283-307.

Girschick, M. A. and Trygve Haavelmo. (1947) "Statistical Analysis of the Demand for Food: Examples of Simultaneous Equations Estimation." *Econometrica* 15, 79-110.

Goldberger, Arthur. (1972) "Structural Equation Methods in the Social Sciences." *Econometrica* 40, 979-1002.

Granger, Clive. (1969) "Investigating Causal Relations by Econometric Models and Cross-spectral Methods." *Econometrica* 37, 424-438.

Granger, Clive and C. M. Elliot. (1967) "A Fresh Look at Wheat Prices and Markets in the Eighteenth Century." *Economic History Review* (Second Series) 20, 257-265.

Granger, Clive and R. F. Engle. (1985) "Dynamic Model Specification with Equilibrium Constraints: Cointegration and Error Correction." Mimeographed. University of California at San Diego Discussion Paper No. 85-18.

Granger, Clive and P. Newbold. (1974) "Spurious Regressions in Econometrics." *Journal of Econometrics* 2, 111-120.

—————. (1977) *Forecasting Economic Time Series.* New York: Academic Press.

Haavelmo, Trygve. (1943) "The Statistical Implications of a System of Simultaneous Equations." *Econometrica* 11, 1-12.

—————. (1944) *The Probability Approach in Econometrics.* Supplement to *Econometrica* 12.

—————. (1947) "Methods of Measuring the Marginal Propensity to Consume." *JASA* 42, 105-122.

—————. (1958) "The Role of the Econometrician in the Advancement of Economic Theory." *Econometrica* 26, 351-357.

Hale, C., R. Mariano, and J. Ramage. (1980) "Finite Sample Analysis of Misspecification in Simultaneous Equations Models." *JASA* 75, 418-427.

Hall, R. E. (1978) "Stochastic Implications of the Life Cycle Hypothesis: Theory and Evidence." *Journal of Political Economy* 86, 971-988.

Hanau, Arthur. (1928) *Die Prognose der Schweinepreise.* Berlin: Reimar Hobbing.

Hannan, E. (1970) *Multiple Time Series.* New York: Wiley.

Hansen, Lars P. and Thomas Sargent. (1980) "Formulating and Estimating Dynamic Linear Rational Expectations Models." *Journal of Economic Dynamics and Control* 2, 7-46.

Hatanaka, M. (1975) "On the Global Identification of the Dynamic Simultaneous Equations Model with Stationary Errors." *International Economic Review* 16, 545-554.

Hatanaka, M. and M. Odaki. (1983) "Policy Analyses with and without A Priori Conditions." *[Japan] Economic Studies Quarterly* 34, 193-210.

Hausman, J. A. (1978) "Specification Tests in Econometrics." *Econometrica* 46, 1251-1271.

Hendry, David. (1980) "Econometrics: Alchemy or Science?" *Economica* 47, 407-422.

————. (1983) "Econometric Modeling: The 'Consumption Function' in Retrospect." *Scottish Journal of Political Economy* 30, 193-220.

Hendry, David and Jean-Francois Richard. (1982) "On the Formulation of Empirical Models in Dynamic Econometrics." In *Annals of Applied Econometrics 1982-83*. Supplement to *Journal of Econometrics* 20, 3-34.

Hickman, Bert ed. (1972) *Econometric Models of Cyclical Behavior*. No. 36 in NBER Studies In Income and Wealth. New York: Columbia University Press.

Hicks, John. (1939) *Value and Capital*. London: Oxford University Press.

————. (1979) *Causality in Economics*. New York: Basic Books.

Hildreth, Clifford. (1960) "Simultaneous Equations Estimation: Any Verdict Yet?" *Econometrica* 28, 846-854.

————. (1986) *The Cowles Commission in Chicago, 1939–1955*. New York: Springer.

Hildreth, Clifford and F. G. Jarrett. (1955) *A Statistical Study of Livestock Production and Marketing*. Cowles Commission Monograph 15. New York: Wiley.

Hill, Bruce M. (1986) "Some Subjective Bayesian Considerations in the Selection of Models." *Econometric Reviews* 4, 191-246.

Hurwicz, Leonid. (1946) "Theory of the Firm and of Investment." *Econometrica* 14, 109-136.

James, W. and C. Stein. (1961) "Estimation with Quadratic Loss." In *Proceedings of the Fourth Berkeley Symposium on Mathematical Statistics and Probability*. Berkeley: University of California Press, 361-379.

Johnston, Jack. (1958) "A Statistical Illusion, Comment." *Review of Economics and Statistics* 40, 296-98.

Jorgenson, Dale. (1963) "Capital Theory and Investment Behavior." *American Economic Review (Papers and Proceedings)* 53, 247-259.

Judge, George et al. (1985) *The Theory and Practice of Econometrics*. 2nd Edition. New York: Wiley.

Kalecki, M. (1935) "A Macrodynamic Theory of the Business Cycle." *Econometrica* 3, 327-344.

Kalman, R. E. (1982) "Dynamic Econometric Models: A System Theoretic Critique." In *New Quantitative Techniques for Economic Analysis*. Edited by G. P. Szego. New York: Academic Press, 19-28.

Katona, George. (1945) *Price Control and Business*. Cowles Commission Monograph 9. Bloomington: Principia Press.

Kendall, Maurice. (1946) *Contributions to the Study of Oscillatory Time Series*. Cambridge: Cambridge University Press.

——. (1960) *New Prospects in Economic Analysis*. London: Athlone Press.

Keynes, John Maynard. (1939a) "The Statistical Testing of Business Cycle Theories." *Economic Journal* 49, 558-568.

——. (1939b) "The Income and Fiscal Potential of Great Britain." *Economic Journal* 49, 626-639.

——. (1940) "On a Method of Statistical Research: Comment." *Economic Journal* 50, 154-156.

Klein, Lawrence. (1943) "Pitfalls in the Statistical Determination of the Investment Schedule." *Econometrica* 11, 246-258.

——. (1947) "The Use of Econometric Models as a Guide to Economic Policy." *Econometrica* 15, 111-151.

——. (1950) *Economic Fluctuations in the United States 1921–1941*. New York: Wiley.

——. (1958) "The Friedman-Becker Illusion." *Journal of Political Economy* 46, 539-544.

——. (1960) "Single Equation vs. Equation System Methods of Estimation in Econometrics." *Econometrica* 28, 866-871.

——. (1966) *The Keynesian Revolution*. 2nd Edition. New York: MacMillan.

Klein, Lawrence, R. J. Ball, et. al. (1961) *An Econometric Model of the United Kingdom*. Oxford: Basil Blackwell.

Klein, Lawrence and Gary Fromm. (1972) "The Brookings Model — A Rational Perspective." In *Problems and Issues in Current Econometric Practice*. Edited by Karl Brunner. Columbus: Ohio State University, 52-62.

Klein, Lawrence and Arthur Goldberger. (1955) *An Econometric Model of the United States, 1929-1952*. Amsterdam: North-Holland.

Kloek, T. and L. Mannes. (1960) "Simultaneous Equations Estimation based on Principal Components of Predetermined Variables." *Econometrica* 28, 45-61.

Koopmans, Tjalling. (1937) *Linear Regression Analysis of Economic Time Series*. Haarlem: De Erven F. Bohn.

————. (1941) "The Logic of Econometric Business Cycle Research." *Journal of Political Economy* 49, 157-181.

————. (1942) "Serial Correlation and Quadratic Forms in Normal Variables." *Annals of Mathematical Statistics* 13, 14-33.

————. (1945) "Statistical Estimation of Simultaneous Economic Relations." *JASA* 40, 448-466.

————. (1947) "Measurement without Theory." *Review of Economics and Statistics* 29, 161-172.

————. (1949a) "Identification Problems in Economic Model Construction." *Econometrica* 17, 125-144.

————. (1949b) "The Econometric Approach to Business Fluctuations." *American Economic Review (Papers and Proceedings)* 39, 64-72.

————. (1949c) "Reply to Rutledge Vining." *Review of Economics and Statistics* 31, 86-91.

————. (1950) "When is an Equation System Complete for Statistical Purposes?" Chapter 17 in *Statistical Inference in Dynamic Economic Models*. Cowles Commission Monograph 10. Edited by T. Koopmans. New York: Wiley, 393-409.

————. (1952) "Comments on a Paper by Guy Orcutt." *Review of Economics and Statistics* 34, 200-205.

————. (1957) "The Interaction of Tools and Problems in Economics." In his *Three Essays on the State of Economic Science*. New York: McGraw-Hill, 167-220.

————. (1979) "Economics among the Sciences." *American Economic Review* 69, 1-13.

Koopmans, Tjalling and William Hood. (1953) "The Estimation of Simultaneous Linear Economic Relationships." Chapter 6 in *Studies in Econometric Method*. Cowles Commission Monograph 14. Edited by T. Koopmans and W. Hood. New Haven: Yale University Press, 112-199.

Koopmans, Tjalling and Olav Reiersøl. (1950) "The Identification of Structural Characteristics." *Annals of Mathematical Statistics* 21, 165-181.

Koopmans, Tjalling, Herman Rubin, and Roy Leipnik. (1950) "Measuring the Equation Systems of Dynamic Economics." Chapter 2 in *Statistical Inference in Dynamic Economic Models*. Cowles Commission Monograph 10. Edited by T. Koopmans. New York: Wiley, 53-237.

Koyck, L. M. (1954) *Distributed Lags and Investment Analysis.* Amsterdam: North Holland.

Kuh, Edward. (1958) "A Note on Prediction from Keynesian Models." *Review of Economics and Statistics* 40, 294-95.

Lawson, Tony and Hashem Pesaran editors. (1985) *Keynes' Economics: Methodological Issues.* Armonk, NY: M. E. Sharpe.

Leamer, Edward. (1978) *Specification Searches.* New York: Wiley.

————. (1982) "Sets of Posterior Means with Bounded Variance Priors." *Econometrica* 50, 725-736.

————. (1983) "Let's Take the Con out of Econometrics." *American Economic Review* 73, 31-43.

Lehfeldt, R. A. (1914) "The Elasticity of Demand for Wheat." *Economic Journal* 24, 212-217.

Leontief, Wassily. (1971) "Theoretical Assumptions and Non-observed Facts." *American Economic Review* 61, 1-7.

Lerner, Abba. (1941) "The Economic Steering Wheel." *The University Review* 7, 257-265.

LeRoy, Thomas F. and Stephen Cooley. (1985) "Atheoretical Macroeconomics: A Critique." *Journal of Monetary Economics* 16, 283-308.

L'Esperance, Wilford. (1964) "A Case Study in Prediction: The Market for Watermelons." *Econometrica* 32, 163-173.

Lipsey, Richard. (1960) "The Relation between Unemployment and the Rate of Change of Money Wage Rates in the United Kingdom, 1862-1957: a further analysis." *Economica* 27, 1-31.

Liu, Ta-Chung. (1960) "Underidentification, Structural Estimation, and Forecasting." *Econometrica* 28, 855-865.

Lovell, Michael C. (1963) "Seasonal Adjustment of Economic Time Series and Multiple Regression Analysis." *JASA* 58, 993-1010.

Lucas, Robert. (1976) "Econometric Policy Analysis: A Critique." In *The Phillips Curve and Labor Markets.* Edited by Karl Brunner and Allen Meltzer. Amsterdam: North Holland.

————. (1987) *Models of Business Cycles.* Oxford: Basil Blackwell.

Lucas, Robert and Thomas Sargent. (1981) "Introduction." In *Rational Expectations and Econometric Practice.* Edited by Robert Lucas and Thomas Sargent. Minneapolis: University of Minnesota Press.

Maasoumi, Esfandiar and P. C. B. Phillips. (1982) "On the Behavior of Inconsistent Instrumental Variable Estimators." *Journal of Econometrics* 19, 183-201.

McAleer, M., A. R. Pagan, and P. A. Volcker. (1985) "What Will Take the Con out of Econometrics?" *American Economic Review* 75, 293-307.

McCarthy, Michael. (1972) "A Note on the Forecasting Properties of 2SLS Restricted Reduced Forms." *International Economic Review* 13, 757-761.

Magnus, Jan and Mary Morgan. (1987) "The ET Interview: Professor J. Tinbergen." *Econometric Theory* forthcoming.

Malinvaud, Edmond. (1966) *Statistical Methods of Econometrics.* Chicago: Rand McNally.

————. (1981) "Econometrics Faced with the Needs of Macroeconomic Policy." *Econometrica* 49, 1363-1375.

————. (1983) "Econometric Methodology: Rise and Maturity." Paper given at the 50th Anniversary Celebration Conference of the Cowles Foundation for Research in Economics, 3 June 1983, Yale University, New Haven, Connecticut.

Mann, Henry B. and Abraham Wald. (1943) "On the Statistical Treatment of Linear Stochastic Difference Equations." *Econometrica* 11, 173-220.

Marschak, Jacob. (1939) "Personal and Collective Budget Functions." *Review of Economics and Statistics* 21, 161-170.

————. (1941) "A Discussion of Methods in Economics." *Journal of Political Economy* 49, 441-448.

————. (1950) "Statistical Inference in Economics." Introduction to *Statistical Inference in Dynamic Economic Models.* Cowles Commission Monograph 10. Edited by T. Koopmans. New York: Wiley.

————. (1951) *Income, Employment, and the Price Level.* Notes on Lectures given at the University of Chicago, Autumn 1948 and 1949. Edited by David Fand and Harry Markowitz. New York: A. M. Kelley.

————. (1953) "Economic Measurements for Policy and Prediction." Chapter 1 *in* Studies in Econometric Method. *Cowles Commission Monograph 14.* Edited by T. Koopmans and W. Hood. New Haven: Yale University Press.

Marschak, Jacob and W. H. Andrews. (1944) "Random Simultaneous Equations and the Theory of Production." *Econometrica* 12, 143-205.

Maxwell, James. (1946) "Gasoline Rationing in the United States." *Quarterly Journal of Economics* 60, 561-587.

Mendershausen, Horst. (1940) "Differences in Family Savings between Cities of Different Size and Location, White and Negro." *Review of Economics and Statistics* 22, 122-137.

Moore, Henry. (1911) *Laws of Wages: An Essay in Statistical Economics.* New York: MacMillan.

————. (1914) *Economic Cycles: Their Law and Cause.* New York: MacMillan.

————. (1919) "Empirical Laws of Demand and Supply and the Flexibility of Prices." *Political Science Quarterly* 34, 546-567.

————. (1925) "A Moving Equilibrium of Demand and Supply." *Quarterly Journal of Economics* 39, 357-371.

————. (1926) "Partial Elasticity of Demand." *Quarterly Journal of Economics* 40, 393-401.

Morgenstern, Oscar. (1950) *On the Accuracy of Economic Observations.* Princeton: Princeton University Press.

Muth, John F. (1960a) "Optimal Properties of Exponentially Weighted Forecasts." *JASA* 55, 299-307.

————. (1960b) "Estimation of Economic Relationships Containing Latent Expectations Variables." Mimeographed. Reprinted in *Rational Expectations and Econometric Practice.* Edited by Robert Lucas and Thomas Sargent. Minneapolis: University of Minnesota.

————. (1961) "Rational Expectations and the Theory of Price Movements." *Econometrica* 29, 315-335.

————. (n.d.) "Short-run Forecasts of Business Activity." Mimeographed. Bloomington: Indiana University.

Nakamura, A. and M. Nakamura. (1981) "On the Relationship among Several Specification Error Tests Presented by Durbin, Wu, and Hausman." *Econometrica* 49, 1583-1588.

Neftci, Salih. (1984) "Are Economic Time Series Asymmetric over the Business Cycle?" *Journal of Political Economy* 92, 307-328.

Nelson, Charles R. (1972) "The Prediction Performance of the FRB-MIT-Penn Model of the U.S. Economy." *American Economic Review* 62, 902-917.

Nerlove, Marc. (1979) "The Dynamics of Supply: Retrospect and Prospect." *American Journal of Agricultural Economics* 61, 874-888.

Neumann, John von. (1941) "Distribution of the Ratio of the Mean Square Successive Difference to the Variance." *Annals of Mathematical Statistics* 12, 367-395.

Orcutt, Guy. (1948) "A Study of the Autoregressive Nature of the Time Series used for Tinbergen's Model of the Economic System of the United States 1919-1932." *Journal of the Royal Statistical Society* (series B) 10, 1-45.

————. (1952a) "Toward Partial Redirection of Econometrics." *Review of Economics and Statistics* 34, 195-200.

————. (1952b) "Actions, Consequences, and Causal Relations." *Review of Economics and Statistics* 34, 305-313.

————. (1952c) "Review of Cowles Commission Monograph 10." *American Economic Review* 42, 165-169.

Orcutt, Guy and S. F. James. (1948) "Testing the Significance of Correlation between Time Series." *Biometrika* 35, 1-17.

Pearson, Karl. (1900) "On Deviations from the Probable in a Correlated System of Variables." *Philosophical Magazine* 50, 152-175.

Perry, George L. (1966) *Unemployment, Money Wage Rates, and Inflation.* Cambridge: MIT Press.

Pesaran, M. H. (1982) "Comparison of Local Power of Alternative Tests of Non-Nested Regression Models." *Econometrica* 50, 1287-1305.

————. (1987) *The Limits to Rational Expectations.* Oxford: Basil Blackwell.

Phillips, A. W. (1954) "Stabilization Policies in a Closed Economy." *Economic Journal* 64, 290-323.

————. (1958) "The Relation between Unemployment and the Rate of Change of Money Wages in the United Kingdom 1861-1957." *Economica* 25, 283-299.

————. (1959) "The Estimation of Parameters in Systems of Stochastic Differential Equations." *Biometrika* 46, 67-76.

————. (1966) "Estimation of Systems of Difference Equations with Moving Average Disturbances." Chapter 9 in *Stability and Inflation.* Edited by A. R. Bergstrom. New York: Wiley, 181-199.

Phillips, P. C. B. (1973) "The Problem of Identification in Finite Parameter Continuous Time Models." *Journal of Econometrics* 1, 351-362.

————. (1977) "Approximations to Some Finite Sample Distributions Associated with a First Order Stochastic Difference Equation." *Econometrica* 45, 463-486.

————. (1983) "ERA's: a new approach to small sample theory." *Econometrica* 51, 1505-1526.

————. (1984) "Exact Small Sample Theory in the Simultaneous Equations Model." Chapter 8 in *Handbook of Econometrics*. Edited by Zvi Griliches and Michael Intriligator. Amsterdam: North Holland, 449-516.

————. (1985) "The ET Interview: Professor J. D. Sargan." *Econometric Theory* 1, 119-139.

————. (1986) "Understanding Spurious Regressions in Econometrics." *Journal of Econometrics* 33, 311-340.

Phillips, P. C. B. and S. Durlauf. (1986) "Multiple Time Series Regression with Integrated Processes." *Review of Economic Studies* 53, 473-496.

Reiersøl, Olav. (1945) "Confluence Analysis by Means of Instrumental Sets of Variables." *Arkiv for Mathematik, Astronomi, och Fysik* 32A, 1-119.

Ricci, Umberto. (1930) "Die 'synthetische Okonomie' von Henry Ludwell Moore." *Zeitschrift für Nationalökonomie* 1, 649-668.

Rothenberg, Thomas. (1973) *Efficient Estimation with A Priori Information*. Cowles Commission Monograph 23. New Haven: Yale University Press.

Rubin, Herman. (1948) "Systems of Linear Stochastic Equations." Ph.D. Dissertation. University of Chicago.

Samuelson, Paul. (1939) "Interactions between the Multiplier Analysis and the Principle of Acceleration." *Review of Economics and Statistics* 21, 75-78.

————. (1983) "Rigorous Observational Positivism: Klein's Envelope Aggregation; Thermodynamics and Economic Isomorphisms." In *Global Econometrics: Essays in Honor of Lawrence Klein*. Edited by F. Gerard Adams. Cambridge: MIT Press, 1-38.

Sargan, Denis. (1958) "The Estimation of Economic Relationships Using Instrumental Variables." *Econometrica* 26, 393-415.

————. (1959) "The Estimation of Relationships with Autocorrelated Residuals by the Use of Instrumental Variables." *Journal of the Royal Statistical Society* (series B) 21, 91-105.

————. (1964) "Wages and Prices in the United Kingdom: A Study in Econometric Methodology." In *Econometric Analysis for National Economic Planning*. Edited by P. E. Hart. London: Butterworths, 25-54.

————. (1980) "Some Tests for Dynamic Specification for a Single Equation." *Econometrica* 48, 879-897.

Sargan, Denis and Alok Bhargava. (1983) "Testing Residuals from Least Squares Regression for being Generated by the Gaussian Random Walk." *Econometrica* 51, 153-174.

Sargent, Thomas. (1971) "A Note on the Accelerationist Controversy." *Journal of Money, Credit, and Banking* 8, 721-725.

————. (1976) "A Classical Macroeconomic Model for the United States." *Journal of Political Economy* 84, 207-237.

————. (1981) "Interpreting Economic Time Series." *Journal of Political Economy* 89, 213-246.

Sargent, Thomas and Chistopher Sims. (1977) "Business Cycle Modeling without Pretending to Have too Much A Priori Economic Theory." In *New Methods in Business Cycle Research*. Edited by Christopher Sims. Minneapolis: Minneapolis Federal Reserve Bank.

Sargent, Thomas and Neil Wallace. (1975) "Rational Expectations, the Optimal Monetary Instrument, and the Optimal Money Supply Rule." *Journal of Political Economy* 83, 241-254.

Schultz, Henry. (1928) *Statistical Laws of Demand and Supply*. Chicago: University of Chicago Press.

————. (1938) *The Theory and Measurement of Demand*. Chicago: University of Chicago Press.

Schumpeter, Joseph. (1951) "Historical Approach to the Analysis of Business Cycles. *NBER Conference on Business Cycle Research*. New York: National Bureau of Economic Research, 149-154.

Shiller, Robert. (1978) "Rational Expectations and the Dynamic Structure of Macroeconomic Models." *Journal of Monetary Economics* 4, 1-44.

Simon, Herbert. (1953) "Causal Ordering and Identifiability." Chapter 3 in *Studies in Econometric Method*. Cowles Commission Monograph 14. Edited by T. Koopmans and W. Hood. New Haven: Yale University Press, 49-74.

Sims, Christopher. (1972) "Money, Income, and Causality." *American Economic Review*

————. (1980a) "Macroeconomics and Reality." *Econometrica* 48, 1-45.

————. (1980b) "Comparison of Interwar and Postwar Business Cycles: Monetarism Reconsidered." *American Economic Review Proceedings* 70, 250-257.

————. (1982) "Policy Analysis with Econometric Models." *Brookings Papers on Economic Activity* 1:82, 107-164.

Slutsky, Eugen. (1937) "The Summation of Random Causes as the Source of Cyclic Processes." *Econometrica* 5, 105-146.

Solow, Robert. (1951) "Review of Cowles Commission Monograph 10." *Review of Economics and Statistics* 33, 358-360.

Stigler, George. (1962) "Henry L. Moore and Statistical Economics." *Econometrica* 30, 1-21.

Stone, Richard. (1947) "On the Interdependence of Blocks of Transactions." *Journal of the Royal Statistical Society* (supplement) 9, 1-45.

————. (1954a) *The Measurement of Consumers' Expenditure and Behavior in the United Kingdom* 1920–1938.! Cambridge: Cambridge University Press.

————. (1954b) "Linear Expenditure Systems and Demand Analysis: An Application to the Pattern of British Demand." *Economic Journal* 64, 511-527.

Stone, Richard, D. Champernowne, and James Meade. (1942) "The Precision of National Income Estimates." *Review of Economic Studies* 9, 111-125.

Strotz, Robert and Herman Wold. (1960) "Recursive vs. Non-Recursive Systems: An Attempt at Synthesis." *Econometrica* 28, 417-427.

Suits, Daniel. (1962) "Forecasting and Analysis with an Econometric Model." *American Economic Review* 52, 104-132.

Theil, Henri. (1953) "Repeated Least Squares Applied to Complete Equation Systems." Mimeographed. The Hague: Central Planning Bureau.

————. (1965) *Economic Forecasts and Policy*. 2nd Edition. Amsterdam: North Holland.

Tinbergen, Jan. (1930) "Bestimmung und Deutung von Angebotskurven: Ein Beispiel." *Zeitschrift für Nationalökonomie* 1, 669-679.

————. (1937) *An Econometric Approach to Business Cycle Problems*. Paris: Hermann & Cie.

————. (1939) *Statistical Testing of Business Cycle Theories*. 2 vols. Geneva: League of Nations.

————. (1940) "On a Method of Statistical Business Cycle Research. A Reply." *Economic Journal* 50, 141-154.

————. (1951) *Econometrics.* Translated by H. Rijken. Philadelphia: Blakiston.

————. (1952a) "Comments on a Paper by Guy Orcutt." *Review of Economics and Statistics* 34, 205-206.

————. (1952b) *On the Theory of Economic Policy.* Amsterdam: North Holland.

————. (1969) "The Use of Models." Nobel Memorial Prize Lecture.

Tobin, James. (1950) "A Statistical Demand Function for Food in the U.S.A." *Journal of the Royal Statistical Society* (series A) 113, 113-149.

————. (1952) "A Survey of the Theory of Rationing." *Econometrica* 20, 521-553.

————. (1958) "Estimation of Relationships for Limited Dependent Variables." *Econometrica* 26, 24-36.

————. (1980) *Asset Accumulation and Economic Activity: Reflections on Contemporary Macroeconomic Theory.* Chicago: University of Chicago Press.

Vining, Rutledge. (1949) "Koopmans on the Choice of Variables to be Studied and of Methods of Measurement." *Review of Economics and Statistics* 31, 77-86.

————. (1956) *Economic Research in the United States.* Paris: UNESCO.

Wegge, Leon. (1965) "Identifiability Criteria for Systems of Equations as as Whole." *Australian Journal of Statistics* 7, 67-77.

————. (1978) "Constrained Indirect Least Squares Estimators." *Econometrica* 46, 435-449.

Whittle, Peter. (1953) "Tests of Fit in Time Series." *Journal of the Royal Statistical Society* (series B), 125-139.

————. (1963) *Prediction and Regulation by Linear Least Squares Methods.* London: English Universities Press.

Wold, Herman. (1938) *A Study in the Analysis of Stationary Time Series.* Uppsala, Sweden: Almqvist and Wiksells.

————. (1943) "A Synthesis of Pure Demand Analysis." *Skandinavisk Aktuarietidskrift* 26, 85-118.

————. (1945) "A Theorem on Regression Coefficients Obtained from Successively Extended Sets of Variables." *Skandinavisk Aktuarietidskrift* 28, 181-200.

————. (1951) "Review of Cowles Commission Monograph 10." *Mathematical Reviews* 12, 431-433.

————. (1980) *The Fix-Point Approach to Interdependent Systems.* Amsterdam: North Holland.

————. (1982) "Soft Modeling: The Basic Design and Some Extensions." In *Systems under Indirect Observation.* Edited by Karl Jøreskog and Herman Wold. Amsterdam: North Holland.

Wold, Herman and Radnar Bentzel. (1946) "On Statistical Demand Analysis from the Viewpoint of Simultaneous Equations." *Skandinavisk Aktuarietidskrift* 29, 95-114.

Wold, Herman and Lars Jureen. (1953) *Demand Analysis.* New York: Wiley.

Working, Elmer. (1927) "What do Statistical Demand Curves Show?" *Quarterly Journal of Economics* 41, 212-235.

————. (1954) *Demand for Meat.* Chicago: University of Chicago School of Business.

Working, Holbrook. (1925) "The Statistical Determination of Demand Curves." *Quarterly Journal of Economics* 39, 503-543.

Wright, Philip. (1915) "Moore's Economic Cycles." *Quarterly Journal of Economics* 29, 631-641.

————. (1928) *The Tariff on Animal and Vegetable Oils.* New York: MacMillan.

————. (1929) "Review of *Statistical Laws of Demand and Supply.*" *JASA* 24, 207-215.

Wright, Sewall. (1921) "Correlation and Causation." *Journal of Agricultural Research* 20, 557-585.

————. (1925) *Corn and Hog Correlations.* U.S. Department of Agriculture Bulletin No. 1300. Washington: U.S. Government Printing Office.

————. (1934) "The Method of Path Coefficients." *Annals of Mathematical Statistics* 5, 161-215.

————. (1984) "Diverse Uses of Path Analysis." In *Human Population Genetics.* Edited by A. Chakravarti. New York: Van Nostrand Reinhold, 1-34.

Wu, De-Min. (1973) "Alternative Tests of Independence between Stochastic Regressors and Disturbances." *Econometrica* 41, 733-750.

Yule, G. University (1927) "On a Method of Investigating Periodicities in Disturbed Series, with Special Reference to Wolfer's Sunspot Numbers." *Philosophical Transactions of the Royal Society* 226, 267-298.

Zellner, Arnold. (1979a) "Statistical Analysis of Econometric Models." *JASA* 74, 628-643.

———. (1979b) "Causality and Econometrics." In *Three Aspects of Policy and Policymaking.* Edited by Karl Brunner and Allan Meltzer. Amsterdam: North Holland, 9-54.

———. (1985) "Bayesian Econometrics." *Econometrica* 53, 253-270.

Zellner, Arnold and Franz Palm. (1974) "Time Series Analysis and Simultaneous Equations Econometric Models." *Journal of Econometrics* 2, 17-54.

INDEX OF NAMES

INDEX OF SUBJECTS